Skills for
RADIO
BROADCASTERS
Third Edition

Curtis R. Holsopple

TAB BOOKS

Blue Ridge Summit, PA

121082

THIRD EDITION
SECOND PRINTING

Library of Congress Cataloging-in-Publication Data

Holsopple, Curtis R.
    Skills for radio broadcasters / by Curtis R. Holsopple. — 3rd ed.
       p.   cm.
    Includes index.
    ISBN 0-8306-2930-0 (pbk.)
    1. Radio broadcasting. I. Title.
PN1991.5.H65 1988
384.54—dc19   87-34276
                                          CIP

TAB Books offers software for sale. For information and a catalog, please contact TAB Software Department, Blue Ridge Summit, PA 17294-0850.

Questions regarding the content of this book should be addressed to:

Reader Inquiry Branch
TAB Books
Blue Ridge Summit, PA 17294-0850

Contents

Dedication

With warmest love and gratitude to my dad, my
mother, my wife, and my son. Your love, support,
encouragement, and prayers kept me going.

Foreword

My very first radio newscast was unforgettable. I'd just landed a job as a part-time announcer at a daytime-only radio station. I had plenty of voice training as an actor in college—I'd even done some television drama already. But when I did that first newscast, I got completely tongue-tangled.

"I'll resign immediately!" I said, stalking out of the newsroom. "That was the worst thing I've ever done in my life."

The program manager just smiled, shook his head and said, "Don't you think we all have to start somewhere?"

I'm glad he didn't let me quit. Within a year of that bumpy start I became the station's chief announcer and news editor at the ripe old age of twenty! Later I served as program manager in the Armed Forces Radio Network in Europe. Eventually I became a correspondent and producer and executive for the NBC Television Network, an assignment that involved me heavily in television coverage of science and politics.

Moving up the ladder in the broadcast industry took skill, determination, and endurance. In 1947 I saw my first television—a tiny three-inch black and white picture of a boxing match in Madison Square Garden. The broadcast was poorly done, and I thought I could do better.

I headed straight for the TV station armed with a full dozen program suggestions, and wound up in a hot little studio for an audition. Those early television cameras needed a lot of light, and the temperature in the studio was well over a hundred degrees. It turned out to be a near-marathon!

They put me through the usual gimmicks. I delivered commercials memorized on-the-spot and ad-libbed interviews with several station employees. Then the director asked me to simply "talk about anything." I described the studio, the lights, the weather, my school background, and my recent newsgathering experiences in Europe.

And then, after about ten minutes, I simply stopped at the end of a sentence, looked squarely at the camera, and said, "If you haven't figured out by now that I can speak well enough, I guess you never will—that's all I plan to do.'' A big voice on the studio speaker boomed with laughter, and the director said, ''You've got the job! How soon can you have your first interview show ready?''

And that, so help me, is how I got my ''big break'' into television—by talking back to the control room. With hard work, preparation, and endurance, you can find a way, too.

Roy Neal, K6DUE
NBC News Aerospace Consultant
Former NBC News Correspondent

Preface

Getting started in broadcasting usually means that your first job will be in a small radio station. It is ironic that the entry-level broadcasting job usually requires a huge variety of skills. Only later, after much advancement, will you have the luxury of specializing.

Major-market radio stations tend to require a high level of skill in specialized areas of the broadcaster's craft, but this narrower range of skill is usually not enough to meet the small station's needs. Aspiring broadcasters should expect to face a wide variety of job responsibilities in radio: announcers also write news copy, the chief engineer takes an on-air shift at times, commercial time sales personnel put in many hours in the production studio, and reporters also do the play-by-play for high school basketball games, watch the automation system, or take meter readings.

A typical day for a combo operator includes the obvious on-air wit and chatter, but it also includes making telephone rounds for news tips, giving tours to station visitors, or even climbing the station's tower to remove a troublesome bird's nest. A broadcaster certainly needs to be a jack-of-all-trades.

This book provides the reader with the basic information required to develop the many talents necessary to get a good start in broadcasting. You'll be ready for your first day on the job as a broadcaster if you combine your broadcast skills with enthusiasm, common sense, and personal integrity.

David L. Hershberger, W9GR

Senior Staff Engineer
Grass Valley Group
a Tektronix Company

Acknowledgments

Most radio and television stations need many people to keep them going. Likewise, each broadcaster is influenced and trained by many dozens of people through exposure to many different broadcast facilities. Dozens of people have given guidance and counsel in helping this book fill the need for an informal but thorough training guide for combo operators.

Several of the names listed are followed by that person's Amateur Radio call sign. Amateur Radio is a fascinating hobby that benefits both the individual participant and the general public. Hams are known for being extra helpful, and these folks certainly lived up to the legend. Check the Glossary for more information about Amateur Radio.

And now, my sincere thanks to the following broadcast facilities and the people that made them tick:

WEHS Radio and Television (closed circuit), Everett High School, Lansing, MI—Gary Dunckel, Rud Hoag, Bob Miller, Al Lokker, N8FEK, and Jim Stroup

WKAM AM and WZOW FM, Goshen, IN—Dan Eckelbarger, Gerry Grainger, and Ron Yoder, W9CG

WGCS FM, Goshen College, Goshen, IN—Dave Hershberger, W9GR, Cal Hess, WA9LJE, Dan Hess, Vernon Schertz, WB9PXI, Jake Swartzendruber, K9WJU, Sandy Swartzendruber, W9JOE, Stuart Showalter, and Roy Umble

WBKE FM, Manchester College, North Manchester, IN—Bob Bowman, Dave Bowman, WA9QPC, Sam Davis, Phil Snyder, W9LVY, Don Starkey, and John Whisler

WAYT AM, Wabash, IN—Lew Middleton, KA9PUB

WBNO AM and FM, Bryan, OH—Jim Glendenning, Mike Moran, Dick Murray, WB8TCI, Bill Priest, and Luke Thaman

WPTA TV and WPTH FM, Fort Wayne, IN—Gary Clem, Casey Drudge, Lynn Peggs, Joe Stovscik, and Mike Wells

WHAS AM, FM, and TV, Louisville, KY—Tyler Barnett, N4TY, Eldon DuRand, III, Gayle Hunt, Mike Myers, WB9GXX, Charlie Smith, and Buster Warner, W4JBA

Some other people deserve special thanks for their specific assistance in the production of this book and/or moral support that has made it all possible:

Mentors, helpers, guides, and teachers—Ray Collins, Kim Tabor and Carl Silverman at TAB Books, Jim Clary, WB91HH, Bruce Kampe, WA1POI, Linda Hershberger Kirk, Merna Latimer, Harold Mahlke, W8QG, Darrell Minnich, Roy Neal, K6DUE, Jack O'Dear, Steve Place, WB1EYI, John Ramsey, N1AKB, Gwen Stamm, Ned Trout, Pam Ward, and Lori Hostetter, our cover model.

Finally, my deepest gratitude goes to my wife, Edith Holsopple, NG1F, and to my parents, Don and Mary Etta Holsopple. They provided the very essential ingredients of counsel, patience, support, and above all, prayer.

Introduction

Skills for Radio Broadcasters is now in its third edition, and it is gratifying to see this manual now being published by TAB BOOKS. Surveying the available books about broadcasting, though, makes one ask, "Who needs *another* book about broadcasting?"

What makes *Skills for Radio Broadcasters* different? Here are some of the primary marks of distinction that set it apart:

1. The realisms of life in a radio station are faced honestly rather than glossed over into some trouble-free ideal.

2. This book is written for the special needs of volunteer combo operators at noncommercial radio stations affiliated with schools and colleges.

3. It does not assume that the reader is a college or graduate student majoring in communications.

4. The material presented is a portrait of the small-station combo operator's duties, responsibilities, and preparations rather than a focus on now-defunct equipment and techniques.

One of the first instructors to teach from this book told his class, "At last! This is a broadcasting book that tells you how things *really* are!" Feedback from this book's users, coupled with my own two decades of broadcast experience, have been invaluable in supplying the information presented here. *Skills for Radio Broadcasters* started as a thesis project for a Master's Degree in Education. It quickly evolved into a college textbook but was written primarily for high school and college students who did not want formal broadcast training. Rather, their main desire was to have a chance to be a DJ while in school—they wanted to know enough to do well and avoid making fools of themselves on the air.

Unit I, "Operating the Equipment," includes Chapters 1 through 5. It is a guided tour of a radio station and its equipment. You'll discover that a radio station's control room contains many things that you already understand, plus a few things you never thought about before.

Unit II, ''Equipping the Operator,'' describes your duties and responsibilities as a radio broadcaster. This section, Chapters 6 through 10, outlines the basic skills required to be a successful radio announcer and control room operator. This is also a guided tour—to help you once you become a real live radio broadcaster!

Unit III is ''Advanced Skills,'' a collection of more advanced information. After you've had a little exposure and experience in radio broadcasting, you'll find yourself asking some questions about techniques and equipment that are beyond what you really need to know, but you've wondered about. Unit III (Chapters 11 through 17) is included as a resource for when you're ready to dig deeper. It provides a necessary foundation for a student who is serious about a career in broadcasting.

Just a note about the cartoons that appear in the book—they are there to illustrate significant points and serve as memory devices. They are also there to entertain the reader and encourage you to keep your sense of humor about a business that can get very intense. Because most radio stations are small operations, the typical little prefab house with a tower out back is featured heavily. Most radio stations use their call letters to make some kind of statement about that station's character or identity; the call letters on the cartoon radio stations follow suit.

The broadcast industry keeps changing and growing, and my ''crystal ball'' gives imperfect images of the industry's future. Therefore, the reader is welcome to direct constructive criticism regarding this book to the publisher's address. All useful comments will be received and considered with appreciation.

Curtis R. Holsopple, K9CH
Newington, Connecticut

Unit I. Operating the Equipment. Experience is the best teacher, and working as a volunteer in a noncommercial radio station is one of the best ways to start gaining experience. (Pictured is Cal Hess of WGCS-FM, Goshen College, Goshen, IN)

UNIT I

Operating the Equipment

This book is intended for beginning broadcast students. Every attempt has been made to give you a real-life view of radio broadcasting. You probably know a little about what happens inside a radio station, but if you learned it from a movie or TV show, your ideas about broadcasting might not be entirely accurate.

Because broadcasting requires a lot of cooperation to get the job done, learning standard procedures and understanding the broadcaster's jargon is important to your success. Build on your experience as a listener, consumer, and user of broadcasting. You are probably familiar with home entertainment equipment such as tape recorders, record players, and radios. Take what you're familiar with, enhance that knowledge, and build on what is familiar to expand your knowledge into unfamiliar areas.

Chapter 1

Introduction to Broadcasting

It's easy to be impressed with people who work amid the electronic wizardry of a radio station. Broadcasters possess the ability to influence many people at once and are connected with the aura of ''show business.'' Broadcasting has its share of glamour, excitement, romance, and high technology. Yet broadcasters are just normal people doing a job that they enjoy.

Skills for Radio Broadcasters was written because many everyday broadcast skills and procedures hadn't been collected together into one easy-to-read manual. Broadcast skills are not hard to learn, if you get the right help. This book cannot replace a good friend or teacher who knows the broadcast trade, but it can provide solid foundation and reference material to help you get off to a good start.

Broadcasters have a specialized vocabulary, and you'll need to learn it to communicate effectively with other broadcasters. New words will be introduced and explained as needed in this text. When you first see a new term, it will appear in *italic* and be defined immediately. All such terms are listed at the end of the chapter where they are introduced. They also appear in the alphabetical glossary at the back of this book.

It's time to get started. Until now you've been a listener. Now you'll get a chance to look behind the radio dial and gain some skills as a radio broadcaster. Get ready to have some fun!

THREE INGREDIENTS TO SUCCESS

Broadcasters who succeed include three major ingredients in their career-building efforts.

Attitude:

☐ Be positive, friendly, caring, informed.
☐ Learn from mistakes and grow.
☐ Think ''can do'' rather than ''no way''.

Knowledge:

☐ Always expand.

☐ Be broad-based in many subject areas.

☐ Be organized, reliable.

Skill:

☐ Know the basics of the craft.

☐ Improve with practice.

☐ Never consider yourself perfect.

WHAT IS A DISK JOCKEY?

First, the terms *DJ* and *disc jockey* are not always appreciated by broadcasters. Sometimes other titles are used:

☐ *Announcer*—The person who speaks on the air

☐ *Engineer* or *Operator*—The person who operates the control room equipment

☐ *Combo Operator*—The person who *combines* the functions of both announcer and operator, performing both sets of duties at once

Don't worry about the title of "engineer." It is used interchangeably with "operator" unless specially modified by *transmitter* engineer or *chief* engineer. Early broadcast operators needed university engineering degrees to operate the primitive, unstable transmitters. Although modern broadcast transmitter operators rarely have advanced engineering degrees, the title is still sometimes used to include nontechnical operators.

COMBO OPERATOR: THE ANNOUNCER/ENGINEER

Sooner or later, the combo operator will do *everything* in a radio station. This is a great way to learn new skills. It keeps the job interesting. You will even have a chance to use some nonbroadcast skills such as woodworking, auto mechanics, gardening and farming, or any other hobby or education you might possess. Don't be afraid to try new things, but also remember that nobody can do all things well. The DJ in Fig. 1-2 has five arms, but most folks get

along with no more than two. You'll have to try different aspects of broadcasting until you find your niche. Eventually you will recognize your strengths and weaknesses and find the particular job situation that suits your talents and needs.

The combo operator is normally found in small- and medium-market radio stations and in many major market ones. The largest stations can afford the extra money to separate the announcing and operating functions into two separate persons working together. The norm is, however, for the radio announcer to also operate the control room equipment.

Whether as a combo operator or a specialist, your broadcast career will advance if you develop the necessary attitude, knowledge, and skill. If you just want to play around in the studio, doing enough to "just get by," your days as a broadcaster will be few and miserable.

You need to know the structure, patterns, traditions, and mistakes of broadcasting. The exercises found at the end of this chapter will guide you toward that end, but reading and observing are not enough. You will learn best when you expose yourself to real radio stations and get personal, hands-on experience.

Make a daily effort to expand your knowledge of all facets of broadcasting. Never assume that you have finished growing. Read the latest broadcast trade magazines. Read the manuals for the studio equipment. Ask questions and visit other stations. Keep exposing yourself to new ideas, equipment, techniques, people, and situations. This will keep your work interesting to yourself and your audience. For a broadcaster, stagnation is death.

GETTING TO KNOW YOUR RADIO NEIGHBORHOOD

You have probably settled into a pattern of listening to two or three radio stations. Ask someone else, and they'd probably list two or three different stations as their favorites. Yet, in most areas of the United States the average listener with an AM/FM radio can hear two dozen or more radio stations.

Set aside your ingrained listening habits for a while. Take some time to explore the radio dial. A

Fig. 1-1. Turning off a listener. A bored sounding announcer can drive listeners away in a hurry.

systematic method for doing this has been provided in the exercises at the end of this chapter. These will help you discover sources of radio entertainment and information that you might not have noticed before.

You'll get valuable background information as a broadcaster when you listen to many different radio stations. You can pick up fresh ideas by listening to distant stations and keep up with the latest tricks being used by the local competition. You can listen to distant radio stations to gather information about weather and highway conditions. In fact, radio stations routinely monitor each other to facilitate emergency communications.

Listening to many different radio stations broadens your own experience as an announcer. You will hear people that you will want to copy, and others whose habits you will want to avoid (Fig. 1-2). If you want a job in a larger station, listening to that station will give you valuable information that is useful in the job interview.

Take the time to listen around. It's especially easy to do when you are traveling, although you can

also listen to *clear-channel* stations from all over North America by tuning around the AM broadcast band after dark. The AM broadcast band "opens up" at night, bringing in distant signals. For now, you just need to know that it happens and that it has a profound effect on the number of AM radio stations that can operate at the same time.

PROGRAMMING AND PROGRAM EVENTS

Radio shows were once divided up into blocks or *programs* devoted to specific types of entertainment and "star performers." Today most radio stations have adopted a different approach to programming: they have now specialized so that each station concentrates on a fairly narrow range of program material that they offer all day. Radio stations no longer air programs in the style expected from television. Radio programming now seems like a continuous stream of music, talk, news, features, and commercials.

Listeners expect a specific kind of programming from each station, such as "all news," "rock music," or "background music." Many small-town sta-

Fig. 1-2. Super deejay. As you gain skill as a combo operator, you seem to sprout extra arms to do several things at once.

tions, however, try to meet the needs of their diverse audience by having a wide variety in their formats. Even among the majority of single-format stations, some variations exist depending on the time of day, and new formats are being developed all the time.

A *program event* is the building block of radio programming. Radio program content can be compared to a freight train (Fig. 1-3). Each radio program event is a separate and individually produced element, just as each railroad car is a distinct and different component of a freight train. Although each event is separate, all must be connected and run in a continuous way, one after another without interruption, like the coupled boxcars of the train.

Each station has its own distinctive *format*, a distinct blend and schedule of program events. As you think about getting a job in broadcasting, learn about different radio formats and choose which ones

you can handle well. Later in this chapter you will study specific radio stations and make a log of the program events you hear. Once you analyze several radio stations, you will recognize the variations in pacing, commercial saturation, and program content.

Program events come in many different types and lengths:

□ *Local news*—Originates at the station, although the newscast may include stories of regional or national importance.

□ *Local sports*—Originates at the station and includes sports news and interviews of local, regional, or national scope. Local events also include sporting events of nearby teams where the broadcast is originated and fed directly to the local station.

Fig. 1-3. A succession of program events. Each program event is separate and different, but radio programming is many events working together just as many freight cars make up one train.

□ *Local weather*—Read by the local announcer or fed from a regional network or weather service office.

□ *Music*—Any type of musical program material, but usually a record or tape available for purchase by the general public, including "oldies" or past recordings.

□ *Musical performance*—Indicates a one-time "concert" performance before a live audience. The broadcast can be carried live or recorded for broadcast at a later date.

□ *Network*—When preceding any of the categories above, indicates that the program material comes from a centralized remote location. Network programming comes to station via tape, telephone lines, radio, or satellite link.

□ *Jingle*—A brief tune or song used in commercials to introduce programs or promote the station or a specific announcer.

□ *Commercial*—A radio announcement intended to sell a service or a product, for which the station receives money.

□ *Public Service Announcement (PSA)*—A radio announcement intended to inform or educate the listener, for which the station receives no payment.

□ *Promotional Announcement (Promo)*—A radio announcement intended to inform the listener about an upcoming radio program or station-sponsored event.

□ *Live Announcer*—A catch-all category for the operator, anytime he or she is on the air introducing records, telling jokes, etc.

WRAP-UP

A radio broadcaster must learn new skills and speak a new language. One especially important skill involves learning to do one thing at a time—and then to keep on going. This is especially important for the combo operator, whose many duties overlap during a normal broadcast day.

Radio programs are divided into program events which are arranged into a systematic pattern, or format. The format will vary from station to station because most stations specialize to reach a specific segment of the audience.

A successful broadcaster constantly absorbs new skills and information and is aware of what other radio stations are doing. Broad awareness of trends in the broadcast business leads to keeping one's professional skills fresh and current.

Exercise 1-1.   "What's on Your Dial"—Daytime AM Stations

Goal: List the radio stations you can pick up easily during daytime hours on the AM broadcast band. This will make you aware of what stations are locally available and their locations on the dial.

Method: Spotting and logging stations.

1. Use an AM radio with a large, well-marked dial. A stereo system with an AM/FM tuner is usually the best.

2. Make a simple diagram resembling the AM dial on your radio and a log page like Table 1-1.

3. Pick out a strong, clear, local AM station and set the volume control at a comfortable level. *Do not reset the volume control again during this exercise.* You are to listen for only those stations that are easy to hear from your location.

4. Dial down to the very bottom of the AM band. Then tune your radio slowly up the band, stopping at any station you can hear plainly. Remember, don't adjust the volume.

5. Every time you locate a station that is loud enough to hear without straining, mark its position on the dial chart on your log sheet. Continue on up the AM band, marking each easily heard station's position on the dial.

6. After you have completed steps 1 through 6, go back and listen again to each station you marked on the "dial."

7. Listen to each station and log the four items of information asked for in the lower part of the log form: *dial location, type of program material,* and if possible, the *city* and *call letters.*

8. Mark the *dial location* as the reading you got directly from the AM dial on your radio, or you can log the station's actual frequency if known.

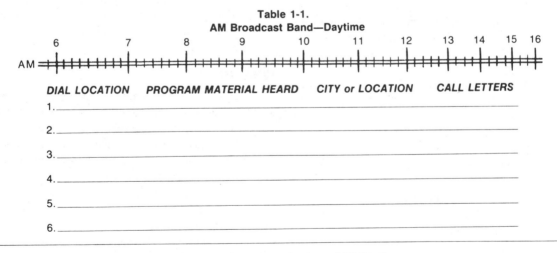

Table 1-1.
AM Broadcast Band—Daytime

DIAL LOCATION	PROGRAM MATERIAL HEARD	CITY or LOCATION	CALL LETTERS
1.			
2.			
3.			
4.			
5.			
6.			

Exercise 1-2.   "What's on Your Dial"—Nighttime AM Stations

Goal: List the radio stations heard at night on the AM broadcast band. Make an effort to listen for radio stations that you are not familiar with.

Method: Spotting and logging stations

1. Use the same procedure as described in Exercise 1-1, marking the stations heard on a log sheet like Table 1-2.

2. You should log at least six radio stations.

3. Log the information for each of the six stations on the log sheet.

Table 1-2.
AM Broadcast Band—Nighttime

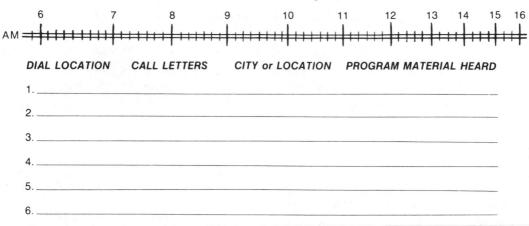

DIAL LOCATION   CALL LETTERS   CITY or LOCATION   PROGRAM MATERIAL HEARD

1. _____

2. _____

3. _____

4. _____

5. _____

6. _____

Exercise 1-3.   "What's on Your Dial"—FM Stations

Goal: List the radio programming available on the FM broadcasting band in your area. Notice the differences in the formats of FM stations as compared to AM stations. Notice also the difference in the overall sound of the FM band compared to the AM band. Listen to the noises made by your receiver when an FM station is not tuned-in properly. Listen to the sounds between stations.

Method: Spotting and logging stations.

1. Use the same procedure as described in Exercise 1-1 to mark the "dial" and log information in Table 1-3 about the FM stations you can hear.

2. Use a portable FM radio or a stereo receiver that is not connected to an outside antenna or cable system. This will give you a receiving capability that is typical for most radio listeners.

Table 1-3.
FM Broadcast Band

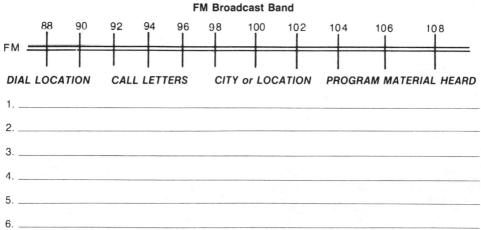

DIAL LOCATION   CALL LETTERS   CITY or LOCATION   PROGRAM MATERIAL HEARD

1. _____

2. _____

3. _____

4. _____

5. _____

6. _____

Exercise 1-4. Comparing AM Daytime, AM Nighttime, and FM Broadcast Band Reception Conditions

Based on your observations in Exercises 1-1, 1-2, and 1-3, answer these questions.

1. About how many miles away was the most-distant radio station in the AM band during the day? AM nighttime? FM band?
2. During which of the three exercises did you have the most trouble with static or fading signals?
3. During which of the three exercises did you have the least trouble with static or fading signals?
4. During Exercise 1-1 (AM daytime), were the stations you heard concentrated close together on the dial or were they spread out? In AM nighttime? In the FM band?

Exercise 1-5. Optional

If you made your FM observation during daytime hours, make another observation using the same receiver setup during the nighttime. If you first observed FM at night, repeat the exercise in the daytime, compare your two FM logs, and note any differences and similarities between them.

Do day/night variations affect AM or FM broadcast bands more? Do formats change at night?

Vocabulary

Each chapter ends with a list of broadcast vocabulary words. Definitions for many words are found in the glossary at the back of the book.

Look over the list of words below. If you do not understand the meaning of any of these words, you might have missed some important information in this chapter.

announcer	live	program
broadcasting	local	program event
combo	log	programming
combo operator	market	promo
commercials	network	PSA
DJ, disc jockey	operator	records
engineer	origination point	script
format	pacing	studio
jingle	production	

Chapter 2

Audio Source Equipment

Radio station control rooms are usually full of racks of equipment. In this chapter, you'll learn how to make sense out of a radio station's control room. You'll discover that you already know a lot about equipment found there.

STUDIO EQUIPMENT

Radio station control rooms vary according to the needs and budget of each radio station. Regardless of the variations, the *control room* is the heart of the station. Much of the program material originates from the control room. Even audio from remote broadcasts must pass through the control room before going on to the transmitter.

When faced with a control room, don't get overwhelmed by trying to understand everything in it all at once. Just look for three main groups of equipment found in radio stations:

- ☐ Audio sources (Chapter 2)
- ☐ Audio control (Chapter 3)
- ☐ Transmission and monitoring (Chapters 5 and 15)

The block diagram in Fig. 2-1 shows that audio flows from SOURCES through CONTROL to TRANSMISSION. When you are faced with a new control room or production studio, look at each individual piece of equipment and put it in one of the three groups. The fellow in Fig. 2-2 is demonstrating a good trick for sorting out the jumble of control room equipment or any confusing situation—it's like the old trick of rubbing your tummy and patting your head. Deal with one thing at a time!

Every radio station has a unique arrangement of equipment. In all cases, however, the audio signal flows from SOURCE through CONTROL to TRANSMISSION. This pattern is the same for *all* stations.

OPERATING THE EQUIPMENT

The vast majority of radio programs involve a control room combo operator who does all of the announcing *and* operates the equipment. This combination announcer-operator might be the only person in the radio station, except during weekday business hours. The combo operator quickly learns all the time-saving shortcuts possible while also learning to

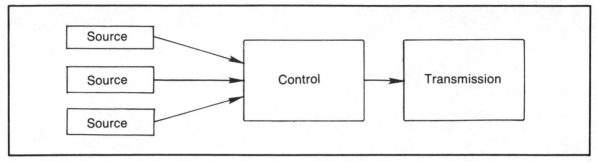

Fig. 2-1. Control room organization. All radio station control rooms function similarly. The audio flows from various *sources* through a *control* console to the *transmission* equipment.

turn out a radio show that is both error-free and artistically pleasing.

When you become good as a combo operator, you'll know your work so well that handling the controls will be second nature. At first, you are likely to be very self-conscious about operating the equipment. Remember, though, that broadcast equipment has been intentionally designed for simple operation, and it will require only a few hours for you to develop automatic operating habits.

Chapter 2 examines each kind of audio source equipment along with some basic operating hints. Chapter 3 deals with how this equipment is interconnected.

MICROPHONES

A microphone is designed to take sound waves in the air and turn them into a varying electrical voltage called the *audio signal*, the tiny electrical current that carries the patterns of the sound waves striking the microphone. A microphone is commonly nicknamed *mike*.

Directional Mikes

Microphones can be designed to be *directional*. They pick up sounds from certain directions while not responding to sounds coming from other directions. Directional mikes are very helpful in broadcast studios, picking up an announcer's voice clearly while rejecting sounds of nearby paper shuffling or equipment operations.

The typical microphone used in control rooms and studios has a *cardioid directional pattern*, named

after the heart-shaped area to which the mike is sensitive (Fig. 2-3). Studio mikes are commonly mounted on adjustable arms, or *mike booms*, so that they don't take up table space.

Notice that the mike is aimed to be most sensitive to the announcer's voice, but it is not sensitive to equipment and script noise coming from the sides and back of the microphone's pickup pattern. The announcer is said to be *on-mike*, but the sound sources from other directions are *off-mike*. Announcers keep their mouths aimed at microphones to avoid the hollow off-mike sound.

Mike placement varies somewhat according to each person's voice. A safe guideline, however, is to place the mike about 9 inches from the announcer's mouth. While the mike must be aimed at the mouth, it can be positioned somewhat to one side (Fig. 2-4) to allow the announcer to have a clear view of scripts and equipment. If the mike is placed too close to the mouth, it will pick up too much *presence* (noises made by lips, teeth, or breath). Yet some presence is required or the speech will sound muffled and hard to understand, as in an off-mike situation.

Testing a Mike

Test a microphone by speaking into it using your normal voice. Read news or commercial copy script. This will be the most accurate test. Do not tap on a mike or blow into it, or you risk damaging the microphone's sensitive components. If you must test a mike in a subtle way without speaking, gently rub or scratch it.

Fig. 2-2. Doing two things at once. This fellow is demonstrating a good broadcaster's trade secret! You can handle many complex situations if you remember to handle just one thing at a time . . . in this case, *first* rub your tummy, *then* start patting your head.

Never kink, walk on, or pull microphone cords. Treat the wires inside the mike cord gently to prevent breaking or intermittent connections. You might see rock singers abusing their equipment, but they can afford to replace it!

TURNTABLES

Turntables in radio stations are a lot like home record players, with a few differences. Broadcast turntables have the following characteristics:

☐ They are simple to operate.
☐ They are rugged and dependable.
☐ They have no automatic record changers.
☐ They handle only one record at a time.
☐ They can handle 33⅓-rpm and 45-rpm records.

Broadcast turntables are easy to use. You must learn how to position a record on the turntable quickly, however, so that the record's first audio begins less than one second after you start the turntable.

Turntable Operation

Getting the record *cued up* is explained in a few simple steps:

1. Place the record on the turntable and select the correct speed.

2. Place the needle on the record in the beginning grooves.

3. Listen to the turntable on the *cue amplifier* so it won't be heard on the air (see Chapter 3).

4. Spin the turntable by rotating it by hand. Be ready to stop it immediately by dragging your finger on the edge of the turntable's platter upon hearing the first audio on the record.

5. Stop the turntable at first audio.

6. Use your hand to manually turn the turntable backwards until you reach the point of first audio, then stop.

13

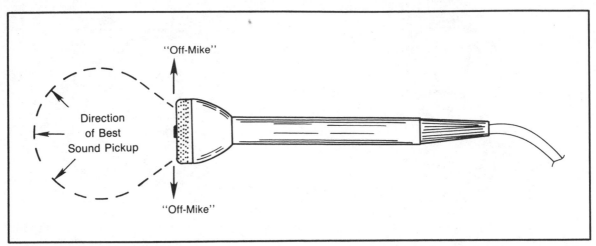

Fig. 2-3. Directional microphone. The typical control room microphone has a *cardioid directional pattern,* so-named because of its heart-shaped area of sensitivity.

Fig. 2-4. Proper microphone placement—top view. The microphone must be aimed at the mouth for best pickup, but it need not be directly in front of the announcer. Positioning it a little off to one side will also work well. (Pictured: Carol Bozena in production studio of WWUH, West Hartford, CT)

14

7. Look at the position of the record label. Use that to guide you in backing up the turntable another 1/2 turn, then stop the turntable gently so you do not bounce the needle off the record.
8. Leave the turntable turned off but set the speed selector for the correct speed (also called *putting the turntable in gear*).
9. The turntable is now set so that the record's first audio will occur about one second after the turntable is started. The one-second cue allows the turntable to come up to full speed before first audio is heard.

Three Precautions About Cueing Records

☐ Because cueing causes extra wear on the grooves, don't turn the turntable too quickly, especially when turning it backwards.
☐ Don't cue the same record more than once an hour if at all possible.
☐ Don't leave the turntable in gear for more than a few minutes with it standing still. Get in the habit of putting it in gear shortly before you need it.

Take some time to compare the labeled illustration in Fig. 2-5 with any turntable available. The parts indicated are found on professional broadcast turntables; home stereo turntables have additional features for automatic record changing.

Broadcast turntables are comparatively rugged, but both the *stylus* (or needle) and the record are delicate and easily injured. Handle a record only by the edge and center label, never touch the grooves. Always store records vertically, on edge, away from heat.

TAPE MACHINES

Broadcast tape recorder/players take three forms: (1) reel-to-reel, (2) cassette, and (3) cartridge. All three will be discussed in enough detail to help you operate them well. It is important to understand a few basic principles of recording and playing audio tapes. The principles are the same for all three types of tape machines.

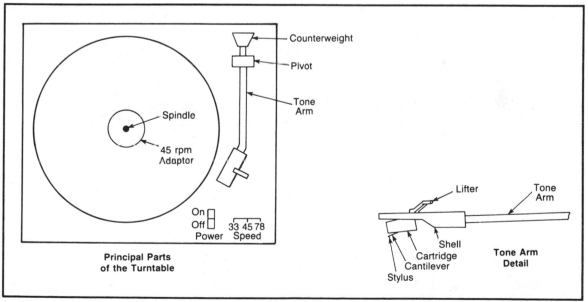

Fig. 2-5. Components of a turntable. A broadcast turntable is very much like a record player used at home, with similar construction and function. Broadcast turntables are much more rugged, however, and do not change records automatically.

How Recording Tapes Work

An audio tape recording uses a magnetic pattern on the tape to hold the information needed to preserve sounds. This magnetic pattern is invisible to the naked eye, but you can get an idea of how it looks by studying a phonograph record.

If you watch a 45-rpm record closely while listening to it, you will notice that the wavy pattern in the grooves is related to the sounds you hear. The record player uses the needle to detect the waves in the record grooves. The mechanical motion of the turntable's needle is changed into an electrical audio signal.

The tape machine uses something called a *tape head* to detect the changing magnetic pattern on the tape, and the magnetic tape patterns generate electrical audio signals in the tape head. The wavy grooves on a record are permanent; they can't be erased. The magnetic patterns on audio tape can remain stable for many years before deteriorating, or those patterns can be rearranged at any time by simply recording over the tape again.

Tape machines have a standard mechanical format. While variations exist, Fig. 2-6 presents the standard layout of the *tape path* of all reel-to-reel tape machines. This is important enough to memorize. Knowing the tape path's layout will be very useful to you as a tape machine operator.

Whether using reels, carts, or cassettes, all tape machines move the tape past the heads in much the same manner. When you play the tape back (refer to Fig. 2-6):

1. The tape enters from the left and is carefully positioned by the tape guide as the tape travels to the right.

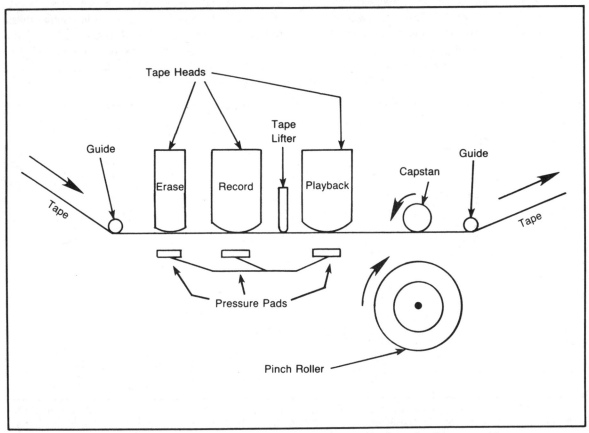

Fig. 2-6. Reel-to-reel tape path. This is the standard layout of the tape path of nearly all tape machines.

2. The tape then passes the *erase head*, which has no function during playback. The tape is held against the erase head by a felt or rubber *pressure pad*.

3. The tape then passes the *record head*, which is also not used during playback operations. A pressure pad holds the tape against the record head.

4. The tape then moves past a *tape lifter*, which is a retractable tape guide. This lifts the tape away from the heads during fast forward and rewind operations to minimize frictional wear to the heads.

5. The tape moves on to the *playback head*. This detects the magnetic patterns on the tape and converts them to electronic audio signals. The playback head also includes a pressure pad to ensure good tape-to-head contact. (*Note:* some machines do not use pressure pads.)

6. The tape is being pulled steadily by a *capstan* that rotates at a precisely controlled speed. A retractable *pinch roller* holds the tape firmly against the capstan during playback operations, but it drops away to per-

mit faster tape speeds during rewind or fast forward.

7. The tape moves on past another *tape guide* and leaves the tape path to the right.

The tape itself is made up of a long ribbon of clear plastic, very much like the plastic used in bread wrappers. One side of the tape is coated with a very fine magnetic powder, called the *oxide coating*, that contains many tiny magnets that capture and hold the sound patterns recorded onto the tape.

When the tape passes the playback head, the magnetic pattern is detected in the head, resulting in electrical audio signals. These audio signals are carried by wires from the head to an amplified output. The tape recorder's output can feed headphones, speakers, or the line connected to an input of the radio station's audio console.

Tape Head Formats

The tape heads scan a certain portion of the tape as it goes by. This scanned area is called a *track*. There are several different tape head formats (Fig. 2-7) *Broadcast standard* tape formats are either full-

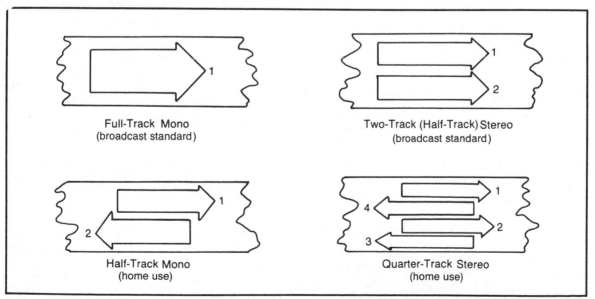

Full-Track Mono
(broadcast standard)

Two-Track (Half-Track) Stereo
(broadcast standard)

Half-Track Mono
(home use)

Quarter-Track Stereo
(home use)

Fig. 2-7. Standard tape head formats. In radio studios, the most common tape head formats are (1) full-track mono and (2) two-track or half-track stereo. The other two formats, (3) half-track mono and (4) quarter-track stereo, are found in consumer equipment for home use but are not broadcast-standard formats.

track mono or two-track stereo. The other two formats are used in home tape recorders.

Full-Track Mono

- ☐ The head scans the full width of the tape.
- ☐ Only one audio track can be recorded on a tape. There is no "side two" on a full-track mono tape.

Two-Track Stereo
(also Half-Track Stereo)

- ☐ The head assembly is subdivided into two separately functioning heads, each of which scans half of the tape during a pass.
- ☐ Both tracks are recorded or played at the same time, or one track can be recorded without disturbing the other.

Half-Track Mono

- ☐ The head scans one half the width of the tape during a pass.
- ☐ The tape can then be turned over and the head can then scan the other half of the tape. Side two is *not* the back side of the tape; it is the other half of it.
- ☐ Two mono audio tracks can be recorded, but only one at a time.

Quarter-Track Stereo

- ☐ The head assembly is subdivided into two separately functioning heads, but each section scans only one quarter of the width of the tape during a pass.
- ☐ The tape can then be turned over, and the head will scan the other two quarters of the tape.
- ☐ Two audio tracks are recorded at a time, but a total of four tracks are available on the tape.
- ☐ Tracks one and two are on "side one," tracks three and four on "side two."

Professional broadcast tape recorders commonly use only two of the above formats: full-track mono and two-track stereo. The other two formats were normally found on tape machines intended for home use, although home reel-to-reel machines have become very rare.

Tape Speeds

Broadcasters have generally adopted one standard speed for moving the tape past the heads: 7.5 inches per second (abbreviated 7.5 i.p.s.). Most tape machines provide for at least one other speed, however. The other tape speeds commonly used are 3.75 i.p.s. and 15 i.p.s.

REEL-TO-REEL TAPE MACHINES

Reel-to-reel machines are often called *tape decks*. Broadcast quality tape decks are divided into two subassemblies: the tape transport and the electronics.

The *tape transport* is the mechanical part of the machine responsible for moving the tape from the supply reel through the tape path to the take-up reel. It includes the tape head assembly and various tape guides to keep the audio tape correctly positioned.

The *electronics section* includes controls for setting volume levels and selecting the record or play modes. Some machines also include tone and equalization controls that adjust the frequency response of the tape machine's audio signal circuits.

In most modern tape machines, the reels run counterclockwise while the tape machine is recording, playing, or running fast forward. When rewinding, the machine turns the reels clockwise. This positions the tape so that the oxide coating is directly in contact with the heads, while the pressure pads are against the plastic backside of the tape.

Broadcast reel-to-reel tape decks have a *pause* or *edit* function that puts the machine into the play mode without any tape motion. The operator then turns the reels by hand to position the tape much like manually cueing up a record. Unlike the cueing of records, tapes are not harmed by repeated cueing unless the tape path itself becomes contaminated or damaged.

The Audio Path

Broadcast machines are not placed in the play or record modes quite as easily as are portable cas-

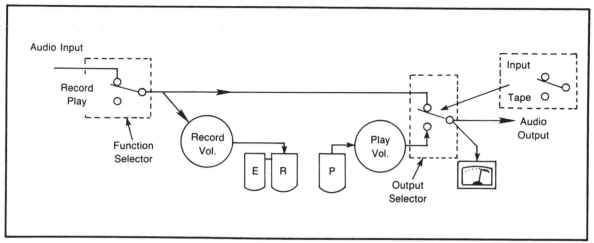

Fig. 2-8. Tape machine audio path. Studio-quality tape machines have two separate function switches: one for the input and one for the output.

sette tape players. The two controls used on most broadcast tape machines allow the operator much more flexibility of operation. (See Fig. 2-8.)

☐ *Function switch*—selects whether the tape machine is in the record or play mode.

☐ *Output selector*—switches the tape machine's meter and output amplifier between the audio coming from the playback head and the audio being fed to the input of the tape machine. Figure 2-8 shows in simple form the relationship of these two controls.

First, consider the play function position. The playback head is always scanning the tape, even when the machine is in the record mode of operation. To hear what is on the tape being played, however, the *output selector* must be switched to tape or play or reproduce (depending on your particular machine), and the play volume should be turned up.

To record, a bit more of the audio path is involved. Switch the function switch to record and the output selector to input. Feed an audio signal into the machine and adjust the record volume for 100% reading on the meter.

Most operators who are learning to use broadcast tape machines are soon confronted with a dead machine for some reason. This is usually due to any

of several circumstances: the volume control is not turned up, the function switch or output selector is set wrong, or (oops!) the power is off!

CASSETTE MACHINES

Cassette recorders are frequently found in home and car stereo systems but haven't been totally satisfactory as broadcast tape machines. Miniature reel-to-reel tapes are encased in a plastic box called a *cassette*. As shown in Fig. 2-9, the tape path for cassettes is quite similar to the reel-to-reel tape path found in Fig. 2-6. Using a cassette makes tape handling and threading extremely simple when compared to the open reels, making cassette systems ideal for small, portable tape recorders.

From the broadcaster's viewpoint there are some disadvantages of cassettes when compared to reel-to-reel machines.

☐ Cassettes are narrower, with thinner tape, making them prone to stretching, folding, breaking, and chattering across the heads.
☐ Cassettes run at a slower speed, giving poorer sound reproduction and more tape noise, with wow, flutter, and tape-to-head alignment problems.
☐ Cassettes are encased in a plastic box, making them much harder to cue up, edit, and splice.

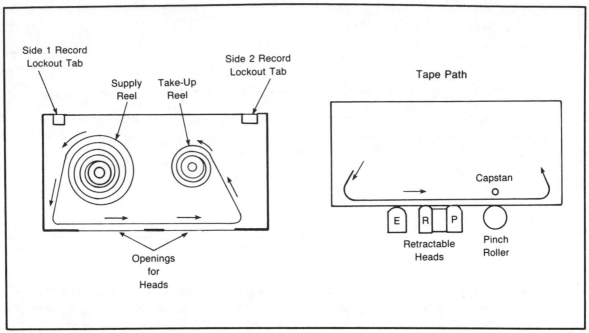

Fig. 2-9. Cassette tape path. A cassette system is a reel-to-reel device with both reels contained in a single plastic box that fits easily into one's hand. The tape is wound with the oxide facing away from the reel hubs because the tape heads are on the outside of the tape path.

Cassette Machines Are Useful

Despite these faults, audio cassettes have steadily improved in quality. They have almost replaced records in home audio systems and have found their place in broadcasting. Their small size and ease of storage make them ideal for making a tape-recorded program log of news programs, when it is important to know exactly what was said on the air.

Compact portable cassette recorders are standard for most broadcast news reporters, who need lightweight and easy-to-use equipment for the immediacy of an on-the-spot interview. The audio from the cassette can be *dubbed* onto the larger reel machines back at the station for precise editing. The audio quality of studio cassette machines has advanced to the point where it is feasible to distribute radio programs on cassette rather than open reel.

Broadcast sales persons find cassette machines helpful in playing commercials for sponsors. These can be specially produced sample commercials,

called *spec spots,* that can demonstrate a certain kind of commercial to a potential customer.

Cassette Tape Path

The operation of cassette machines is very much like that of reel-to-reel machines (see Fig. 2-8). In most cases the tape moves from the supply reel on the left to the take-up reel on the right, passing the erase head, record and playback heads, and the capstan/pinch roller in the same sequence as with the open reel machines.

In cassettes, the tape is wound with the oxide coating facing out, away from the reel hubs. The head assembly is mounted below the tape, rather than above it. Cassettes have the useful feature of including a tab that can be removed to prevent recording over the tape. There is one *record lockout tab* for each side of the cassette.

Portable cassette machines usually have a record/play head that is combined into one. These lack some of the operational flexibility of the studio models. Because of their small size, cassette machines and the cassette tapes are somewhat delicate. Always insert and remove the tape from the machine with care. Careless handling of the cassette can damage the tape and cause misalignment of the tape heads.

Cassette machines have only two head formats: mono and stereo. All cassette tapes are interchangeable when properly recorded and played on machines in good working condition.

CART MACHINES

Currently, the most heavily used tape machines in broadcasting are the cart machines. The word *cart* is short for *tape cartridge.* A broadcast cartridge is similar to the 8-track tape found in older home and car stereo systems. It uses ¼-inch magnetic tape like that used on the open-reel machines, but the tape is enclosed in a plastic case. The cart is larger and shaped differently from the cassette, and the tape is handled in different ways.

Construction of a Tape Cartridge

The unique feature of a tape cart is the reel arrangement inside the case of the cartridge itself (Fig. 2-10). The tape does not shuttle between two reels, as is the case in the other tape machines. The cart contains one continuous loop of tape wound in a spiral around a single hub.

Like the cassette, the tape in the cart is wound with the oxide facing away from the hub. Figure 2-10 shows that the tape passes the heads and the capstan (the pinch roller retracts for cart removal and insertion). Then the tape goes around the corner post and is wound onto the outside of the reel of tape. As the reel revolves, the layers of tape slip past each other. The tape makes an ever-decreasing spiral until it has reached the hub. Then it is pulled out of the center of the spiral, past the hub, over the other layers of tape on the reel, and into the tape path past the heads.

Carts require some special considerations. One is the need for specially lubricated tape to permit the slipping of the layers of tape. Another special feature is that the tape cartridge cannot be rewound. The fact that the tape only goes in the forward direction is not a major handicap, however. The cart for a 60-second commercial is typically no more than 70 seconds long.

The cart machine automatically recues the tape loop to the beginning of the recording after it has

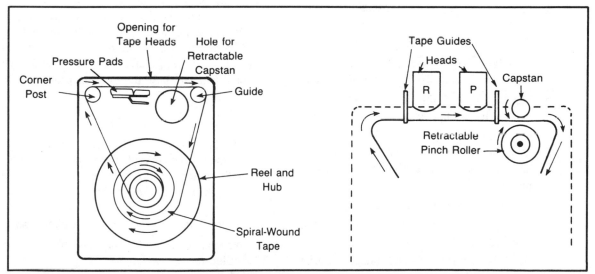

Fig. 2-10. Cartridge tape path. A tape cartridge uses a single reel and a continuous spiraling loop of tape. With this arrangement, no rewinding is necessary.

been played. Some of the more expensive cart machines include a *fast cue* mode for quick cueing to the beginning of the tape. Carts vary in length according to how much tape is in the loop. Tapes come in various standard lengths ranging from 10 seconds to more than 5 minutes. Extra large carts can hold much more tape, but these are rare in broadcast applications.

Operation of cart machines is very simple, probably one of the most foolproof tasks required of a broadcast operator.

To Play a Cart

1. Insert the cart into the slot, also called the *gate*, on the front of the cart machine.

2. Push the play button.

3. When the cart is done, it will run around to the beginning of the recording and stop automatically.

4. Remove the cart after it has recued and stopped automatically.

To Record a Cart

1. Select a cart slightly longer than the material to be taped.

2. Bulk erase the cart slowly and completely.

3. Play the cart for several seconds, then erase again to ensure that it is fully erased.

4. Play the cart until the *splice* in the tape loop passes the heads (some cart recorders will find the splice automatically).

5. Stop the machine and push the *record set* button to put the machine into the record mode.

6. Set the recording volume level.

7. Cue up the material to be recorded with a one-second back cue.

8. Start the cart machine and source material at the same time.

9. When the program audio ends, stop the cart

machine and play until it recues automatically.

10. Be sure to put an appropriate label on the cart according to your station's format for cart labels.

Bulk Erasing a Cart

All radio stations have a device that looks like a brick with a push button and electric cord. This device is called a *bulk eraser* (Fig 2-11), and it generates a strong magnetic field that completely erases everything on a tape, cart, or cassette. Turn on the bulk eraser, then pass the tape over it slowly two or three times on both sides. The tape is now completely blank and ready for recording. *Note:* move the tape away from the eraser before turning the eraser off.

COMPACT DISC PLAYERS

In the mid-1980s, a new type of playback machine became commonly available: the compact disc player. This new device plays small discs about the size of the palm of your hand. Microcircuits and computer technology allow a compact disc player to perform search and repeat functions. It has an excellent sound quality, and the discs themselves are not affected by stray magnetic fields, moderate heat, or dust. A compact disc player is also very easy to operate. If your radio station has one, you'll have no trouble learning how to handle it properly.

REMOTE AUDIO SOURCES

Program material can come to the studio from various audio sources outside the station. These remote audio sources are connected to the control room through one of three means:

□ Regular dial telephones with a *phone patch*

□ Special dedicated broadcast phone lines called *broadcast loops*

□ *Radio links*, including satellite receiving dishes

Fig. 2-11. Using bulk erasers. A bulk tape eraser can wipe out all program material on a cart, cassette, or reel of tape in a matter of seconds. Be sure to hold the tape *away* from the eraser while turning it on and off. It's also a good idea to keep other tapes, watches (both electronic *and mechanical*), and magnetic-striped credit cards away from the bulk eraser at all times.

In most cases, use of remote audio sources requires a bit of extra skill from the broadcast operator in the control room. The records, tapes, and mikes in the studio can all be controlled by the operator, including control over timing of each program event. Remote audio, however, comes into the studio according to some previously arranged schedule, and the operator must comply with the schedule. This allows virtually no room for error! The operator simply cannot get behind schedule when dealing with a remote or network source, or part of the program material won't get on the air. Remote broadcasts are discussed further in Chapter 13.

WRAP-UP

Control room equipment can be divided into three groups: (1) audio sources, (2) audio control, and (3) transmission. Virtually all program material originates in the control room, or passes through the control room.

The combo operator uses microphones, turntables, various tape machines, phone lines, remote audio sources, and radio links to bring together the program material heard on the air. Broadcast equipment in general is designed to be rugged and easy to operate, although care is required to keep equipment operating at peak performance and reliability.

Exercise 2.1.   Microphone Technique Observation

1. A common problem experienced by novice announcers is the *popped P,* the blast of air leaving the mouth when the letter *P* is formed. This makes an annoying blast of air in the mike and is intolerable on the radio.

   Use a lit candle in place of a microphone and read aloud while watching the flame flicker:

   ☐ Position the candle in front of you from 6 to 9 inches away from the mouth. Read aloud.

   ☐ Try positioning the "mike-candle" 45 degrees to one side, varying the distance again. Read aloud. Note the lessened flickering when the candle is off-center.

   ☐ Place the candle directly in front of you again and practice reading aloud while trying to avoid making the candle flicker. Concentrate on clearly pronouncing the words while not building up excessive pressure in the mouth.

2. Make frequent tape recordings of yourself while reading aloud. Once you are "on the air" as a radio announcer, continue monitoring yourself with a tape recorder. Listen later for any undesirable vocal habits, such as lip smacking, saliva crackle, popped P, dropped consonants (an', goin', etc.), slurred or overlapping words, gulping, etc. These problems get worse if the microphone is placed too closely to the mouth.

3. Watch for good and bad microphone techniques anytime you observe someone else using a microphone, as in public speeches, television interviews, etc.

Exercise 2.2.   Turntable Operation

Goal: Develop proper record and tone arm handling techniques to permit quick and safe operation.

Method:

1. Practice getting a record out of the jacket and placing it on the turntable while handling it only by the edges and the center. Repeat until you can do this quickly, without fumbling.

2. While listening to your turntable, place a record on it and practice putting the needle on the record and removing it.

3. Lift the tone arm from beneath so that you don't force the stylus down into the record.

4. Work on accuracy and carefulness first, then practice for speed.

Exercise 2.3.   Tape Machine Observations

Goal: Become familiar with the tape path of the various types of tape machines by looking for each major part as listed below.

Method: Use the following list to locate components on reel, cassette, and cart machines:

reel spindles
erase head
record head
playback head
capstan
pinch roller
tape guide

pressure pads
record lockout tab and probe (cassette only)
retractable pinch roller (cart only)

Exercise 2-4.   Discussion Questions

1. If you were a radio combo operator in a station that had a strict music format of the Top-40 hits plus 40 selected old-time songs, which equipment would you prefer for playing the music? You can choose between turntables, cart machines, cassettes, and reel tapes. Explain the advantage of the type of equipment you prefer, considering quick cueing, easy access to specific songs, and preservation of old and rare recordings.

2. Portable tape recorders and radio links have created *electronic journalism*. This brings a strong element of immediacy and realism to broadcast news. List and explain some of the problems involved in reporting the news as it happens in the case of auto accidents, disasters, court cases, city council meetings, or the U.S. Congress.

Vocabulary

boom	flutter	reel to reel
bulk eraser	gate	rewind
capstan	hub	satellite link
cart	loop	shuttling
cart machine	magnetic tape	source
cassette	mike, microphone	spec spot
cassette machine	monitor	spindle
console	needle	starting groove
copy	off-mike	stylus
cue, cueing, cued-up	on-mike	supply reel
cue system, cue amp	on the air	take-up reel
dedicated line	open reel	tape lifter
desk stand	pause	tape path
directional mike	pinch roller	telco
edit	platter	telephone lines
erase head	play, playback	tone arm
erasing	playback head	volume
fast forward	pressure roller	wow
first audio	radio link	
floor stand	record head	

Chapter 3

The Audio Console
and
Studio Support Equipment

The focus of the control room is the *audio console*. The operator uses the audio console to select audio sources and control volume levels. Typical audio consoles, or *boards*, also provide many auxiliary functions that aid the operator in controlling the audio signals and the studio equipment. Once the audio leaves the console, the support equipment processes and routes the audio to several destinations.

Concentrate on smooth, accurate operation of the console and studio equipment. After you gain confidence and proficiency in reaching for the right switch or knob, you will be ready to make good use of more-intimate knowledge of the equipment.

THE AUDIO CONSOLE

Most radio station control rooms have several tape machines, turntables, and microphones, but only one audio board. With few exceptions, every audio signal that reaches the transmitter passes through the board. It is up to you, the operator, to use the console to get the right audio source on the air at the right time with the correct volume. You must use good engineering practices, meet legal requirements, and still make it all come together in an artistically pleasing way.

The first few times you sit in front of the audio board, you will probably need to think out every move. The day will come, however, when your hands will make swift, smooth adjustments without your conscious attention. Board operation will become as automatic as walking, chewing gum, reading street signs, and humming a tune to yourself all at once.

A well-designed audio console is arranged for ease of operation with a minimum of error-producing problems. Overall, the audio console should get an audio signal "from here to there." The main control room console's functions are:

☐ Getting the required audio source on the air

☐ Metering audio signal volume

☐ Cueing sources not currently on the air

- ☐ Audio monitoring the console output
- ☐ Signal routing
- ☐ Intercommunicating between studios
- ☐ Controlling the remote start/stop of equipment

Audio-handling functions include the program channel, the audition channel, the cue channel, the meters, and the monitor.

Program Channel. The route taken by the audio signal from the source to the transmitter is the program channel. It provides full volume control and metering capabilities to ensure faithful signal handling with minimum distortion.

Audition Channel. The audition channel often duplicates the program channel in all functions. The audition channel can be used as an emergency backup for the program channel. It can be used to route signals from a source to a recorder, telephone line, or radio link without involving the program channel or the transmitter. It is used to control program material that is different from what is on the air.

Cue Channel. Nearly all audio consoles have a simple sound system for in-studio listening to audio sources, as when cueing a tape machine or turntable. That's why it is called the cue channel. It generally has no metering and might have poor audio quality (which does no harm). It feeds nothing else but the cue speaker in the control room.

VU Meters. The loudness of signals passing through the audio console is measured and displayed by a VU meter (Fig. 3-1). The letters *VU* stand for *volume units*, a measure of loudness. VU meters are used by the operator to regulate the volume levels so that all audio sources are balanced. VU meters are used to ensure that the transmitter is being fed audio signals that are neither too loud nor too soft.

Monitor or "House Monitor." The house monitor sound system can accept signals from the program channel, audition channel, and an on-air

Fig. 3-1. VU meter. A DJ's constant companion, the volume unit meter measures loudness of audio signals.

monitor receiver and feed them to speakers all over the radio station. It is usually of high quality with excellent speakers to give the operator a true indication of signal quality.

Audio consoles take many different forms. The simplest portable consoles will not include all of the features listed above, while the most advanced boards might have several program channels. Regardless of how many features a given board has, someone will wish for just a few more. The truly skilled operator will learn to use the available equipment to the limits of its capability, without going beyond the limits or abusing the equipment.

VU METERS, LEVELS, and MODULATION

Radio stations must keep the volume of audio signals reasonably constant. Large or sudden variations in volume greatly annoy the listeners (Fig. 3-2). Overly loud audio will overload the transmitter, causing distortion of the transmitted sound. This not only sounds bad but also causes interference with other radio stations. If the audio is too soft, the effective range of a broadcast transmitter is reduced—this irritates the listeners! (You don't want to do that!)

The *Federal Communications Commission* (the *FCC*) requires that radio stations maintain their audio volume peaks at a specified level. The loudest distortion-free audio signal level is defined as *100% modulation*. The rules dictate that all stations must maintain volume peaks between 85% and 100% modulation as measured at the transmitter.

The control operator uses a meter on the control room audio console to measure volume levels. This VU meter guides the operator to adjust the volume to the proper level, a procedure called *riding gain*. (The word "volume" can be replaced with *level* or *gain*.)

The VU meter has two sets of markings (Fig. 3-3). One set indicates modulation percentage, and the other set indicates *Volume Units*, calibrated in *decibels*. One decibel is defined as the smallest change in volume detectable by the human ear. The decibel markings on the VU meter are not particularly useful for the everyday board operator. They are necessary when broadcast engineers run performance tests on the station's equipment, however.

The board operator normally watches the meter scale marked for modulation percentage, riding the gain to bring volume peaks into the 85% to 100%

Fig. 3-2. Maintaining audio levels. Proper audio levels must be maintained for the convenience and comfort of the listener. Too soft material will go unheard, while too loud audio is annoying to the listener and can even cause interference to other radio stations.

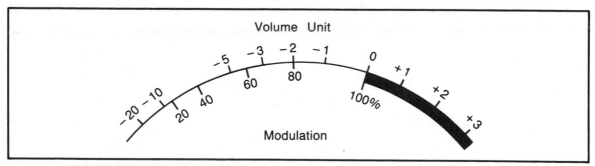

Fig. 3-3. VU meter scales. All VU meters are marked in units called *decibels*. The reference point (zero) is at about two-thirds scale, a bit to the right of center. Some VU meters also have a modulation percentage scale, with 100% modulation equalling "zero VU."

range. You should know, however, that 100% modulation is the same as the *zero VU* mark. That might be confusing, but memorize it anyway!

Think of zero VU as the mark to hit; the other plus and minus dB marks show how far away you are from the target point. The zero VU point is also the 100% modulation point. Both modulation percentage and the number of "dB down" are used to describe the loudness of an audio signal.

SIGNAL FLOW THROUGH THE CONSOLE

Operators who understand their equipment are highly valued in the broadcast industry. To see how an audio console is put together, look at the block diagram in Fig. 3-4 that shows the function of each section of the console and the relationship between sections. The console is divided into five main sections, with the audio flowing through each section:

1. The *input selector* selects which of several audio sources are connected to a particular pot.

2. The *pot* (short for *potentiometer*) or *fader* varies the audio signal level from the input.

3. The *channel selector key* routes the audio signal from the pot to any of the channel amplifiers.

4. The *channel amplifier* (audition, cue, or program channel) raises the audio signals from the channel selector key to the standard power level that results in a 100% modulation level at the transmitter.

5. *Outputs* for any of the three channel amps can include the following:

    □ Speakers
    □ Headphone jacks
    □ VU meters
    □ Line outputs from the board to other studio equipment

THE CONSOLE LAYOUT

If you spend several hours operating an audio console, you will probably memorize the location of all the knobs and switches without really trying. If you then use a different audio console, you will immediately be familiar with how most of it works, although the arrangement will be somewhat different. Audio boards, like automobiles, are standardized in most ways, while still leaving room for variations.

The standard 8-pot studio audio console is usually about 2 to 3 feet long, 10 inches high, and 1 foot deep: (Consoles are classed by the number of pots.) Broadcast consoles vary from 4 to 16 pots wide, while recording studio consoles can have over 30 faders side by side! Each pot is numbered from left to right across the console, and the pot, along with its associated input selectors and channel keys, is referred to as a *mixing channel* or simply *channel*.

A simplified 5-channel board much like one used in a small production studio or newsroom is shown in Fig. 3-5.

□ The *Channel 1 pot* is for the studio mike and nothing else.

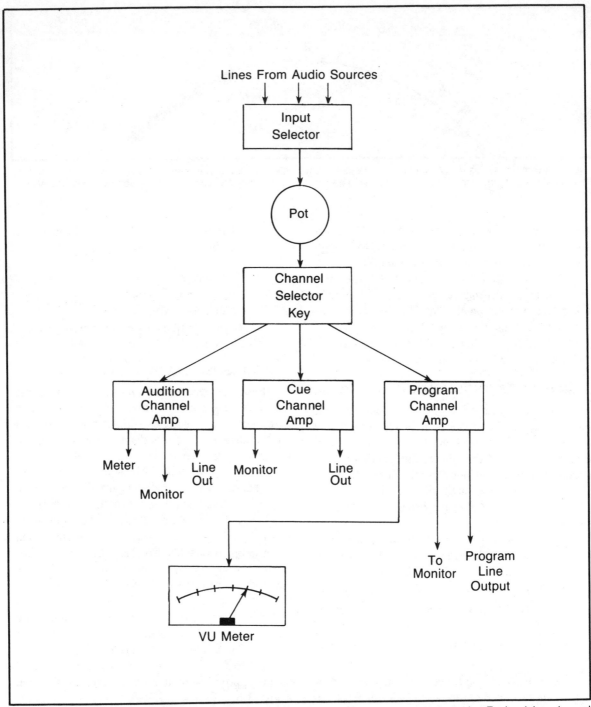

Fig. 3-4. Mixing channel block diagram. An audio console has several identical mixing channels. Each mixing channel can connect with different audio inputs, control the volume level with a "pot" (potentiometer), and then route the audio to either the audition channel, cue channel, or program channel.

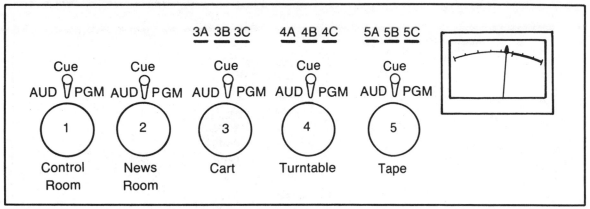

Fig. 3-5. Audio console front panel layout. Most broadcast studio consoles provide separate mixing channels for the control room and newsroom mikes. Other channels can be shared among several audio sources.

- ☐ The *Channel 2 pot* is for the news room mike.
- ☐ The *Channel 3 pot* is for playback of the cart machine.
- ☐ The *Channel 4 pot* is for the turntable.
- ☐ The *Channel 5 pot* is for the reel-to-reel tape machine.

Such a board is simple to operate because each source has its own pot, and each pot controls only one source. Many times, however, having one pot connected to only one audio source isn't practical. In most control rooms, only some pots will be dedicated to one source (such as the control room mike, each turntable, or the newsroom). Other pots must handle several possible audio sources.

Pots that control several audio sources are connected to input selectors that choose among the sources, allowing you to pick just one. The loudness of the audio signal is adjusted by the pot, and the audio is routed from the pot to the correct output channel by the *channel selector key*.

Several mixing channels are set side by side in the console to allow many separate audio sources to be mixed together into one composite audio output signal. Some boards select the *cue* position with the pot itself by turning the pot all the way down to zero. The audio automatically is fed to the *cue amp* in this arrangement.

You should memorize this signal path through each mixing module. If you ever have a *dead board* where you suddenly lose all audio signal, check at each control and switch, making sure it is correctly set. Most equipment failure turns out to be operator error!

Program Channel Mixing and Master Volume Control

After the audio signal is routed from the channel selector key to the program channel, it is mixed together with other audio signals. These signals are all combined into one composite audio signal. Then they are routed to the board output intended for broadcast. The program channel amplifier includes its own single volume control, called the *master volume control* (Fig. 3-7).

Regardless of the settings of any mixing pots, the master pot can cut the program channel volume down to zero. All mixing pots feed into the master pot. In normal board operation, the master pot is set at about the 2 o'clock position, and the mixing pots are used to set all levels.

Only rarely will the master be adjusted. Some audio consoles even have the master volume inside, and it can only be changed by the station's chief engineer. If you are using a board with the master pot on the front panel, make sure it is set at 2 o'clock (or at some indicated level) so that the program line

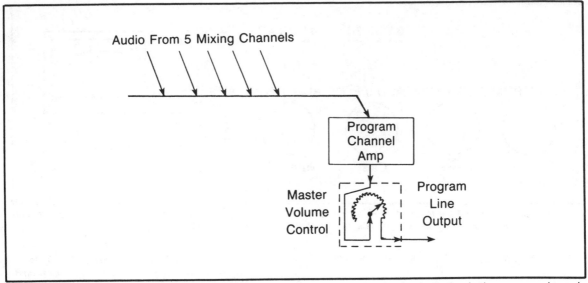

Fig. 3-6. Master volume control. Audio from a board's many mixing channels are mixed together in the program channel amplifier. The combined output of the program channel is controlled by the master volume control.

will operate. *If the master pot is turned all the way down, the board will be dead.*

Monitoring

Once the audio signal leaves the program channel amp, it is monitored in two ways: (1) the VU meter and (2) the program monitor speaker and headphones.

When you send an audio signal to the transmitter or to a tape recorder, set the volume level for peaks at 100% according to the board's VU meter. You should also listen to the air monitor speaker.

Inexperienced board operators often cause *dead air* by thinking they have put a tape or record on the air but were not observing the VU meters or listening to the air monitor. Anytime you put a new audio source on, double-check to make sure you have indeed put it on the air. Listen to the monitor and watch the VU meters!

Some boards have separate meters for the program channel and audition channel. Some boards share one meter for both with a switch provided to select between metering program or audition. Other

boards meter the program channel only, with no metering provided for the audition channel.

Virtually all audio consoles provide a separate, full-time amplifier and speaker for the cue system. Then one other high-quality amplifier and speaker system is provided for the other monitoring. The control room monitor speakers are switched between *audition, program,* and *air* (or *external*).

Most audio consoles provide a front panel switch for selecting the audio going to the control room speakers. They also have a volume control for the board operator's convenience in adjusting the monitor volume up and down.

Most radio stations have *air monitor* speakers set up in the lobby, offices, even the restroom so station personnel can hear the air monitor at all times. Otherwise, if the transmitter goes off the air, the operator might be the last to know!

Putting It All Together

The block diagram in Fig. 3-4 shows only one mixing channel, while Fig. 3-7 shows five mixing channels set side by side in an arrangement typical for a small control room console. For the sake of

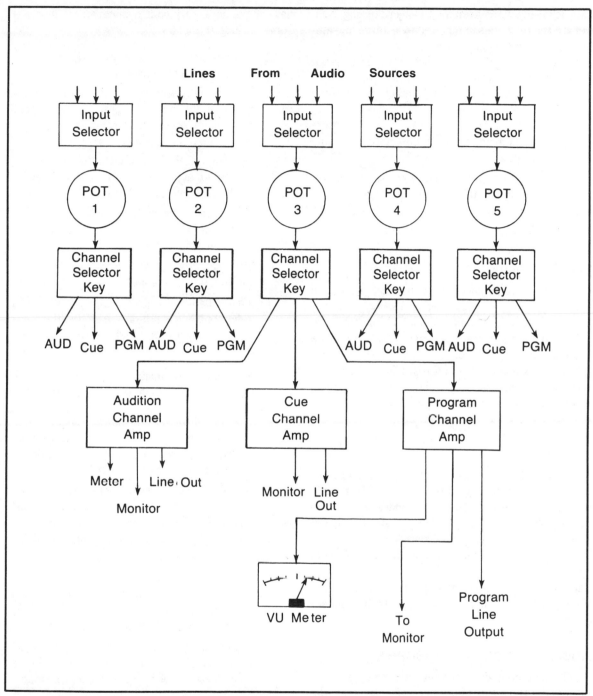

Fig. 3-7. Five-channel board block diagram. Five mixing channels like the one depicted in Fig. 3-4 are connected side by side to make a typical multichannel audio console. For simplicity, only mixing channel #3 is shown connected to the audition, cue, and program channel amplifiers.

simplicity, the wires from the Channel 3 mixing channel are the only ones completed to all three line amplifiers (audition, cue, program). The other channels are connected in the same way, although it is not shown in this drawing.

Notice again the following characteristics of the console:

☐ Some mixing pots handle more than one source.

☐ The output of each pot can be fed to any of three lines (audition, cur, or program).

☐ Only the program channel normally feeds an audio signal to the transmitter.

Warning Lights

When an announcer is on the air, the studio must be quiet to prevent unwanted sounds from being transmitted. Broadcast audio consoles are equipped to automatically turn on warning lights when a microphone is turned on. The lights indicate that there is a *live mike* in the studio. (A live mike is turned on and picking up audio.) Each microphone mixing channel operates a separate set of lights so that only the affected studio's lights come on.

Speaker Muting

Coupled to the warning light system is an automatic means of turning off the studio speaker when a live mike is present. This avoids undesirable *acoustic feedback* (a loud squealing sound). When the combo operator turns on the control room mike, the red warning light comes *on*, and the control room speaker goes dead. The combo operator must wear headphones to hear what is happening. It is very poor practice to operate the board with no headphones.

AUDIO CONSOLE ACCESSORIES

Radio station control rooms are busy, crowded places. Getting the operating controls of all the equipment within arm's reach of the operator is a task like solving a jigsaw puzzle. Control room and console designers have used many approaches to

have all the necessary controls nearby. Such accessories include the following:

☐ *Remote start/stop controls*—Operates the turntables, tape decks, and carts.

☐ *Headphone selectors*—Connects the control room headphones to program, audition, cue, remote, or other audio sources.

☐ *Studio routing switchers*—Used in stations where more than one control room might be on the air or when a studio can feed audio to the AM and/or FM transmitters.

☐ *Intercom*—In the audio console; allows operators and announcers to talk to each other from separate studios.

☐ *Automated tape machine controls*—Regulate the function of computer-operated studios.

☐ *Phone patch*—Controls selection of which telephone line is put on the air and the feeding of control room audio to the telephone line.

In addition to these many extra controls, several other things should be easily seen by the operator:

☐ *Bulletin alarm lights*—Indicate special messages are being received on the newsroom teletypes, the weather monitor radio, or the Emergency Broadcast Receiver.

☐ *Telephone light*—Indicates incoming calls by flashing a bright light in the control room; replaces the ringing bell on the telephone.

☐ *Studio warning lights*—Flash when a microphone is on in the studio.

☐ *Automation video terminal*—A TV screen showing what program events have been programmed into the computer that operates automated tape machines and audio mixers.

☐ *Transmitter meters*—Required by the FCC for monitoring purposes; it must be visible from the control room operating position.

Memorize the location of every switch and knob on the audio console you are working with. Try operating it while looking at the wall or ceiling.

THE PROGRAM LINE

The output of the program channel amplifier ultimately sends audio signals to the transmitter. After the program channel audio leaves the console, however, it must first go through the *distribution amplifier* and the *audio processor* (Fig. 3-8).

The distribution amplifier (also called the *DA*) is used to feed (or distribute) program line audio to several destinations at once. As shown in Fig. 3-9, each output of the DA is isolated from the others. Making or breaking connections at any one output will not change the signal level at any other output.

Program audio must be kept at a specific standard level (100% or zero VU) to ensure proper modulation of the transmitter. No other equipment should siphon off the program audio. Therefore, the DA feeds separate audio lines to the transmitter, each tape recorder, the lines to studio monitor amplifiers, and the phone patch.

In the normal operation of a control room, the operator is not concerned with the DA in any way unless it fails to operate. Never turn off the power to a DA, unless specifically instructed to do so by the chief engineer. Turning it off or adjusting it can disrupt the audio to the transmitter or other important pieces of equipment.

THE PATCH PANEL

Even a combo operator in the best-planned radio station can run into unforeseen circumstances. A special program or sudden equipment failure can require quick reconfiguration of the control room equipment. Constant rewiring is out of the question because it is slow, expensive, and impractical.

A permanent wiring setup that still permits quick, temporary changes is provided by the *patch panel*, (Fig. 3-10). This looks very much like an old-fashioned telephone operator's switchboard. The patch panel is made of rows of audio connectors, or *jacks*. The inputs and outputs of all studio equipment are connected to this jack field. The jacks automatically connect together in pairs when no patch cords are in place, and the audio source equipment is said to be *normalled through* to the board inputs when the audio is following its normal path.

If the occasion arises when a special interconnection of equipment is required, the patch panel allows the operator to do that quickly and simply. For instance, if an operator needs to transfer some music from record to tape without going through the board, a patch cord is connected from the "turntable out" jack to the "tape recorder in" jack. The audio then flows directly from the turntable to the tape recorder. If the patch cord is removed, the turntable once again is connected to the board input, and the recorder input is restored to the program line output.

There are several ways to organize the placement of the jacks in a patch panel. Standard practices exist, although they might not be used in every radio station.

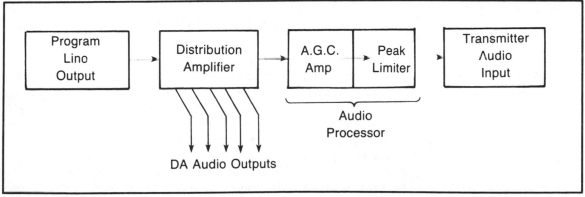

Fig. 3-8. Radio studio program line block diagram. Once the audio signals leave the control room audio console's program line output, the signals pass through a distribution amplifier, followed by an audio processor, and finally on to the transmitter's audio input.

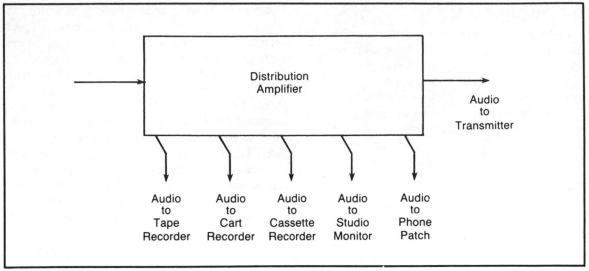

Fig. 3-9. Distribution amplifier. A distribution amplifier allows the single program line to feed many different audio lines without affecting each other.

Audio Flows from Top to Bottom

Refer to Fig. 3-10 to see how a typical patch panel is interconnected with an audio console. The audio sources are connected to the upper row of jacks, the upper row of jacks are normally connected to the bottom row of jacks, and the bottom row of jacks are connected to the inputs of the board. This automatic interconnection of outputs to inputs is called a *normalled through* connection. If a patch cord is inserted, the normal connection between jacks is broken, and audio is routed through the patch cord.

Order of the Jacks

There are two popular ways of arranging the jacks: (1) left to right in the same patterns as the board inputs or (2) grouped by types of equipment. In Fig. 3-10, the patch panel's jacks are arranged in the same order as the input selectors on the audio console.

The patch panel is connected between the audio source equipment and the inputs to the board itself, as shown in Fig. 3-10. This layout is a 5-channel board. Channels #1 and #2 are not routed through the patch panel because mike channels have to be reserved for full-time use and include the warn-

ing lights and studio speaker muting functions. Channels #3, #4, and #5 all have input selector switches, allowing these three mixing channels to handle a total of nine audio sources. The input selector switches are so constructed, however, that each mixing pot can handle audio from only one audio source at a time.

Patch panels also appear in other locations around the radio station. Special arrangements for temporary audio signal routing might be needed in the newsroom, production studio, and transmitter room.

The Routing Switcher

The plug-and-jack patch panel arrangement can be replaced with an array of push buttons called a *routing switcher*. This device can take many forms, but all models handle the signal routing function just described for patch panels. Routing switchers are very convenient and easy to operate. Some can even be computer-controlled.

Take plenty of time to get familiar with the arrangement of the jacks on the patch panel—someday you might find yourself in an emergency situation and your quick, deft patching will save the day. Do

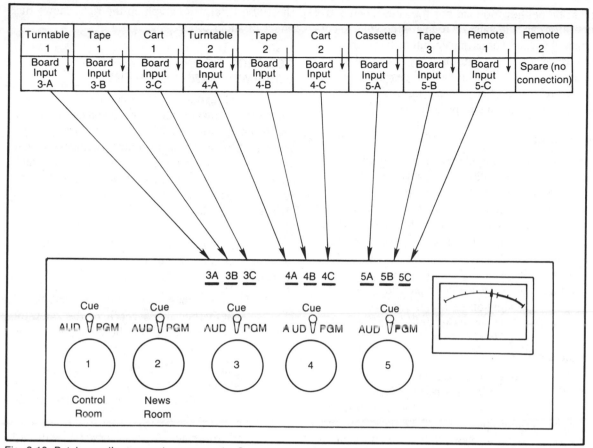

Turntable 1	Tape 1	Cart 1	Turntable 2	Tape 2	Cart 2	Cassette	Tape 3	Remote 1	Remote 2
Board Input 3-A	Board Input 3-B	Board Input 3-C	Board Input 4-A	Board Input 4-B	Board Input 4-C	Board Input 5-A	Board Input 5-B	Board Input 5-C	Spare (no connection)

Fig. 3-10. Patch panel's connection to console. Some audio patch panels are arranged in the same order as the inputs to the audio console. Audio sources appear in the top row of jacks and are normally connected internally to the corresponding audio console inputs. If a jack is inserted, the "normal" connection is broken, and a new temporary hookup can be established.

you want to look good? Get to know your patch panel well!

Warnings About Patching

1. Insert and pull out all patch cords by the body of the plug only. Do not place any mechanical strain on the cord, or the wires might break.

2. Always keep notes for other operators, explaining the patches you make. Include the following information:

   ☐ Patched from where
   ☐ Patched to where
   ☐ When the patch is no longer needed
   ☐ Name of person who made the patch

3. When you come on duty in the control room, check the patch panel immediately. If there are any patches, make sure they do not interfere with the operation of studio equipment you will need. If you find a patch with no tag on it, you are probably free to pull out the patch cord. If there are any engineers working nearby, ask them before removing the patch.

AUDIO PROCESSING

The audio signals being fed to the transmitter

must be neither too loud nor too soft. The control operator can ride gain, or regulate the volume constantly by hand, but having an automatic volume control is very useful. Automatically maintaining constant volume is done in two stages using (1) the automatic gain control amplifier (also called the AGC amp) and (2) the audio peak limiter.

AGC Amp

An AGC amp is placed in the program line to hold the average audio signal levels constant so that the peaks are near 100%. Some AGC amps are only compressors that turn down the volume if it gets too loud. Other AGC amps compress loud audio and also expand audio that is too soft, bringing it up to full volume.

More-elaborate AGC amps separate the bass, midrange, and treble audio frequencies, and control the gain separately on each of these three bands of frequencies. They are called *split-band AGC amps*.

Peak Limiter

An alert board operator and a good AGC amp are still not enough to prevent overmodulation. Sudden audio peaks are held to 100% with a peak limiter. As the graphs in Fig. 3-11 show, any audio less than 100% is allowed to pass through unaffected, but the output of the peak limiter is never louder than 100%. The left graph shows the audio signal from the board steadily rising until it passes the 100% level. The graph on the right shows the effect of audio processing.

CONTROL ROOM EQUIPMENT ARRANGEMENT

Physical layouts of radio control rooms vary. There are many considerations involved in arranging the equipment, and needs vary according to the station's format, available control room space, and the personal preferences of the station's staff. Therefore, there is no one best way to lay out a control room. There are, however, several guidelines that are helpful. Most control rooms may look something like the arrangement shown in Fig. 3-12.

Architects of radio studios often incorporate several common convenience factors into their designs:

☐ The horseshoe shape puts the most equipment within arm's reach of the operator without requiring that he or she leave the seat.

☐ Turntables are located forward enough to allow the operator to see the records. In a fast-paced show, this prevents starting the wrong turntable.

☐ Cart machines are also forward, with cart storage close by. At times, operators must make quick changes in carts, requiring minimum movement.

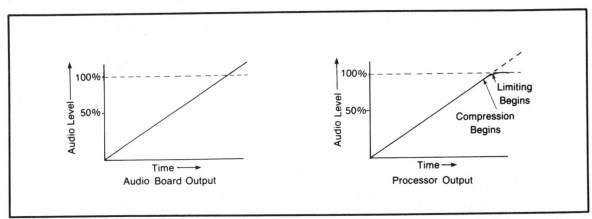

Fig. 3-11. Results of audio processing. As the signals from the audio board get louder, the signals from the processor also increase. As the program line volume approaches 100%, however, the processor starts leveling off the volume peaks, allowing none louder than 100%.

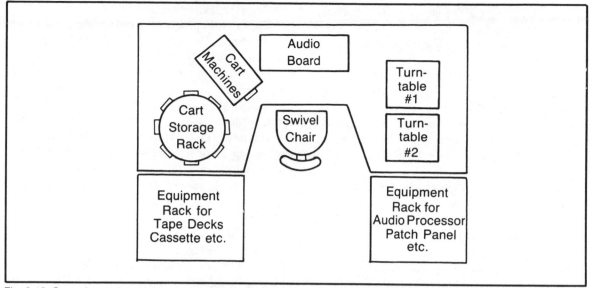

Fig. 3-12. Control room layout. No one studio layout is best for all situations. Most studios, however, wrap the equipment around the operator in an **L-** or **U**-shaped console to keep equipment within arm's reach.

☐ Other seldom used equipment is placed to the rear, though still within arm's reach of the seated operator.

The audio board is central to any control room and occupies the space directly front and center. Most consoles are less than 1 foot high, so it is convenient to mount a small easel or copy stand on top of the console. This puts scripts, notes, and record jackets directly in front of the operator's face. Often the copy stand is made of clear plastic, allowing the operator to see through it to a clock or to a window into an adjacent studio.

The control room must be designed with enough open space for good acoustics. The announcer and microphone should not be placed too closely to a studio window or a large flat surface. The sound reverberation can make the announcer's voice sound hollow and muffled.

If possible, the announcer either faces a sound-absorbing wall or is as far as possible from the studio windows. The microphone should not be aimed toward the studio window, or the reverb will be easily picked up. Relatively small changes in the mike placement can reap huge improvements in sound quality.

Likewise, the cart and tape machines must be mounted to minimize mechanical noise pickup by the studio microphone. Controls and switches are specially designed to operate with little or no noise. Any custom-made studio equipment must also be solidly built and silent in operation.

Control rooms should be arranged to allow easy access to the back sides of all equipment for servicing. If this access is possible without forcing the operator to move out of the operating position, so much the better. Unfortunately, many low-budget radio stations with small studios overlook the need for easy access to the equipment. Servicing and repairs are frustrated as a result.

It is very important to keep all control room wiring neat, orderly, and well marked. A sloppy layout wastes time in an emergency when people are trying to effect repairs. You might never be directly involved in studio construction or remodeling, but if you ever influence your station toward orderliness, you will have done your employer a good deed.

WRAP-UP

The audio board contains controls for selecting audio sources to be aired, controlling the volume level of the audio signals, routing and mixing the audio, and monitoring the results. The audio from the pots or faders can be routed by the channel selector switches to any of three line amps: audition, cue, or program.

VU meters provide an accurate means of measuring the loudness of an audio signal. Federal regulation and good broadcast practice require that audio peaks from all audio sources be in the 85% to 100% range to avoid sudden changes in volume. The studio speakers and house monitors help the operator keep track of what is on the air.

The audio console also provides for studio warning lights to notify people when a microphone has been turned on. It automatically turns off the studio speaker to prevent feedback. Other accessories can be incorporated into the board to allow for remote start/stop of equipment, intercom, phone patch, and headphone audio control. Other studio accessories include bulletin alarm lights, telephone lights, and

possibly a computer terminal.

The board's program channel audio leaves the board and goes through an audio distribution amplifier. This allows the program channel to be fed to the transmitter without undesirable effects from the house monitor, phone patch, or tape machine inputs.

The program line from the DA to the transmitter undergoes audio processing to ensure that the transmitter gets the proper audio signal levels. Processing involves automatic gain control (also called compression) followed by peak limiting of extra loud audio signals and can include split-band processing of bass, mid-range, and treble frequencies separately.

While many factors influence how a specific control room is arranged, the major goal is to provide the operator with convenience and efficiency. Ease of servicing the equipment by the engineering staff is also important.

Exercise 3-1   Audio Console Experiences

Goal: To develop awareness of the operational routines used by the combo operator by performing several simple drills with the console controls.

Method: In each case, work on accuracy first, then speed.

Input Selector Drill

1. "Clear the board" so that no inputs are selected and all pots are at zero.
2. Have an associate call out the names of each audio source in random order (tape 3, cart 1, turntable 2, etc.).
3. Operate the input selector, mixing the pot and channel selector to get the source on the air.

Riding Gain

1. Use a record in which the song ends by fading out gradually.
2. Play the end of the record, starting several seconds before the conclusion.
3. When the fadeout occurs on the record, use the mixing pot to hold the volume peaks at 100% as long as possible.

Crossfades

1. Play two records: one with the level at 100% and the other completely "potted down" to zero.
2. Operate the gain pots simultaneously, fading one down while fading the other up. Keep the meters peaking at 100% all through the crossfade.
3. Practice crossfades at different rates, some fast and some more slowly.

Clipping Short

1. Play a recorded speech or newscast on a tape machine.

2. At the end of a sentence, quickly pot down before the next sentence begins.

3. Try again, but flip the channel selector key off the program line to the audition channel at the end of the sentence instead of potting down.

VU Meter Action

1. Play a hard rock record with the audio peaks at 100%.

2. Watch the movement of the meter and try to relate its movements to the sounds coming from the record.

Exercise 3-2.   Audio Processor Observations

Goal: Become familiar with the effect of the audio processor on program audio. Note the gradual volume reduction (or compression) as the board levels approach 100% and the clipping action for levels over 100%.

Method:
1. Watch the meters on the AGC amp when normal-volume program material is playing through it.

2. Make the following observations:

   a. Note that the AGC amp meters are at rest during silent or low-volume passages.

   b. Note that during loud program material, the meters kick up, indicating that automatic gain reduction is taking place.

Exercise 3-3   Patching Practice

Goal: Become familiar with the layout and use of the patch panel in your studio so that you can make patches quickly and accurately.

Method: Caution! Do not make any patches that will affect the station's ability to stay on the air!

1. Patch a turntable so that it appears on a board input marked for a tape machine. Play a record to verify that you have successfully made the patch.

2. Patch a remote line into the board, using any pot that is available on the patch panel.

3. Use the patch panel to connect the phone patch to a tape recorder input. Record yourself picking up the telephone and speaking briefly into it. (Note. It is illegal to record a telephone conversation without the permission of the person at the other end!)

Exercise 3-4.   Studio Equipment Sketches

Spend at least one hour in a radio station control room while making the following drawings. One hour may be insufficient to complete all of these drawings. Don't rush!

1. Draw a view from above the control room showing the placement of the operating desk, audio console, turntable, and equipment racks and any other major components in the room.

2. Make a sketch of each equipment rack in the control room showing what pieces of equipment are in each rack.

3. Sketch the patch panel showing what each jack is for (just write in what each label says).

Exercise 3-5.   Studio Observation Program Event Logs

Spend at least one hour observing a combo operator during an air shift.

1. Make a program event log similar to the one described in the exercises at the end of Chapter 1.
2. Note the audio source of each program event (announcer, turntable 1, turntable 2, cart 1, cart 2, reel 1, reel 2, remote, newsroom, etc.).

Vocabulary

accoustic feedback	FCC	output
air monitor	gain	overmodulation
AGC	input	patch
AGC amp	input selector	patch bay
amp, amplifier	jack	patch panel
audio processor	jack field	peak limiter
audition channel	layout	phone patch
balance	level	pot, potentiometer
board	limiter	production studio
channel selector keys	load down	program channel
clipped audio	mixing channel	riding gain
compression	modulation	signal
copy stand	modulation percentage	signal routing
crossfade	monitor	split band
dead air	mono	stage
decibel (dB)	noise	stereo
distortion	normalled connection	VU, volume unit, VU meter
distribution amp, DA	on duty, off duty	watt
fader		

Chapter 4

Handling Program Materials

Any job in broadcasting requires that you handle the program materials properly. This involves much more than just blowing the dust out of the record grooves. You need to know what program material to put on the air, when to air it, where you can get it, how to handle it, how to label it, and where to put it when you're done.

This chapter covers these aspects of handling program materials and focuses on several categories:

☐ *Format*—Guidelines used by a station to decide what to air and when to air it.

☐ *Handling*—The right and wrong ways to physically use records, tapes, and scripts (Fig. 4-1).

☐ *Filing*—Organizing tapes, records, and scripts within the radio station so that the correct program material gets on the air.

☐ *Labeling*—Identifying each tape, record and script for quick recognition by all station personnel.

☐ *Distribution*—Sources of program material, how programs get to the station, and disposal of used materials.

A whole book could be written about each category. For now, however, you only need to absorb the main points. Once you begin working in a radio station, you will quickly find that each station has its own special way of doing things. Remember, these methods for dealing with program materials are sensible, efficient, and involve a minimum chance for error.

FORMAT

Decades of broadcasting have led to the development of some traditional ways of doing things. The listeners have become accustomed to these traditions where they affect the arrangement of the radio program material heard on the air. Some of these traditions include:

1. Station identification by call letters and city at the top of each hour

Fig. 4-1. Proper handling. Be careful to hold loose reels of tape up on edge. Laying it flat can send you for a loop!

2. Newscast at the top of each hour
3. Weather forecast at the end of every newscast
4. Frequent information updates during morning and evening rush hour or drive time
5. Development of the combo operator's radio personality so that he or she becomes part of the entertainment
6. Musical selections played from tapes and records rather than live performances

Some of these traditions are now required by law, while others have evolved over many years of trial and error by radio programmers. Because variations in practice occur within these traditions, do not cast your ideas in concrete. The "traditions" are presented as guidelines to help orient you to general broadcast practice.

Tradition #1: Station Identification ("ID")

The FCC has established that all radio stations must identify themselves clearly. The FCC assigns *call letters* to each radio station. Each set of call letters is unique to each station. FCC rules require that the radio station announce its call letters and city at the top of each hour.

Stations can make the *ID announcement* more often than hourly and need not identify at the top of the hour if it would interrupt a program. If not done at the top of the hour, however, the station ID should come at the next possible break in the program.

When you are the on-air combo operator, you must remember to make the station's ID announcements. It is required by law and is good for the station's public image. Call signs are discussed in more detail in Chapter 10.

Tradition #2:
Newscasts at the Top of the Hour

Predictability. Dependability. Both are words that should be associated with all radio broadcast operations. Nearly all radio stations offer newscasts as a part of their formats, and the most likely time to catch radio news on the air is at the top of the hour. In most cases, the newscast begins immediately following the hourly station ID announcement.

Some stations program a five-minute newscast beginning at five minutes before the hour, particu- if they also offer a network news service at the top of the hour. Some stations have their news at another time, such as at the bottom of the hour or every other hour. The listeners expect news at the top of the hour.

Tradition #3: Weather Forecasts

Very few parts of the world have weather so boring that the local radio station finds it unnecessary to broadcast the weather predictions. Nearly every radio station features regular weather forecasts during its broadcast day. As with news, the listeners are accustomed to hearing the weather at certain times. Local newscasts commonly begin with a very brief look at the local weather. If the weather itself is a major news item, that story generally runs first in the news.

A full weather forecast is always included in a local news segment. If the local news program runs longer than five minutes, the first five-minute segment often ends with a brief weather forecast before continuing with more news. A newscast of any length should always end with the current temperature and the latest weather forecast. The pie chart and format list in Fig. 4-2 mention where weather updates might occur in a typical 15-minute period.

As a service to the listeners, most radio stations also have regularly scheduled weather forecasts at other times, such as 15 minutes after the hour, the bottom of the hour, and 15 minutes before the top of the hour. Other stations broadcast the weather during the newscast, at 20 minutes past the top of the hour, and again at 20 minutes before the top of the hour.

Tradition #4: Drive-Time Information Updates

North Americans rely heavily on the automo-

bile for transportation to and from work; therefore, the car radio has become an important part of many people's lives. Radio stations recognize this fact and pack the morning and evening drive times with extra information. Weather, time and temperature, traffic information, and frequent news headlines are popular ingredients of radio at these times of the day. The listener has learned to expect it. A station that ignores these needs presents a radio program that might seem incomplete.

Tradition #5:
The Combo Operator as a "Personality"

A radio announcer must never detract from a radio show, but a good announcer can add to it by injecting his or her personality, assuming it is done in a friendly or appealing manner. Truly skilled radio personalities have high value as entertainers, and the music or information they present is secondary. Successful radio personalities know what the audience wants to hear.

Tradition #6: Recorded Music

In the early days of radio, the recording industry was also in its infancy. Broadcasters relied heavily on "live" talent, including the employment of studio orchestras. When high-quality records of musical performances became popular and available, radio stations made good use of these records as program material, and studio orchestras slowly faded away. Now most music heard on the radio is distributed by record or compact disc, although the radio station can transfer its records to tape to avoid the wear and damage caused by repeated use.

The Format is the Station's Character

Bringing all of these traditions, as well as others, into proper coordination requires that a radio station decide upon a *format*. A format is a set of guidelines used by a station to decide what to air and when to air it. This list of standard radio station formats, indicating the wide variety of formats used, is from the *Broadcasting and Cablecasting Yearbook—1987* (pages F-68 to F-96).

Adult Contemporary	Country and Western	Gospel	Portugese
Agriculture and Farm	Disco	Greek	Progressive
Album-oriented Rock (AOR)	Discussion	Hardcore	Public Affairs
Alternative	Drama/Literature	Inspirational	Reggae
American Indian	Easy Listening	Italian	Religious
Beautiful Music	Educational	Jazz	Rock/AOR
Big Band	Eskimo	Light Rock	Sacred
Black	Ethnic	Middle of the Road (MOR)	Soul
Bluegrass	Finnish	Native American	Spanish
Blues	Folk	News	Talk
Chinese	Foreign Language/Ethnic	New Wave	Top 40
Christian	Free Form	Nostalgia	Underground
Classical	French	Oldies	Urban Contemporary
Classic Rock	German	Other	Variety
Comedy	Golden Oldies	Polish	
Contemporary Hit/Top 40	Good Music	Polka	

(From the Broadcasting/Cablecasting Yearbook 1987. Reprinted by permission.)

A radio station's general format refers to the dominant kind of programming it offers. Some stations are all-news and some play hard rock. Others are country and western music-oriented. "Format" takes on a slightly different meaning when specifically applied to a station's schedule of programs and individual program segments during the broadcast day. Then the format is a highly structured schedule of exactly what happens when. Some radio stations go so far as to collect these schedules, or program formats, in a book.

If a format is used frequently, a large chart can be drawn up and posted on the studio wall for quick reference. Two different kinds of format charts are used:

1. *Format list*—Names each event and gives specific instructions as needed.

2. *Pie chart*—A round graph divided up into sections showing how much time is devoted to each event.

Both are illustrated in Fig. 4-2, giving the format for a 10-minute radio newscast. Take the time to read everything in both examples, then decide which is more specific and precise, and which is easier to refer to at a glance. The pie chart format is very graphic, but not much information can be crammed into it. The format list must be read with a bit more care, but it contains specific and accurate information. In broadcast practice, either kind of chart can be used, depending on the specific situation.

The pie chart is especially helpful when the music director of a radio station wants the music arranged in a certain way, as in Fig. 4-3. This helps the combo operator select specific songs to play so that they coordinate well with other program events during the broadcast day.

The music format pie chart in Fig. 4-3 shows that the first song following a newscast is always fast-paced and energetic. The next song is a current Top-10 hit record. Following the weather forecast, the DJ plays an *oldie*, a song more than five years old, and plays another oldie just before the sports at 40 minutes past the hour. The last record before the newscast is an instrumental, which can be faded out to keep the start of the newscast on schedule. The other sections of the chart show where commercials go, and the remaining music is optional or chosen by the combo operator. The pie chart allows the music director to determine the mix of music, including how many oldies get played every hour versus how many current hit records.

Figure 4-4 is another kind of pie chart that indicates what not to do. The music director might want to avoid certain clashing kinds of music. The combo operator uses this chart to see what kinds of records should not be played in sequence. So long as the two records chosen are not adjacent on the pie chart, and fit into the format chart, the combo operator is free to play them.

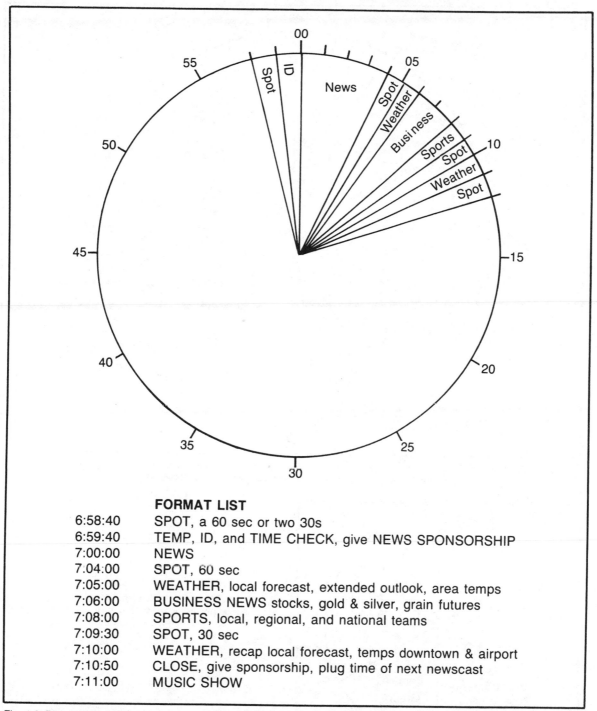

FORMAT LIST

6:58:40	SPOT, a 60 sec or two 30s
6:59:40	TEMP, ID, and TIME CHECK, give NEWS SPONSORSHIP
7:00:00	NEWS
7:04:00	SPOT, 60 sec
7:05:00	WEATHER, local forecast, extended outlook, area temps
7:06:00	BUSINESS NEWS stocks, gold & silver, grain futures
7:08:00	SPORTS, local, regional, and national teams
7:09:30	SPOT, 30 sec
7:10:00	WEATHER, recap local forecast, temps downtown & airport
7:10:50	CLOSE, give sponsorship, plug time of next newscast
7:11:00	MUSIC SHOW

Fig. 4-2. Pie chart and format list. The pie chart shows patterns of programming at a glance, while the format list is better for showing detailed format information.

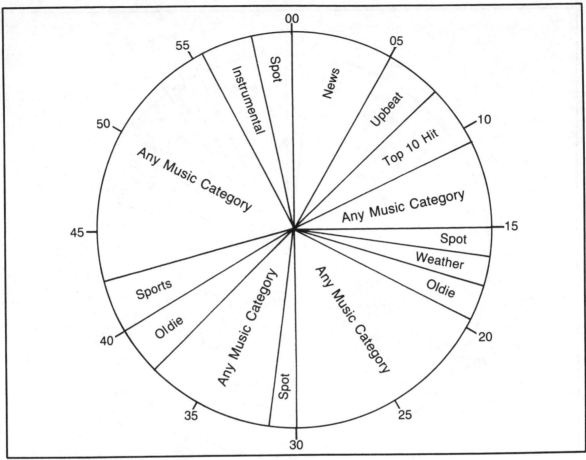

Fig. 4-3. Music format pie chart. A broadcast hour is mapped out here, showing what kind of music to play during different segments of the hour. Scheduled breaks for commercials, weather, sports, and news also appear.

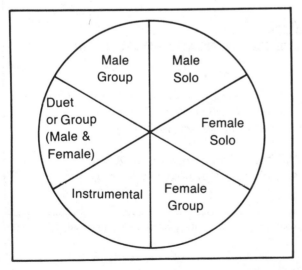

Fig. 4-4. Music mix pie chart. Some stations control the mixture of songs played by using this format to show what *not* to do: *don't* play two songs back-to-back if their descriptions on this chart are next to each other.

Some stations have very strict formats that must be followed carefully by the on-air personalities. Other stations use pie charts and formats just to give the staff a general guideline. Other stations merely restrict the available records, letting the operators use their own judgment on what music to play. Be sure to find out what the format policies are in any station you work for so that you can help promote the station's chosen image.

HANDLING

The tapes, records, carts, and scripts used in radio stations are the lifeblood that keeps the stations going. You must treat these materials carefully to avoid damage, loss, or confusion. With all of these you should:

- ☐ Avoid dropping, bending, entangling, or marking them.
- ☐ Avoid contaminating them with food, drinks, or dirty hands.
- ☐ Label everything clearly.
- ☐ Store them correctly in the proper place, with the title or label oriented for easy reading.
- ☐ Always put away records, tapes, and scripts so that the next person can find them.

Keep records in their paper, cardboard, or plastic dust jackets, and cleaned with a special cloth or record-cleaning brush. Be careful when placing the stylus on the record and also while cueing and removing the needle so that the record is not damaged. Never lay a record down flat on a table or place anything on top of a record.

Do not crush open reel tapes or the reel will break, causing damage to the edges of the tape. Hold reels upright—Fig. 4-1 shows what happens if you don't! Thread the ends of the tape smoothly into the reels. A sloppy threading job will crease each layer of the tape, which will be heard on the air in the form of *dropouts* or momentary lost audio.

Never drop, throw, or crush a cart. Some carts have pencil leads glued inside as a part of the reel surface. Dropped carts can loosen the pencil leads, which can cause the cart to jam and stop suddenly. Carts that have been crushed or broken in some other way also become very troublesome. Both carts and reel-type tapes must be clean to deliver a good performance. If you must touch the tape itself, wash your hands first to remove dirt and grease that could damage the tape surface.

Do not fold or mark in any way that would make them harder to read. Refile them when not in use. While some stations permit you to mark on the scripts, do so with light pencil marks so your notes don't confuse the next announcer.

FILING

During each broadcast day, several hundred tapes, records, and scripts pass through the hands of each announcer and engineer. It is vitally important that all of this material be organized. The *copy book* is a notebook with all commercial scripts filed inside in alphabetical order by the name of the sponsor.

The *day book* is a variation on the copy book in which only the scripts needed for a particular day are inserted. The day book can be organized alphabetically but is usually arranged in consecutive order according to the program schedule for the day. If one script is needed more than once during the day, several copies are made with one at each required location in the book.

The *daily play bin* is a large compartment for each day of the week containing all the records, tapes, and scripts needed for that particular day. Some radio stations have play bins for each day of the month.

The *card box* is a collection of very short scripts for public service announcements, community events, etc. These can be dropped in at the announcer's discretion.

Computerized scripts from inexpensive word processing computers are now in many radio stations. The announcer can display scripts on a video screen to replace the day book and card box in everyday use. Computers can fail, however, so *hard copy* is usually available in a notebook somewhere close by.

Personal bins are compartments for each announcer where he or she can store records, tapes, and scripts temporarily. It can also serve as an employee mailbox.

Program bins are assigned for storage of specific program tapes or records. If the station plays a taped program every week, the tape is held in the program bin until the day it is aired, then the program director relocates it to the daily play bin.

Records can be stored in several ways in a radio station's music library. They can be arranged:

- [ ] *Alphabetically* by artist's name
- [ ] *Numerically* by record company and number
- [ ] *Categorically*, either alphabetically or numerically, but grouped by "female vocal," "male vocal," "vocal group," "instrumental," or any other category desired

Regardless of what record filing system exists at your station, use it to refile all your records.

LABELING

All program materials need to be labeled clearly so that all staff members can locate what they need. As a combo operator, you are most likely to label tapes and carts that you have recorded. Scripts and records will most likely be labeled by someone in the station who is trained specifically for the job, following a long-standing format. If you need to label any of these materials, use other previously labeled scripts or records as a guide.

Labeling Tapes (Open Reels)

When you are responsible for recording something—whether it is a commercial, a *feed* from the network, or a recorded program intended for airplay later—you should pay close attention to the proper labeling of the tape. A well-recorded tape that is *lost* is useless.

Assuming you have just recorded a 15-minute interview program called "Focus on City Hall," here are the steps you should take to label it properly, resulting in something that looks like Fig. 4-5.

```
FOCUS ON CITY HALL
recorded May 10
15 min
```

Fig. 4-5. Proper tape labeling. Put a self-stick label on the tape reel of a program you have recorded for later broadcast. Keep it simple and clear.

- [ ] Put a self-stick label on the tape reel.
- [ ] Put a similar label on the outside edge of the tape box.
- [ ] Fill out a cue sheet with full recording information and place it inside the tape box.
- [ ] Remove any other labels on the reel and box, or cross them out so that only the current labels are readable.

The Cue Sheet

If a tape has only one *cut*, such as the 15-minute program "Focus on City Hall," the cue sheet only needs to identify the title, participants, record date, play date, and technical information. Assume, instead, that "Focus on City Hall" is a five-part series of five-minute programs, all on one tape. Then the cue sheet should include all of the previous information plus a rundown of the contents of the tape, either written below, on the back, or on a second page (Fig. 4-6).

The main purpose of the cue sheet is to instantly identify what is on the tape and any information required to ensure its proper playback. Be sure you write clearly and accurately.

Here is an explanation of the cue sheet shown in Fig. 4-6:

Reel #—Some radio stations assign each reel of tape a house number that aids in keeping inventory.

Title—Identifies the program content on the reel of tape.

Rec date—The date the program was recorded.

Airs—The date the program is scheduled for airplay.

Participants—Gives names of everyone involved on-mike.

Speed—The tape machine recording speed, in inches per second.

Full/half track—Indicates record head format; recording engineer should cross out whatever does not apply.

Stereo/mono—Cross out whatever doesn't apply.

Original/Copy—The original tape gives the best sound reproduction. Keep the original in a safe place and use copies in everyday situations.

Save/Reuse—Check appropriate blank. Even a "reuse" tape should be saved for a few days after the air date.

Recorded on tape machine #—Knowing what machine was used is helpful if later editing is re-

quired. The same machine can then be used for that particular tape. This gives the most consistent audio quality.

Recording engineer's initials—Always note the name or initials of the recording engineer. This is good to know if there are questions about the recording.

Length—Be sure to write down the program length accurately in minutes and seconds.

Cut—In multiple recordings on the same reel of tape, the cut number is important information for keeping things straight. Number each segment. Count any false starts or errors as a separate cut and indicate them on the cue sheet.

Contents—Give the formal title for the program or a brief description that distinguishes each cut from the others.

End cue—(not shown in Fig. 4-6)—This

REEL # 28   TITLE Focus on City Hall

REC DATE May 10   AIRS May 13-17

PARTICIPANTS Mayor Joe Smith, Bill Jones

SPEED 7½   FULL/HALF   STEREO/MONO

ORIGINAL/COPY   SAVE/REUSE

RECORDED ON TAPE MACHINE: Pro Studio # 3

RECORDING ENGINEER'S INITIALS: EBH

PROGRAM LENGTH:

Cut	Contents	Length
1	New Town Park	4:58
2	Flood Damage	5:01
3	New Ambulance	4:55
4	Police + Fire Contracts	4:57
5	Town Census Projections	5:00

Fig. 4-6. Tape cue sheet. The cue sheet lists essential information about the contents of a reel of tape.

can also be written as "Q.") The cue sheet is also used to warn the operator of the presence of a test tone at the beginning of the tape. Include a special warning if the tape has been made *tails out* (rewind before playing).

Cart Labels

Tape carts have very little space for labels but usually need less information on them. The label sticks onto the edge of the cart opposite the opening for the tape heads. A typical cart label is shown in Fig. 4-7. Here is an explanation of the information shown on the sample label:

C-84—The cart's house number, similar to the reel number on tapes. This cart contains a commercial, and it is cart number 84.

Grants—The name of the store buying commercial time.

Air cond—The abbreviation indicates that this spot is about air conditioners. There might be other Grants spots for other kinds of products, so this extra information is helpful and significant.

:60—The spot is exactly 60 seconds long and can be written :60 or 1:00. The time stated on the cart label must be accurate *to the second*. If the spot is 59 seconds long, mark the time on the label as :59; do not round it off to :60.

Copy—Look in the copy book for additional instructions about this spot, possibly a live tag announcement.

Kill 5/16—Means that you must not play this spot after May 16.

CRH—Write the initials of the in-house announcer on the label. Sometimes the combo operators wants to avoid playing two spots back-to-back using the same announcer's voice.

| C-84 | GRANTS air cond | :60 |
| copy | kill 5/16 | CRH |

Fig. 4-7. Cart label. The end of a tape cart is labeled with simple information describing the spot.

Record Labels

Records are labeled by the manufacturer. Close inspection reveals a wealth of information including: song title, length, composer and lyric writer, any famous backup artists, and the music licensing company that owns the copyright to the record.

The radio station's music director will probably add labels to the records with additional information, such as, when the record was received at the station, which cuts are recommended for airplay, and record library catalog number (for easy refiling). Single records might be marked to show point of first audio.

DISTRIBUTION

Radio program material comes to the station on any of several media. Most music is distributed on disc, although stations that subscribe to a special music *syndication* service probably receive their music on large reels of tape.

Compact discs are promising media for program distribution in the future because they offer the possibility of the cuts being played in user-selected order. The random access capability of compact disc players makes them ideal for automated radio stations.

Besides the music, radio stations receive other kinds of programs on disc and tape. Careful recording techniques allow one LP (long-playing) record to hold two programs of 30 minutes each or four, 15-minute programs. Several weekly features and programs are distributed this way. The record is played once and discarded. Other programs are distributed on tapes that are usually mailed back and reused.

Communications satellites have revolutionized network program distribution. Formerly, all network affiliated stations received network programs on special dedicated telephone lines. More stations are now erecting satellite receiving dishes and picking up their network programs directly from network headquarters via satellites orbiting in space.

WRAP-UP

Program materials are the lifeblood of any radio station, and all station employees should know how to ensure the safety and quality of program materials. This is accomplished by carefully selecting format and by properly handling, filing, labeling, and distributing all program materials.

Formats, procedures, and guidelines exist because the listener expects dependable, predictable broadcast operations. Your first goal is to serve the needs of the audience. Once you understand your particular station's procedures, then you might consider offering suggestions for improvements.

Exercise 4-1.   Making Pie Charts

Goal: Generate pie charts to demonstrate that different radio stations have different formats.

Method: Go back and look over the Program Events exercises at the end of Chapter 1. Use the information you gathered there to make a pie chart showing each station's format. Make additional observations and program event logs if need be. Then answer the following questions based on the stations *you* observed.

1. When during the hour were the newscasts run?
2. How long was each station's newscast?
3. Did all stations have local news?
4. Did all stations have network news?
5. Besides news, what other information was included in the newscast (such as sports, business news, recreational information, etc.)?

Exercise 4-2.   Weather Forecast Formats

Use a tape recorder to record a radio station's weather forecast. Now record the weather forecast from a different radio station. Play the tape back as many times as necessary to answer the following questions.

1. Make a list of the kinds of weather information that was included in each forecast: weather conditions, wind direction and speed, likelihood of rain or snow, high temperature, low temperature, current wind, barometric pressure, and temperature.
2. Were any special weather-related conditions mentioned in association with the weather forecast? (Look for items such as tanning index, air quality alerts, snow depth, how much rain fell during the past 24 hours, or when high and low tides will occur.)
3. What time periods were covered by each forecast? How far into the future was the weather predicted?

Exercise 4-3.   Drive Time Information

Goal: Use a specialized program event chart to measure whether a radio station emphasized drive time information.

Method: Listen to a specified kind of radio station, using a copy of the chart in Table 4-1 to note each time certain information is mentioned. Repeat the exercise for each of four different kinds of radio station. For example:

☐ Small-market local AM station
☐ Major-market AM station
☐ FM rock or country music station
☐ FM easy listening station

Table 4-1. Drive-Time Information Log

Observer's Name:

Date of Observation:

Station Call Letters and Frequency:

Time Observation Began:

Listen to each station for 20 minutes during drive time on a weekday morning or afternoon. (You can record the broadcasts if you wish.) List the time in minutes and seconds that each kind of information is given.

Current Time Given	Current Temperature Given	Weather Forecast Read	Traffic Conditions Reported	Station ID or Slogan Announced

Based on your observations of each station, answer the following questions:

1. Which station gave information the most frequently? Which gave it the least?
2. What kind of format was used by the station that gave the most information? (Use the list of standard formats given in this chapter.)
3. What kind of format was used by the station that gave the least information?
4. Compare the small-market station observations with the major-market station. What differences do you notice in the kind of information given?

Exercise 4-4.   Use Of Radio Personalities

Goal: Make a simple program log to note how often the live announcer is used as a program event. Compare announcer use of radio stations having different formats.

Method: Listen to a specified kind of radio station, using a copy of the chart in Table 4-2 to note each time certain information is mentioned. Repeat the exercise for each of four different kinds of radio station. For example:

☐ Small-market local AM station
☐ Major-market AM station
☐ FM rock or country music station
☐ FM easy listening station

Table 4-2. Announcer Program Event Log

Observer's Name:

Date of Observation:

Station Call Letters and Frequency:

Time Observation Began:

Listen to each station for 20 minutes during drive time on a weekday morning or afternoon. (You can record the broadcasts if you wish.) List the time in minutes and seconds that each kind of information is given.

Current Time Given	Gives News, Sports, Time, or Weather	Makes Comments About Music	Delivers Commercials	Other Announcing

Based on your observations of each station, answer the following questions:

1. Which station (give call letters) used a live announcer the least frequently? Which used the announcer the most?
2. What kind of format was used by the station that used the live announcer the most? (Use the list of standard formats given in this chapter.)
3. What kind of format was used by the station that used the announcer the least?
4. Compare the small-market station observations with the major-market station. What differences do you notice in the kind of information given?

Exercise 4-5.   Labeling Records

Goal: This is an "open-ended" exercise in which you will discover various facets of organizing and using a record library. This exercise assumes that you have access to a radio station.

Method: Answer the questions to determine how your radio station's record library is organized. An all-news radio station is not suitable for this exercise.

1. What kind of music is played on your radio station?
2. When the DJ plays the music, what kind of program material does he/she handle? (Examples: 45 rpm, LP albums, CD discs, carts, reel-to-reel tapes)
3. Who chooses the specific music selections to be played; the DJ, the music librarian, the music director, or the program director?
4. Who is responsible for pulling the music from the music library and collecting it for airplay?

5. Who is responsible for returning and refiling the music in the library after it has been played?

6. Some record libraries subdivide the records into sections much like the pie chart in Fig. 4-4. How are the records subdivided in your record library?

7. Within a subgroup, how are the records organized? (Example: numerically by record company catalog number, alphabetically by recording artist's last name, or by an assigned index number?)

8. Does your record library have some kind of indexing system? If so, what kind? (Example: index card, notebook, computer)

9. If your record library has an indexing system, list each way you can sort the records listed. (Example: by artist's name, by composer's name, by song title, etc.)

Vocabulary

after the hour	drive time	oldie
before the hour	dropouts	personality
bottom of the hour	format	prerecorded
call letters	hit record	radio personality
copy book	ID	Top 10
cue sheet	local news	
day book	LP record	

Chapter 5

Broadcast Transmitters

As a combo operator, you will probably be required to keep an eye on the transmitter. Do not be afraid of transmitters, just respect them. They contain lethal high-voltages inside but can be safely operated by nontechnical persons. Routine transmitter operation requires very little skill and time, as long as the operator follows proper operating procedures.

WHAT THE COMBO OPERATOR IS EXPECTED TO KNOW

Routine operation of a broadcast transmitter is no more complex than keeping an eye on the dashboard gauges of your car. In the case of broadcast transmitters, however, you might have to write down some numbers periodically. This involves looking at various meters and writing their readings into a log book. Meter readings require less than five minutes of your time and are taken at least once every three hours. You will occasionally adjust the output power, switch antenna patterns (if you work for an AM directional station), or turn the antenna heaters on and off. Some transmitters are very de-

pendable and might even be computer controlled, requiring no human supervision unless they signal for help.

Transmitter duty is not very time-consuming, but the operator must be alert to any small problems before they turn into big ones. Never make any unauthorized adjustments to the transmitter. Only make adjustments and repairs that the chief engineer has specifically instructed you to make. You can cause serious damage and destruction to transmitting equipment if you engage in random or uninformed knob twisting. Call the chief engineer if you suspect that the transmitter is in trouble.

THE FUNCTION OF A TRANSMITTER

A *transmitter* is an electronic device that combines relatively weak audio signals with powerful radio frequency signals. The combined audio and radio signals are then fed to an antenna and radiated out into space for reception by listeners. The block diagram of a radio transmitter in Fig. 5-1 shows the major functions. There really isn't a lot happening

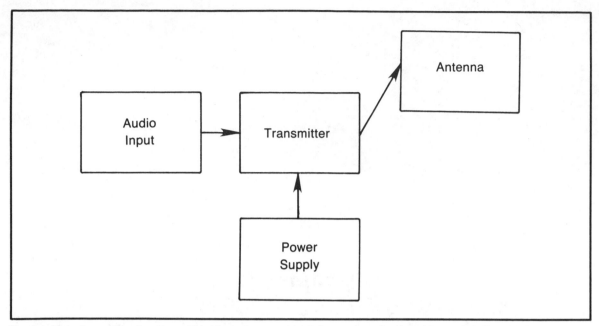

Fig. 5-1. Major transmitter functions. This block diagram shows that a transmitter combines relatively weak program audio signals with powerful radio wave signals and feeds them to the antenna.

inside the transmitter compared to other pieces of equipment in a radio station. Any transmitter engineer, electronic technician, or ham radio operator could quickly tell you that many things have been left out of this diagram. As the nontechnical combo operator, however, you need to know only these four main transmitter stages:

☐ *Audio input*-receives the audio signals from the control room via the program line and feeds it into the transmitter.

☐ *Power supply*-takes commercial electricity and converts it to the proper voltages needed by the transmitter to make radio signals.

☐ *Transmitter*-makes radio frequency signals and combines them with the audio input signals into a modulated radio signal.

☐ *Antenna*-is a metal structure that takes the modulated radio signal from the transmitter and sends the electromagnetic radio waves into space.

Any transmitting setup includes these basic functions. TV transmitters and stereo AM or FM transmitters have additional inputs, however.

THE AUDIO INPUT: MODULATION

The process of combining the audio signals with the radio frequency signals is called *modulation*, defined as "the process of change." When no audio signals are being sent to the transmitter, the radio frequency signals are steady or unchanged, and only silence or *dead air* is being transmitted. When the transmitter is on the air transmitting dead air, it is called an *unmodulated carrier*.

If the audio being fed from the control room has peaks at the 100% level on the audio console meter, and all other program line audio levels are correct, the transmitter receives audio signals that cause 100% modulation. The transmitter is fully modulated. This means that the transmitted signal has the least distortion, is the loudest possible, and travels the farthest while causing the least interference with other radio stations.

TRANSMITTER OUTPUT POWER

A typical small-town AM radio station probably has a power output of 500 to 1000 watts. A small-town FM transmitter runs with an output power level of 2000 to 10,000 watts. Such transmitters typically reach out to receivers up to 15 or 20 miles away—enough to cover a county or a large city if terrain permits.

The FCC license granted to the station states the output power for the transmitter. The station is then required to maintain that output power. If a station is assigned an operating power output of 1000 watts, the operators should check it regularly to make sure that the output power has neither gone down nor up. A small variation is permitted by the FCC because no transmitter is absolutely stable.

Note: For AM and FM broadcast transmitters, the FCC's allowance is 10% below or 5% above the assigned power level. A transmitter can deviate by these percentages from the licensed power stated on the station license.

The operator has a simple control for raising or lowering power so that the licensed power level can be maintained (Fig. 5-2). If you are not able to bring the transmitter back to the licensed power level with this control, contact the station's chief engineer immediately!

It is permissible to operate the transmitter at reduced power in an emergency situation. If this must continue for more than a few days, the chief engineer must notify the FCC of the reason for the reduced power operation and what steps are being taken to restore normal transmitter service.

Under no circumstances is it legal or advisable to operate a transmitter at *higher than normal* power levels (Fig. 5-3). This causes interference with other radio stations and puts a dangerous strain on the components inside the transmitter. Damaged transmitter parts can easily cost several hundred dollars to repair or replace. If certain parts of a transmitter fail, the cost could run into thousands of dollars. So maintain licensed power!

Fig. 5-2. Maintaining output power. The transmitter operator uses a simple control to raise and lower the power.

Fig. 5-3. Maintain licensed power. Never run a transmitter at higher than the licensed output power. Keep the transmitter room well ventilated on hot days.

TRANSMITTER METER READINGS

If you are required to read the meters on the transmitter, you will be instructed by the radio station personnel on the exact procedure to follow. There are several general guidelines that apply in most cases.

☐ Read the meters regularly, at least as often as required by station policy.

☐ Read the meters immediately when you come on duty so you know how the transmitter is currently behaving.

☐ Write meter readings in the log book *clearly* so that you or anyone else can easily read the entries.

☐ Check the transmitter frequently between scheduled readings, especially during bad weather, but once or twice extra during your shift in any event. Just look over the meters (without writing things down) to make sure everything is normal.

☐ Don't ignore trouble or unusual transmitter activity. Odd meter readings, strange noises, or any difficulty in operating the transmitter should be reported to the chief engineer *immediately*.

☐ Check log sheets at the end of your shift to make sure you have filled in all required information. Sign your name at the required locations on the log sheets.

The Transmitter Operating Log Book

Each radio and TV station is required to keep written notes on the performance of the transmitter. This is required by the FCC, but it is also a good practice in ensuring trouble-free transmitter operation. The chief engineer relies on your accurate meter readings as one way of tracing the source of a problem or predicting trouble before it occurs.

The log book is a collection of data recorded by the transmitter operators. Typically, each page of the log represents a full broadcast day (Fig. 5-4). Meter readings are taken according to FCC rules and local station policy, although many stations read more frequently than the bare minimum of once every three hours. Most stations require meter readings hourly or once every two hours.

When to Read the Meters

Besides the regular meter reading schedule, write down readings under any of the following circumstances:

- [ ] When a new transmitter operator comes on duty
- [ ] After adjusting the output power back to the normal level
- [ ] Anytime the transmitter is put on the air, such as at sign-on or after any unscheduled interruption caused by power failure, equipment trouble, or weather-related interruptions
- [ ] As requested by the chief engineer or station manager

WGCS - FM 91.1 MHz
Goshen College Broadcasting Corporation
Goshen, Indiana

Transmitter Operating Log

Time On Duty	Operator's Signature	Time Off Duty

Day: _____

Date: _____

All Times Are In EST / EDT

EBS Messages

Received Via _____

Time Received _____

Time Sent _____

Time	Feed Line psi	IPA K amps	PA Fil volts	PA Current amps	PA Voltage kV	Power Out kW	SWR	Remarks	Opr Initials

Remarks:

Fig. 5-4. Sample log sheet. Transmitter operators were once required to take meter readings twice an hour. Modern transmitting equipment requires less frequent attention, and transmitter logs can even be kept automatically by a computer.

The transmitter operating log is a useful place for recording other information:

☐ E.B.S. tests

☐ Results of transmitter tests

☐ Description of changes or additions to the equipment

The log book is a narrative of the station's operation from the technical viewpoint. Keep it in a safe place and preserve it in good condition. Because each radio station has its own procedures for logging the transmitter's meter readings, the details of transmitter operations won't be discussed here. Chapter 15 covers generally accepted logging procedures and other transmitter and antenna basics.

ANTENNA DE-ICERS

Many stations, particularly FM and TV stations, have electrical heating elements built into the antenna system. A special meter on the transmitter, called the *SWR meter* (see Chapter 15), warns the transmitter operator to check the tower for ice build-up. If ice is present, the operator throws a switch to turn on the heaters. Within an hour or so the ice melts off and the antenna once again accepts full power.

Don't worry about the tower falling down and killing you because of ice buildup. You're more likely to die from drinking the coffee made by the chief engineer at 4 A.M.!

OPERATING A TRANSMITTER

Proper transmitter operation requires that the transmitter be allowed to warm up for a few minutes before going on the air. Likewise, it should cool down after going off the air before being turned completely off. This avoids sudden changes of temperature that could damage the components inside the transmitter.

Signing a Transmitter On the Air

Here is a typical procedure for signing a transmitter on the air at 6:00 A.M.

TIME	PROCEDURE
5:30 A.M.	Arrive at station. Turn on transmitter by pushing button marked STAND BY, FILAMENTS ON, or WARM-UP. At this point one or two of the transmitter's meters should jump up to near-normal readings, although most will remain at zero. If the transmitter has an internal cooling fan, it will probably start up at this point. The transmitter is not yet on the air.
5:50 A.M.	Put the transmitter on the air by pushing the button marked ON AIR, PLATES ON, or CARRIER ON. The remaining meters should immediately rise to near-normal levels. The transmitter is now on the air.
5:51 A.M.	Give a simple legal station I.D. announcement while watching the modulation monitor to make sure audio is reaching the transmitter.
5:52 A.M.	Take meter readings to make sure the transmitter is working properly.
5:58 A.M.	Begin the station's formal sign-on message and scheduled broadcast activities.
6:15 A.M.	Check transmitter meters again and adjust power output if necessary.
	Check output power frequently during the first hour of operation. Most older transmitters will vary quite a bit until fully warmed up.

The early sign-on is a good practice so that any trouble will be caught before you begin scheduled programming. Be sure to follow the sign-on procedure stated by your chief engineer!

Adjusting Transmitter Output Power

Many transmitters drift around a bit because of temperature changes or commercial power fluctuations. Most older transmitters are not able to self-adjust to maintain the correct output power. Check the meters frequently.

Power output is most likely to vary during the first hour or two of operation. It is also likely to change at sunrise, sunset, during the morning get-up-and-go-to-work times, as well as supper time in the evening. The transmitter power level is especially likely to drop around 4:30 to 6:00 in the afternoon on summer weekdays when people come home from work and turn on their air conditioners, TVs, and microwave ovens. The extra electrical load on the community power system causes the voltage to drop in your transmitter and the power output to also drop. Two or three hours later, the houses have cooled, the ovens are off, and the load goes off the power lines. Your transmitter can now deliver more output power. Watch for these regular changes in power output so that you will not run too much or too little transmitter output power.

Adjusting the power output on most transmitters is simple. Some transmitters have a knob that you twist much like adjusting the volume control on a receiver. Other transmitters have a pair of push buttons marked RAISE and LOWER to adjust the output power up and down. *Watch the output meter while changing the power level.*

If you are raising power and the output meter stops rising, do not continue to try to raise power—the transmitter is giving you all it can. When you adjust power, however, you might not see an immediate response. Some transmitters change power a few seconds after you make the adjustment.

Taking the Transmitter Off the Air

At the conclusion of the broadcast day, air the sign-off message. At that point, take one last set of meter readings before turning off the transmitter.

Assuming a sign-off after the 11:00 P.M. newscast, here is a typical transmitter shut-down schedule.

TIME   *PROCEDURE*
11:00 P.M.   Newscast.

11:05 P.M.   2-minute sign-off announcement.

11:07 P.M.   Take final meter readings.

11:08 P.M.   Take transmitter off the air by pushing PLATES OFF, or CARRIER OFF. Most meters (especially POWER OUTPUT) should fall to zero; some meters will fall gradually while others will drop immediately. Let the transmitter's fan (if any) run for 5 to 10 minutes to allow the transmitter to cool down.

11:15 P.M.   Completely shut down transmitter with FILAMENTS OFF or POWER OFF.

If you are the sign-off engineer, take the responsibility to make sure everything is ready for the next broadcast day:

☐ Put away old logs and get out new ones.

☐ Leave notes about any equipment trouble.

☐ Clean up the control room.

Don't feel too bad if transmitter meter readings are somewhat meaningless to you. It will take time before you begin to get a feel for what normal meter readings look like. After you have logged about 10 hours of transmitter operation, you will start to feel at home. If you work part-time, especially if you work just a few hours a week, it will take somewhat longer for you to feel comfortable. See Chapter 15 for a thorough discussion of transmitter meters and how to read them.

If you ever feel insecure or uncertain about your meter readings, be sure to consult the posted typical meter readings and look back at previous log pages to see what normal readings should be. Don't copy someone else's log entries! It is illegal and a waste of time.

MONITORING EQUIPMENT

The FCC requires that stations make sure their equipment is operating according to "good engineering practice." This means that the chief engineer must know that all is well. This information of transmitter performance is provided on a continuous basis by several pieces of monitoring equipment.

The Air Monitor

One of the simplest ways to check on transmitter performance is to have some means of feeding a radio receiver output back into the control room. This special receiver is called the air monitor. Distortion, hum, program line trouble, or a transmitter that has suddenly died will be noticed quickly if you listen to the air monitor at all times.

Listening to the air monitor lets you know what the listeners at home are hearing. You can adjust the volume of the air monitor, however, without affecting what goes out to the listeners. Most audio consoles have a monitor amp with an input selector switch. This switch selects between audio coming from audition, program, and air (or external.)

The Modulation Monitor

Another very reliable way to inform the control room operator of transmitter performance is to have

Fig. 5-5. Overmodulation. The modulation monitor's meter cannot always keep up with sudden loud sounds. Therefore, the modulation monitor has a flashing light to make sure you notice when the really big ones sneak through!

the air monitor audio fed into a carefully adjusted VU meter. This meter shows the results of the modulation process.

In addition to a moving meter indicating modulation percentage, a modulation monitor is equipped with a flashing light. The flasher is usually set to light up if the modulation exceeds 100%. Some kinds of sounds will cause momentary overmodulation (Fig 5-5), even though the meters don't read too high. Harsh sounds, such as cymbal crashes, scratches on old records, and hard-sounding letters (k, x, s, t, etc.) can cause the overmodulation flasher to light, but they happen too quickly for the meter to respond.

Because the audio going into the transmitter has been through audio processing equipment, the modulation monitor's VU meter will probably not agree exactly with the VU meters on the control room audio console.

The Frequency Meter

It is important for any radio station to remain precisely on the licensed frequency. The transmitter and antenna are very finely tuned, and an off-frequency transmitter will perform very poorly.

The air monitor receiver is designed to control a frequency meter or a digital readout frequency counter. This allows the operator to know exactly what the transmitter's true operating frequency is.

If the transmitter gets too far off frequency, notify the chief engineer immediately. In practice, broadcast transmitters stay on frequency with good stability, and this is one area of the transmitter that very seldom gives trouble.

WRAP-UP

Transmitters are not fearsome beasts, and their operation is generally routine and simple. The best safeguard for avoiding transmitter troubles is for the operator to memorize normal meter readings and transmitter noises so that anything unusual will be noticed immediately. Notify the chief engineer if you ever think that the transmitter is behaving oddly.

The FCC licenses each radio station to operate at a specified power output level with a certain operating frequency. The operator is expected to read and write down meter readings at regular intervals as a way of making sure the transmitter is functioning correctly.

The transmitter operator should follow established procedures for transmitter sign-on, power adjustment, and sign-off to ensure that the transmitter is not put under any severe strain. Accurate, regular meter readings ensure proper transmitter operation. Various kinds of studio monitoring equipment provide the transmitter operator with constant information to keep the broadcast operation within the bounds of good engineering practice.

Exercise 5-1.   Modulation Fundamentals

Check your comprehension of the concept of *modulation* by answering the following questions.

1. Define the term *dead air*.
2. When the transmitter is delivering the loudest undistorted signal possible, this is indicated by what modulation percentage?

Exercise 5-2.   Transmitter Fundamentals

Check your comprehension of basic broadcast transmitter facts by answering the following questions.

1. List at least three instances when it is good practice to log the transmitter's meter readings.
2. Ice buildup on an FM broadcast antenna will probably result in what kind of an SWR meter reading? Higher than normal or lower than normal?

Exercise 5-3.   Broadcast Monitoring

Check your comprehension of the fundamentals of monitoring your broadcasts by answering the following questions.

1. If you are also responsible for the transmitter, what should you listen to to make sure you're still on the air? A program channel, audition channel, or air monitor?

2. If you adjust the volume of the air monitor, does that affect what the listeners at home hear?

3. If the modulation monitor's flasher lights up, what is probably true about the peak modulation percentage?

Vocabulary

air monitor	interference	SWR (Standing Wave Ratio)
AM broadcast band	log book	sign-off
chief engineer	meter	sign-on
distortion	modulation	warm-up
FM broadcast band	modulation monitor	

Unit II. Equipping the operator. Many AM radio stations use several towers to radiate their signals to a specific service area. Shown is the impressive array at WSVA-AM and WQPO-FM, Harrisonburg, VA.

UNIT II

Equipping the Operator

Assuming you've read and understood the material in Unit I of this book, you can see already that you'll never listen to a radio broadcast the same way again. Instead of hearing a steady stream of music and talk, you can now picture the DJ busily flipping around tapes, carts, and records while also twisting knobs and pushing buttons.

Now that you've had a peek at the radio station's equipment, let's take a closer look at *you*, the combo operator. Many new skills are needed for you to know how to operate as a radio broadcaster instead of just a member of the audience.

Chapter 6

Announcing and Operating

The combo operator has plenty to do. When you sit in the control room chair, your voice and mind must be ready to say the right things at the right time in a way that will please the listeners (or at least not annoy them). Yet, as the combo operator, you are also responsible for operating the studio equipment and handling the tapes, carts, records, and scripts with precision and artistry. Does that sound too hard?

Remember that you can balance on a bicycle, pedal it, steer it, whistle a tune, scratch behind your ear, and read street signs all at the same time. Given enough time and practice, most people become dependable, enjoyable combo operators.

You can observe a more experienced operator make a sudden dive for the board and give a flawless announcement with no apparent preparation. That is like driving your car on the wrong side of the road—sooner or later, it will get you into big trouble. You will save yourself a lot of panic and error if you plan ahead and prepare yourself for upcoming announcements and equipment operations.

A good announcer/operator must plan ahead. Don't ever be ashamed of writing down notes or even a full script of what you need to say. Likewise, feel free to write out notes to yourself. Make reminders of what audio source is next, typical pot settings, or anything else that will help your operation be smooth, flawless, and pleasing to the audience. This kind of preparation makes your job less hectic, and you will sound better on the air—that will please your boss.

DEVELOPING A SMOOTH ANNOUNCING STYLE

The secret ingredient in smooth announcing is experience. Your goal is to sound relaxed, confident, friendly, and believable. If you know what you're doing, and are familiar with what you are saying, much of the required self-confidence will be there (Fig. 6-1).

Naturally, the seasoned veteran of many years in broadcasting has developed some habits and has a mental file cabinet of stock phrases for all occa-

Fig. 6-1. The voice of confidence. Know what to say, when to say it, and how to say it.

sions just waiting to be called up. That is how good newscasters can describe a major news event without a script or rehearsal. They call upon their experiences of the past to guide their words.

Even as a newcomer to the control room, you can also open the mike and speak from experience! How? Use this simple three-step procedure for developing a smooth announcing style:

1. Know *what* to say.

2. Know *how* to say it.

3. Know *when* to say it.

Before you speak on the microphone, consciously ask yourself if you are prepared in these three ways.

What to Say

What do you say on the air? Work with the following:

☐ Program events just ended, just beginning, or coming up

☐ Time, temperature, weather

☐ Station slogans

☐ Interesting background facts about popular songs and performers (but keep it short)

☐ Scripted material as required by the station's format (spots, promos, news, and sports).

You might have heard disc jockeys of popular music stations who seem to be a fountain of cute remarks, funny stories, or humorous lead-ins to records. While the style of delivery might be very informal, the success of such announcers hinges on their careful preparation ahead of time. While their remarks might not be completely scripted, in many cases they do come to the studio prepared with an *ad-lib sheet* filled with notes and outlines of what they plan to say.

Scripts, notes, and cue cards aren't enough, especially when you are a new announcer. It is very important to take the time to rehearse your lines out loud. Listen to yourself, time yourself with the clock. Look for words or combinations of words that will be hard to pronounce or not easily understood. Rewrite your script if necessary. Remember, the goal is to give the listeners what they want to hear and to deliver it in a way that the audience finds attractive.

Another word about what to say, or what not to say. Avoid holding conversations with off-mike studio guests and especially avoid *inside jokes* with members of the station's staff. These remarks, intended mainly for someone who is not a member of the audience, usually don't make sense to the listeners. Inside jokes and half-there conversations make for bad radio and are quite unprofessional. When you are on the air, direct your efforts to the on-air product.

Worse than the inside jokes is when the air personality gets mad at the boss and starts complaining on the air. It is possible to entertain the audience with jokes about your life as a radio announcer, but be careful. If the audience or your boss thinks that you're just blowing off some built-up anger on the air, you will soon be looking for another job.

How to Say It

Your voice can be trained, strengthened, and improved like any other part of the human body. The voice itself should be exercised (Fig. 6-2). Try singing or talking during the half hour before you go on the air, especially if you have the morning sign-on shift. Sing your favorite song (even if you don't sing well). After each verse, start over again, singing in a higher pitch. Repeat until you are too high to sing comfortably. Restart at your normal pitch and sing each verse lower until you can't go lower.

Fig. 6-2. Voice warm-ups. It's best done on your way to work, unless you carpool with someone else!

Stretch and exercise the mouth, tongue, and jaw muscles by overpronouncing the words. Try singing or speaking very slowly, then very quickly, but always working on accuracy and clarity. (It helps if you travel alone so that nobody has to listen to this!)

Take a look at the two combo operators in Fig. 6-3. Operating the board while poorly seated (left) pulls the body into a curled-up position. This collapses the chest, ruining the natural resonance of the chest cavity. The slumped-over announcer at left can't breathe very deeply, and the voice will be very thin. Insufficient breath to power the voice results with many words ending in an annoying croak instead of a normal downward inflection. A particularly bad problem here is that the announcer has his head tilted back onto his shoulders, which puts tension on the throat muscles. This ruins the possibilities for a relaxed, flexible vocal style.

The right-hand example in Fig. 6-3 is seated in a way that holds the head level, the shoulders back, chest expanded, stomach flat, and the throat muscles relaxed and ready for the serious business of operating his beautiful voice. This position is the best

way to sit for maximum voice performance. The voice can only use the body to full benefit if it is standing, however, and some of the major market announcers always stand while speaking on the air.

As a part of your warm-up routine, make an effort to breathe deeply and get a little exercise to cause some hard breathing. This will possibly cause you to do some coughing, which is the whole point—get those lungs cleared out, the chest walls expanded, and the whole body toned up.

Some people think that they have to use a special radio voice when announcing. This is only partly true. You should follow the same expression patterns that you use when conversing with someone, but with less variation in the loudness. Try speaking conversationally into a microphone while watching a VU meter. Don't put on a special golden throat voice that sounds phoney, but do try to maintain the volume peaks in the 85-100% range.

Some people's voices get too soft when faced with a microphone, and words get lost, particularly at the end of a sentence. Other people almost sing each word, and their voices become unnaturally in-

Fig. 6-3. Posture affects the voice. If you slump, your voice will sound shallow and cramped. Sitting up straight helps give your voice a full, pleasing quality.

flected. Others develop far too much up-and-down inflection, exaggerating the normal pitch changes in the voice.

Smile while you're announcing. Even though nobody can see you do this, smiling gives your words a bright, clear sound. It is easier to understand and more pleasant to the listener's ear.

When to Say It

First turn on your brain, then start your mouth. Nothing sounds worse than a radio announcer stumbling around for words. Many beginning announcers find themselves speechless in front of an open mike because they forgot to be fully prepared. Uncertainty leads to hesitation, mistakes, stuttering, and a weak voice. If an announcer does this very much, the listeners quickly start complaining, or they find a better radio station. Be ready when that mike comes on! Go through these few steps of preparation before each on-air announcement:

1. *Script:* Write down exactly what you will say.

2. *Rehearse:* Practice out loud and listen for any words or phrases that are hard to say.

3. *Rewrite:* Write the script over if necessary.

4. *Breathe:* Take several deep breaths just before your mike comes on; this relaxes your chest and helps you get through long sentences.

5. *Smile:* This helps you speak clearly and distinctly.

6. *Slow down:* Don't rush over words, especially hard ones.

7. *Be yourself:* Relax, be friends with the audience.

If you know what you are going to say, know you can say it, and say it as if you care about it, you'll have an audience. Don't forget that the station manager is part of the audience.

WHAT DOES THE AUDIENCE WANT?

A frustrating little proverb states, "If you don't say it the way they want to hear it, you haven't said it." Radio depends on the ear of the listener to re-

ceive the product of the radio station. The announcer should pick words and phrases carefully, asking what the audience likes, wants, or cares about. If you speak with the golden voice of a network news commentator, but use empty or meaningless words, you will be a failure. You need to know enough about your audience that you can meet its needs in an intelligent way.

Written scripts are very helpful in delivering high-quality radio announcing. Naturally, newscasts are written out because of the requirement for accuracy and consistency. Commercials are also written out in most cases, at least to cover the specifics of the product or service being advertised. The control room and studio walls can hold poster-sized scripts listing station slogans or catch phrases like "This is FM 91-derful, WGCS in Goshen" or "Advertisers put their smart money where our mouth is . . . KOIN, Portland."

The radio personality who announces several dozen records each day quickly memorizes a variety of ways to get the job done. The audience wants to know the name of the song and the name of the performer, but if you always deliver this information in exactly the same way, it will get stale in a hurry. The creative announcer works in remarks about the time, temperature, a quick weather forecast, a plug for an upcoming newscast, a promo for the station's contest, or facts and background remarks relating to the song or artist on the record. Resist the urge to load up each live announcement with too many frills. It is better to say little and do it well.

A well-scripted, well-rehearsed commercial or newscast won't please the audience if the announcer has some irritating voice trait. If the audience isn't pleased, radio dials get twisted to other stations—bad news. The good news is that most people can improve their vocal skills with:

☐ **Warm-up**—Get the voice and lungs ready for work.

☐ **Control**—Use your voice accurately, like any good tool.

☐ **Confidence**—Be relaxed and ready to speak.

These tricks of the trade are used by any public performer, particularly singers or public speakers. You could enroll in a class that teaches good diction and voice control. Another good way to develop your voice is to sing in a choir, especially one that has a good director who demands careful pronunciation.

SMOOTH OPERATING

Experience brings smooth announcing and steady hands on the controls. The combo operator must become so familiar with the studio equipment that the hands automatically move tapes, records, scripts, knobs, and switches to keep the program flowing smoothly. This requires some good manual coordination and the ability to memorize the exact location of everything in the control room.

Once you get into full-time radio work, you will have plenty of opportunities to operate the equipment. If your broadcast work is only part-time, especially if you work on the air only one or two days a week, your ability to develop automatic operating skills is reduced. Use every opportunity to improve your skills and accuracy.

Cue Records and Tapes Quickly

The actual procedures for tape and record cueing were discussed in Chapter 3. Beyond the sheer mechanics of it, though, you need to develop speed. The combo operator in most radio stations almost never has more than two minutes to do anything. When you are a beginner, you will need most of the time available during one song to get the next record ready. A seasoned veteran can cue a record during a 30-second spot with time to spare.

Tape cueing can be done in gradual stages. During one record you can go to the play bin and bring the tape to the operating position. During the next record you can get the tape threaded onto the machine. Later you can locate the beginning of the program scheduled for airplay, and still later you can do the precise cueing of the tape.

Work on your accuracy first. As your experience and confidence grow, you will discover that you can cue records and tapes quickly, often without looking. Your hands will memorize the necessary movements. The day will come when you will cue records and tapes while reading the log.

Maintain Correct Audio Levels

VU meters and modulation levels were discussed in Chapters 3 and 5. You must be conscious of the audio levels and VU meters, however, to maintain the proper levels automatically.

Constantly check and recheck the VU meters on the board and modulation monitor. Always keep one ear tuned for the air monitor speaker. Notice sudden audio level changes immediately. Dead air should make you respond instantly!

Once you develop an ear that is sensitive to audio levels and dead air, you will automatically stop talking when a studio speaker goes dead—unless, of course, you are the announcer on the air. It is humorous to watch experienced radio announcers stop speaking in mid-word when the background music stops in a public place. It also shows the depth of their professional skill.

Keep Accurate Logs

The FCC has relaxed log keeping requirements for some kinds of broadcast stations. Accurate program and transmitter logs are still legal proof of the performance and operation of the radio station, and most radio stations still require the operators to keep correct logs. Commercial radio stations get their money from spots that have been successfully aired. The program log serves the dual purpose of informing the combo operator what spots to air and when to air them. This allows the station's bookkeeper to verify that the sponsor's ads actually ran, and then collect the money for them.

Well-kept transmitter logs are required by the FCC under many circumstances, and they are very important to the chief engineer. The engineer can look at a set of meter readings and quickly be warned of possible transmitter trouble.

Anytime you must write in a log book, make an effort to write clearly and legibly. Someone else has to read it!

Observe and Operate
the Transmitter Properly

Try to schedule a short session with the chief engineer for transmitter training. Notice any special instructions or cautions he or she might mention. As you operate the transmitter, listen to the noises it makes. If you work for a station that has an all solid-state transmitter, unusual noises will be especially noticeable because solid-state transmitters are normally almost silent.

You need to learn what sounds normal and looks normal for your particular transmitter and its meters. Once you are sensitive to the sounds of the equipment around you, you'll notice problems very quickly by the change in the sounds (Fig. 6-4). I kept track of the operation of six videotape machines just by listening to the sounds in the TV station tape room. A machine that was out of adjustment just sounded different!

If anything out of the ordinary happens, feel free to contact your chief engineer or another ex-perienced operator. Failure to correct problems can result in expensive damage to the transmitting equipment.

DEAL WITH THE PUBLIC CONSTRUCTIVELY

Many radio announcers report this same occurrence: the studio phone rings, they answer it, and the person on the other end of the line either has some stupid question or just wants to talk. This happens because radio station personalities are a part of the popular show business mystique admired by many people. Yet, unlike movie stars or TV personnel, radio broadcasters are accessible to the public. Radio stations use this to promote interest in the station and the station's sponsors.

Many radio stations openly encourage the members of the audience to call in and talk to the announcers. Others have remote studio facilities built into a trailer or mobile motor home and put the combo operator out in shopping centers and other public places. Remember, these people of the audience ad-

Fig. 6-4. Avoiding transmitter trouble. Don't ignore unusual sounds coming from the transmitter room!

mire you for your special skills and personality. They want to be your friend, and they want you to notice them and to be friendly toward them. Sometimes it is hard to always be warm and happy to visitors when you're a busy combo operator, but that's part of the job.

When an on-duty combo operator must also deal with the public, the loyalties and responsibilities become divided. When you find yourself in this position, remember that you can ask a phone caller or studio visitor to keep quiet and wait while you perform some of your on-air duties. Just tell them politely, "Hang on while I take care of something, then I'll get back to you." When you need to end a conversation, just thank your visitor or caller for making the contact and tell them good-bye. If they keep talking anyway, just say "Look, I'm real sorry, but I've got to clear this phone line." Then, just hang up—gently.

While in conversation with a listener, you might be asked all kinds of questions about radio stations and your glamorous life as a DJ. Some questions can be highly technical in nature, but very poorly phrased. Don't put someone down for the ignorance of their question. Just go ahead and give the best answer you can. If you are also ignorant on the subject, feel free to laugh and explain, "Wow, I don't know how that works either!"

AUDIO PRODUCTION

Most commercial radio stations require that each announcer also perform in commercials and other announcements. This requirement should be no problem for the announcer because audio production is usually very interesting work. In some cases, audio production is just plain fun.

Audio production refers to the process of preparing and recording program material prior to broadcast. This includes making commercials, promotional announcements, public service announcements, features, and special programs.

Studio skills are put to the extreme test during production sessions because creativity is very important. This means that unusual or even physically difficult operating procedures are being used. Advanced production techniques are discussed in more detail in Chapter 12.

WRAP-UP

The combo operator must perform many duties at once—including announcing, equipment operating, transmitter operating, and answering the telephone—while accurately preparing and broadcasting various records, tapes, and live announcements.

Successful combo operation requires that you plan ahead, rehearse, and be prepared. This means that you need to know what to say, know how to say it, and know when to say it. While the announcing duties are being performed, the studio equipment must also be operated in a way that is professionally acceptable.

The sign of a good combo operator is this: the listener can hear and appreciate a radio program without being conscious of the announcer or equipment operations.

Exercise 6-1.   Smooth Announcing Style

Goal: Answer the following questions to indicate your understanding of the basics of good announcing.

1. What is a simple three-step procedure for having a smooth announcing style?

2. List at least four kinds of remarks an announcer can make besides telling the audience the name of the song just played.

3. What is an inside joke?

4. What are three ways to improve your vocal skills?

5. Why is it important to smile while announcing? (After all, nobody can see you!)

Vocabulary

ad-lib

audio production

cue cards

frills

inflection

inside joke

lead-in

program log

resonance

transmitter log

Chapter 7

Writing for Broadcast

Radio broadcasters have developed a reputation for being dependable. The public relies on the information the broadcaster gives them, and the radio personality becomes a trusted friend in the listener's home or car. Therefore, when you deliver any kind of information over the air, be both consistent and accurate (Fig. 7-1). In this situation, it is best to read from a written script.

Broadcast scripts are written with two special considerations:

☐ The script must be easy to read aloud.
☐ The material must be easy to listen to.

The listener has no immediate control over the radio announcer's delivery. Once something is said, it is gone. Broadcasters use a few tricks to make their writing and announcing easier to understand.

Even if you consider yourself a good writer, you might find that the habits you learned for print media are not necessarily the best for radio scripts. Print-media writing styles tend to use complex sentences. Large numbers, graphs, and data tables are print-oriented devices. None of these are of much use when all the information must be delivered through the spoken word.

Broadcast writing relies heavily on short, simple sentences. Complex numbers are simplified, rounded off, or compared to something else. Effective broadcast writing:

☐ grabs the attention of the listener.
☐ sets the scene.
☐ delivers important information.
☐ triggers the imagination.
☐ uses simple, self-contained sentences.
☐ summarizes.

ATTENTION GETTERS

The first line of a news story or commercial should say "Listen! This is what I'll talk about next." The first line, or *lead-in*, might not make

Fig. 7-1. Script writing. Careful preparation of radio scripts ensures accuracy and high quality. (This is Carol Bozena of WWUH-FM, West Hartford.)

complete sense by itself, but it is used to raise the interest of the listener. The lead-in is also a *throw-away* because the listener might not hear or understand it at first. Its main function is to prepare the listener for the story or announcement that follows.

The lead-in is not always a grammatically correct sentence, but you should *not* try to write lead-ins that sound like newspaper headlines. Lead-ins tend to sound unnatural and very odd when spoken. When writing a lead-in, try saying it out loud. Does it sound interesting? Will the audience have some idea of what comes next? Will the listener want to hear more?

Think also of the radio announcer. Are there any difficult to pronounce words? Are any of the word combinations hard to say? How does the lead-in sound?

SET THE SCENE

Radio commercials are very short, typically lasting either 30 or 60 seconds. The script for the 60-second spot fills about one typewritten page, double-spaced, and many news stories are shorter than that. Therefore, each sentence must count, and every word must be carefully chosen to deliver the desired information.

Following the lead-in line, the next line or two must explain the intent or significance of the spot or story and can include significant information. In some cases, the lead-in is a question which is answered in the second line.

DELIVER IMPORTANT INFORMATION

What does the listener want to hear? What does the audience want to know? Your radio script contains only a few short sentences, yet in that brief space you must arouse interest and curiosity, then supply the information that satisfies these desires.

Rotating Spots

Avoid overloading one story or spot. Too much information delivered in a short time span can confuse the listener and obscure the message. When producing commercials, one common method of dealing with this situation involves producing two or three *rotating spots*.

In rotating spots for one client, the sponsor's information is divided up and produced into several spots that are then all recorded onto one long tape cart. This automatically gives each spot equal airplay, and a regular listener to the station will eventually hear them all. Each spot is simpler, easier to understand, and more effective than one spot loaded down with a high-speed announcer straining to get it all said.

Keeping News Fresh

Newscasters avoid overloading a single story by rewriting for each newscast, bringing in additional facts each hour. Stale information is dropped, while new facts are worked in to keep the story fresh.

Handling Numbers and Prices

Be careful with numbers! Before you include them in a spot or story, decide exactly what the audience needs to know. If a commercial must deliver specific price information, then this should be included. But news stories can often be more understandable and interesting if numbers are simplified or put into general perspective. Look at the examples below.

Specific prices are sometimes necessary, but too many of them in one spot fills the listener's head with a swirl of numbers. Sometimes it is simpler and more effective to make a general statement:

ALL PRICES HAVE BEEN REDUCED 35 PERCENT. SHOPPERS, YOU CAN BUY ANY SHIRT IN OUR STORE FOR LESS THAN TEN DOLLARS.

When including numbers in a news story, sometimes accuracy is less important than simplicity and clarity. The news writer could be accurate but confusing in this statement:

STATE HIGHWAY FUNDS TOTALING $234,805 WILL BE SPENT ON THE BRIDGE RENOVATION PROJECT.

The long number is hard for the announcer to say, and is difficult for the listener to fully comprehend. It is much simpler in a less complicated form:

A QUARTER-MILLION DOLLARS OF STATE HIGHWAY FUNDS WILL BE SPENT ON THE BRIDGE RENOVATION PROJECT.

The large number is now stated in understandable and easily pronounced language, making the story more effective.

Names in the News

If you expect to write news stories, you must be well informed about the news. Make a point of absorbing common names of people and places, both locally and at the world level, especially the pronunciation of these names. Listeners tend to get very upset over mispronounced names that are well known to them.

If you find yourself confronted with a person's name that is difficult to pronounce, there are some ways to get around that problem:

- ☐ Use pronunciation guides supplied by the news wire service.
- ☐ Ask someone else, particularly the news director or an older, more-experienced announcer.
- ☐ Use dictionaries; larger ones include place names and some include famous people.
- ☐ Avoid the name if you can't say it, and simply refer to the person by his or her title or position.

The suggestion of avoiding the name completely is a last-ditch measure to be used in case all others fail. This does put the person into context, and the listener will find this informative. Prepare yourself to occasionally be caught saying a name wrong. When this happens, you will be corrected (sometimes not very kindly) by someone who knows the correct pronunciation. Human nature makes this a bit hard to live through, but try to learn from these corrections. You can be sure that your improvement will be noticed and appreciated.

If you must read a news story that you did not write (such as copy that came from the newswire teletype), take the time to read it before broadcasting it. If at all possible, rehearse out loud. Feel free to write on the news copy, making any necessary notes to help you get through difficult names, words, or phrases. Rewrite the whole story if necessary.

TRIGGER THE IMAGINATION

The radio audience is not limited by the spoken word because words can cause the listener to imagine visual scenes that go along with what is being said. Good radio relies heavily on the mind's eye (Fig. 7-2) to give color, motion, smell, and feeling to the announcer's words.

Traditional news writing works with the facts of the story, yet the best news reporting makes people imagine that they are on the scene. During World War II, CBS Radio News correspondent Edward R. Murrow used vivid but factual language to describe bombs being dropped on the city of London by German warplanes. Listeners were mentally transported to the scene by Murrow's clear-cut accounting of the events and their meaning to the people of Lon-

Fig. 7-2. Word pictures. Make them *see* it in their mind.

don. Likewise in your reporting, try to make the raw facts come alive but do not distort them.

Radio commercials and public service announcements permit much more creative freedom in the use of language. The scriptwriter is free to develop miniature dramas. With a few voices, some sound effects, and music, a few basic facts about the sponsor's product are delivered. This can be done in a way that the audience's imagination fills in the gaps, broadening the impact of the announcement.

Such scriptwriting relies heavily on using key words or phrases that the audience is familiar with. Slang expressions and current jokes are very useful when one word must carry the weight of a hundred. The writer must be careful, however, to use words and phrases that truly do carry meaning for the audience.

Effective use of sound effects, music, and extra voices in a commercial can do much to make it more interesting and memorable. If the audience remembers the sponsor's commercial, the product advertised will also be remembered. A detailed discussion of commercial production techniques is found in Chapter 11.

USE SELF-CONTAINED SENTENCES

State things simply. Broadcast language avoids long, complex sentences. Somebody has to read that script out loud, which means they must stop to breathe sometime. Long sentences are difficult to deliver and can be difficult to understand.

Try to complete a thought within one sentence. State a concept simply, then use additional sentences to expand, clarify, or modify that concept. Don't write lung-busters like this one:

THE GOVERNOR, WHILE SMILING AT REPORTERS IN HIS OFFICE, SIGNED THE BILL INTO LAW WHICH FREED THE FUNDS THAT WERE BEING HELD BY THE LANDMARK COURT DECISION MADE LAST YEAR BY THE STATE SUPREME COURT.

This is very hard to read without gasping for air in the middle. The audience is left reeling as well!

Let's take the same information, but break it down to the one-concept, one-sentence formula:

THE GOVERNOR WAS SMILING TODAY. REPORTERS WATCHED WHILE HE SIGNED THE SO-CALLED ''FROZEN FUNDS BILL'' INTO LAW. LAST YEAR, THE STATE SUPREME COURT DECIDED THAT THE FUNDS SHOULD NOT BE SPENT, CALLING ON STATE LAWMAKERS TO DRAFT NEW LEGISLATION. THE ''FROZEN FUNDS'' COURT CASE WAS CALLED A ''LANDMARK DECISION'' BY LEGAL EXPERTS.

In the second example, each phrase delivers a concept or fact without being interrupted and is about one typed line long. Notice that the lead-in line arouses interest but carries no important information. Punctuation is used liberally to help the announcer with expression and breathing.

SUMMARIZE THE STORY

Both news and commercials benefit from a summary at the end. Listeners frequently miss the beginning of an announcement, and some kind of repetition helps deliver the most important parts of the message. Commercials often end with the name of the sponsor and the location of the business. News stories are generally not summarized within the story, but a long newscast often includes a headlines-only summary at the conclusion.

End a radio spot with the sponsor's slogan, an attention-getting phrase or music jingle that is easy to remember. Another method is to use a full-length musical jingle, which helps the listener remember (in a general sort of way) who or what was just advertised.

USING THE NEWS WIRE

Local radio stations use written news stories that are provided by regional and national news networks through automatic printers called *teletypes*.

Both United Press International (UPI) and the Associated Press (AP) provide this service. The data is distributed from national headquarters, through state or regional bureaus (which add in regional news), to local subscribers at radio and TV stations. Both of these *wire services* have similar offerings:

☐ 24-hour daily service

☐ Hourly headlines and short news stories

☐ Hourly regional weather conditions data

☐ In-depth news stories several times a day

☐ Detailed weather forecasts and bulletins from the weather bureau

☐ Sports stories and scores

☐ Farm and business news

☐ Feature and human interest stories

☐ News analysis and commentaries

☐ Pronunciation guides for names currently in the news

Regardless of the technology involved in delivering the news to your station, most news stories intended for broadcast still arrive in the studio in printed form on paper. (Some stations have, however, converted everything over to computer screens with a paper backup in case of computer failure.) The printing itself is generally in CAPITALS ONLY, not the mixed upper and lowercase print found in this book. You might find all caps a bit difficult to read at first, but it will eventually seem normal as you gain news reading experience. The uppercase on a teletype is used for numbers and punctuation, while the letters are considered to be lowercase.

When you are preparing a newscast, you must look through yards of printed teletype paper to find the stories you need. Wire services do a good job of formatting their printed page to help you find what you need quickly. Take some time to scan the headlines or given titles to look at all the different kinds of information offered. News bulletins are especially well marked, and emergency messages are set apart with several blank lines of paper followed by: "X X X X X X X" across the page.

The news wire is very helpful to the local radio stations by providing information that the individual news directors would not be able to get unassisted. When you read news copy, be on the look out for mistakes. This stuff is not perfect, and errors do creep in. You should always proofread any wire copy and rehearse it out loud if possible. Don't be afraid to edit, rewrite, or even drop a story as needed.

When you proofread wire service material, select and edit each story with this in mind:

☐ Does this story have local interest?

☐ Does this story have actual news value?

☐ Do the contents of this story stay within locally accepted bounds of good taste?

Watch out for the following problems in each story:

☐ Excessive length

☐ Needless repetition

☐ Material offensive to the audience

☐ Typographical errors

☐ Difficult words or phrases

Feel free to rewrite any story to suit your speaking style or your station's format and news policy. If you write a local news story that you feel might be interesting to listeners outside of your station's coverage area, you can submit that story to the wire service for distribution over the state or national networks.

If your station uses a mechanical printer (and many still do), you must learn how to change the paper and ribbons so that the news copy can continue to be received. Instructions are usually printed inside the lid of the machine. Ask the chief engineer or an experienced employee at the station for a brief training course on teletype ribbon and paper maintenance—they'll be only too happy to stick you with the job thereafter! Maintaining the news wire is not one of the most pleasant jobs around a radio station, but it is part of your job. A few messy fingers are a small price to pay for the knowledge that you are helping your station provide a reliable news service.

WRAP-UP

People expect reliable and consistent information from their radio, which makes the written radio script very important. Broadcast scripts are written with equal attention to how announcers speak and how audiences listen. The choice of words and sentence structures must result in good communication between the broadcaster and the listeners.

Several factors enter into good broadcast writing: use of attention-getters, setting the scene with vivid language and important facts, delivery of further important information, the use of the listener's imagination to help carry the message, the use of simple sentence structures, and summaries to review the material. Broadcast writing should sound like natural speech patterns, and the writer should constantly give attention to how the written words will eventually sound on the air.

Most radio stations subscribe to news services that distribute material via wire or satellite networks to printers called teletypes. Local stations are free to edit and rewrite wire service copy and can also submit stories to the news service for state or national distribution.

Exercise 7-1. Painting Word Pictures

Goal: Write a commercial. (This is a creative exercise with no necessarily correct answers.)

Method: Make up all of the ''facts'' needed to write a 60-second commercial. Use the following checklist to ensure that all necessary information has been included:

- ☐ Sponsor's name (name of business)
- ☐ Sponsor's address
- ☐ Hours store is open
- ☐ Sponsor's slogan (if any)
- ☐ Kind of product
- ☐ Why listener should want or need this product
- ☐ How it works or how it is used
- ☐ Situations where use of this product is necessary or desirable
- ☐ How much it costs
- ☐ How you can pay for it (credit, financing, payment schedule, etc)

Exercise 7-2. Painting Word Pictures

Goal: Rewrite the commercial from Exercise 7-1. (This is a creative exercise with no necessarily correct answers.)

Method: Take the 60-second commercial from Exercise 7-1 and make a 30-second version. If you can't cram in all the essential information, sort out what information is essential and must be kept or make two rotating spots.

Vocabulary

Associated Press, AP

delivery

edit

fresh news

lead-in

news copy

rewrite

rotating spots

script

slogan

stale news

teletype

throw-away lines

United Press International, UPI

wire service

Chapter 8

Control Room Survival Skills

Broadcasters use a collection of tricks and shortcuts to keep from going crazy on the job, but you won't find much information about "control room survival skills" in most books about the broadcaster's craft. Like ancient legends and superstitions, many of these trade secrets are passed along verbally during production studio bull sessions. Survival skills go beyond the obvious techniques used to operate equipment successfully. There are other skills equally necessary to the successful broadcaster (Fig. 8-1).

Little problems can arise in any job, but the combo operator has the added stress of knowing that there is an audience listening when disaster strikes in the control room. You should expect trouble, plan for it, cope with it, and move on as quickly as possible. The problems and solutions discussed in this chapter are not going to cover all the possibilities. Use this material as a starting point, then seek out your own best solutions based on personal experience. Try to learn from each situation. Even a major problem is useful if you take the time to analyze it later.

For now, it is enough to deal with four main areas of broadcast skills to help get you started:

- ☐ Get the most out of your studio time.
- ☐ Build good relationships with people.
- ☐ Develop your creative talents.
- ☐ Be ready for trouble.

The broadcast profession is an interesting combination of electronic hardware, social science, and commercialism. Almost any skill or bit of knowledge you have can be used during your radio career.

GET THE MOST OUT OF YOUR STUDIO TIME

Experience is an excellent teacher. Books, lectures, and observation can only prepare you in some ways. Actually getting hands-on experience quickly shows you much more. The radio station control room or production studio is your workshop, and the equipment and program materials are your tools. If you don't use your studio time wisely, you will face problems, delays, and frustrations.

Fig. 8-1. Control room survival. Keep the area neat and uncluttered with the program log in plain view at all times. (The Bloomfield, CT, WGAB-AM studio is manned by John Ramsey, Chief Engineer.)

Listen to Your Station. You are a part of a team of broadcasters. Listen to the other members of your team so that you can fit your work into the whole product.

Arrive Early. Never be late. When you arrive early, the other station employees know you will be ready. This helps them relax, allowing them to do their best work.

Read the Logs in Advance. Be prepared by reading the program log before you come on the air. This helps you know what will occur during your show and gives you good material for plugging the programs that will be on later that day. Make special note of any network programs or difficult situations that will occur.

Pull Your Materials. Locate your records, tapes, carts, and scripts before you go on the air. Put them in the order of use and arrange them

neatly. Take good care of your program materials. Put everything back where it belongs when you're done with it, too.

Preview Recorded Materials. Plan for some time in the production studio to listen to each cart and the start and finish of each tape. Read through your scripts out loud. Your familiarity with the program materials helps make a good radio show.

Study the Format. Become familiar with the procedures. Be sure you understand how to handle each program event on your show. Follow your station's guidelines about choice of music, announcing style, newscast formats, etc.

Set Up Early. Stay ahead as much as possible. Load your cart machines, tape decks, and turntables, and keep them loaded. Never wait until the last minute to cue up program materials. Early setups help you be ready for emergencies.

Once you are set up and ready, recheck everything just before air-time to make sure all controls are properly set. Don't try to start a tape machine that you forgot to turn on—it won't work!

Ask Questions. When you come on duty, ask the people already there if you need to know anything. Ask about equipment trouble, special unscheduled broadcast events, or important news developments. Check the staff bulletin board and your employee mailbox for recent notes and messages. Once you have prepared for your time in the studio, be sure to ask for help if you don't know how to handle something.

Check and Double-Check. Make sure you have the correct record, tape, cart, or script. Make sure tapes and records are correctly cued. Look out for leaders on tapes, especially tapes that contain several cuts. Don't mistakenly cue up the announcement intended to tell you when a program should be aired—listen to beginnings of tapes for about a minute. Constantly monitor remote audio lines during the last hour before broadcasts to verify that no problems have developed. Review the locations of all program materials so that you use the correct ones. Take another look at all control settings before using an audio source. Look at the VU meters and modulation monitor several times each minute.

Is all of this a lot of extra work? No. It is part of your job. Nobody is perfect, but a broadcaster should try to be. Make every effort to do your job well, then look for ways to do it better.

BUILD GOOD RELATIONSHIPS WITH PEOPLE

Broadcasters do not work alone. Your broadcast career will put you in contact with many different people, giving you the opportunity to polish each other smooth.

Learn from Others. Observe your co-workers. Think about how other people do their work, learning from their successes and failures. Ask for advice and listen carefully when it is offered. You don't need to agree with everything you are told but use all information available when you make a decision.

Help Others Do Well. Look for ways to help the other station employees do a good job. Don't interfere with them or their chosen methods and don't leave problems that will slow them down. Make sure you have allowed all carts to recue. Rewind all tapes (unless directed otherwise) and refile all program materials correctly and neatly. Clean up the studio before you leave. Avoid unprofessional behavior that will annoy or interrupt someone else's work.

Share the Tough Jobs. Because small market radio stations rarely employ more than twelve people, all employees should be ready to help with some extra duties: empty wastebaskets, change teletype ribbons, clean up spilled coffee, or mow the grass in the transmitter field. Be ready to help cover work shifts when other people are unavailable because of vacation, illness, or special events. Broadcasting is a continuous effort—and someone has to work nights, weekends, and holidays.

Stupid Inefficiency. Sooner or later you will encounter something that seems all wrong to you. Be careful about forcing your bright ideas onto other people; it requires careful preparation of both the idea and the people who will hear it. Avoid making critical remarks because this just makes people mad. Instead, look for an opportunity to suggest a change that would help everybody in the station. Write your proposal down, listing the nature of the problem, your solution, the advantages (and disadvantages), and what is involved in the change you are proposing. Stay calm and don't get mad if things move slowly. Sell your idea!

Make Sure the Carts are Cued

Because radio stations depend heavily on carts, they are often a source of trouble and embarrassment. The most common problem is usually an uncued cart. When you pull your program materials before your air shift, take a moment to play all of the carts once (called *cycling the carts*). It's best if you listen to each one, but the main point is to make sure that all carts have cued automatically to the beginning.

Why cycle the carts? Sometimes you need to stop a cart manually before it recues itself. When you stop a cart yourself, take it out of the machine and lay it *upside down* right in front of you, so you won't forget to recue it later. When you recycle a cart, make sure the cart machine you're using is not live on the air.

Another common problem with carts is that you might play one, then forget you played it and play it again. Always note in the program log when you have played a spot. Some stations require that you write down the exact time each scheduled program event is aired. Other stations have the log divided into 15-minute blocks, and you need only make a check mark after each item is broadcast. You can also prevent playing the same cart twice by removing it from the cart machine as soon as it recues.

"The Boss" and You

Your work supervisor, "The Boss," expects you to do a good job. You are welcome to ask questions so that you can do your job well, but you are also expected to be able to think for yourself. Anything you can do to give The Boss confidence in you will be very helpful.

Try to follow instructions and listen carefully to constructive criticism. Arguing is a waste of time. The Boss is not always right, but probably has more experience than you do, so he or she just might know something that you don't! If you know The Boss is wrong, be patient and diplomatic, just as you wish to be treated. Be ready and willing to take on new responsibilities. Learn about the station's operation from as many angles as possible. This makes you a more valuable station employee.

"Can do" should be your attitude. "No way" is a poor response to a challenge. When confronted with a problem, tell The Boss you'll handle it. Some station managers don't want to take the time to discuss work assignments, so you will have to learn how to get additional information and help from another station employee if you need it.

Your Job Contract

Any station employee, including volunteers and student interns, should have a clear idea of his or her job responsibilities. These are sometimes explained in a detailed work contract. Many small market radio stations relay this information verbally, and

there isn't always a written list of job obligations available. Encourage your employer to provide you with a written job description. Explain that you want to know what duties you are expected to perform, and the contract will help you do your job well. Make your employer feel free to communicate with you.

Specifics in your job description should include:

☐ Your wage (stated hourly, monthly or yearly)

☐ What your normal working hours will be

☐ Under what circumstances you can earn overtime pay

☐ The station's policy regarding pay for working on holidays

☐ The station's vacation and sick leave policies

☐ Fringe benefits (health and life insurance)

☐ Educational benefits

If you are prepared to ask these questions, and write down the information in the presence of your employer, you will appear to know what you are doing. Most employers respect that.

Labor Unions

Some radio stations have formal labor union contracts. This means that a representative from an outside agency, the labor union, handles all of your contract negotiations for you. In fact, you *must* work through the union negotiator if you are working under a union contract. Labor unions have been very helpful in improving working conditions, job benefits, and wage scales. For this service to the station employees, unions charge a fee that each employee must pay. These *union dues* are sometimes a fixed dollar amount paid each month or can be calculated based on the actual earned income. Union contracts offer many benefits but also have the disadvantage of protecting some lazy employees while underpaying people who have extra talents and energies.

Part of developing your broadcasting career is developing a good job record. Any experience in broadcasting is a good start, including unpaid volunteer positions. Look for any opportunity to get additional experience and keep a written record of it for later reference.

DEVELOP YOUR CREATIVE TALENTS

Any broadcast-related experience is helpful in advancing your career. Creative people seem to have a free flow of ideas on all kinds of subjects. Much of this comes from a breadth of experience and a willingness to try anything. Here are some ways to enhance your creative abilities.

Read the local newspaper, news magazines, novels, books, broadcast trade publications, warning labels on boxes . . . in short, read anything you can find that will expand your knowledge of the world around you. Select the best TV shows to watch. View programs that will keep you informed and expand your knowledge. Enroll in college, trade school, or an adult education program, taking any class that will help you in your work, or seems interesting to you. This extra mental exercise will help to keep your mind alert, and the knowledge you gain will eventually be useful in your career.

Try New Techniques. Watch other radio people do their work. Arrange to visit and observe different radio stations. Listen at home, noting special program events that you want to understand from the combo operator's viewpoint. Then visit the studio and take notes that answer your questions. Look for ways to incorporate your new knowledge into your own studio work. Feel free to try new tricks but don't overload your spots with them.

Establish Good Contacts. Keep a file of names of people you meet. These other broadcasters might be able to help you find special resources that will help you in your work. They might even help you get a better job when the time comes to move on.

Be a Diplomat. If you have a creative idea, be sure to use it in a way that benefits the station. If you have the ability to write creative multivoice commercials, try involving some of your co-workers. It makes everyone look good and develops better working relationships.

BE READY FOR TROUBLE

Be ready for trouble by avoiding it in the first place. Don't overlook simple precautions (Fig. 8-2). Think things through carefully before you act. This applies to your whole life as a broadcaster, both at work and away from it.

Audience Relations. You need the friendship and loyalty of the audience. Work at developing that friendship. It should show through in your voice and attitude on the air, in the quality of your studio production work, your friendly and helpful attitude when answering the station's phone, and whenever you are out in public.

Care for the Equipment. Be careful with the tools of your trade. Do not abuse or misuse the studio equipment. Also do not allow yourself to be careless, or you could cost the station money and inconvenience through damaged or lost equipment and program materials.

Your Trouble Reports. When a problem occurs, be sure to write out a clear and informative trouble report. Give the station manager or chief engineer all possible usable information. Be sure to attach a note directly to any malfunctioning equipment. Avoid being critical or sarcastic; just report the facts.

Controlling the Control Room. If anyone enters the studio and disturbs your work, do whatever is necessary to restore order. Tell them to be quiet, tell them to go stand in the corner, or tell them to leave, if required. Never sit there and allow someone to distract you from your work. Even the station manager or owner should respect this rule. Keep the control room neat and clean up your pop bottles, coffee cups, and papers before the next shift begins.

Cart Handling Hints. Tape carts are very important to combo operators. Their convenient size and uses make them very valuable. Handle them gently. Make sure they are properly labeled. If you must leave a cart uncued temporarily, place it face down on the table as a reminder to recue it later. If you drop one, inspect it carefully for damage.

Electrical Safety

Properly installed broadcast equipment is safe, but you should observe the following extra precautions:

☐ Know the location of power switches and circuit breakers.

Fig. 8-2. Stay informed. Don't overlook simple precautions, such as keeping tabs on current weather conditions.

☐ Never reach inside equipment that is turned on or plugged in.

☐ If someone is receiving an electrical shock, *do not touch the shock victim directly*! Pull the victim loose with a loop of cloth, a rope, a microphone cord, or a dry wooden stick.

☐ Know how to contact an ambulance quickly.

☐ Never allow yourself or anyone else to work on the transmitter or tower without another person around.

☐ Insist on safe and reliable wiring in the studios.

☐ Never attempt to repair equipment without proper tools, training, and preparation.

Fire and Smoke

Use Class C (carbon dioxide) fire extinguishers for studio and transmitter fires.

Never use a water-type (Class A) fire extinguisher on or around electrical equipment. The wa-
ter will conduct electricity, and you could be killed by electrical shock. Class B or dry chemical fire extinguishers are effective in putting out fires, but the chemical causes severe damage to electrical circuits and components.

Equipment fires are rarely very bad because there is little combustible material inside. A serious fire hazard exists if the fire spreads to paper, wooden desks, curtains, carpet, or paint. If you experience a fire at the radio station, avoid breathing the smoke. Some electrical components contain chemicals that are extremely dangerous at high temperatures. Lung damage from smoke inhalation is only one kind of hazard. The smoke might also contain PCB, a flame-retardant chemical that causes permanent damage to the reproductive system resulting in tragic deformities, miscarriages, or total sterility.

Stay low and crawl on the floor if you must because the air usually will be cleaner there. Get out of the smoky area, then call for help. Try to stop small fires immediately but call for the fire department as soon as possible. Let the professionals handle larger fires. Inexperienced people could easily be injured or killed.

Weathering the Storm

Radio stations use tall towers to radiate their signals. Proper installation of the transmitting equipment assures a high degree of safety to the people working in the station. Avoid touching the transmitter during thunderstorms, however. Never climb on or go near the tower during storms. Don't touch metal studio equipment any more than necessary during storms.

Heavy snowfall can cause a huge static buildup on the antenna system, which may cause arcing and sparking around the station. Heavy snow and ice can build up on the tower and building (Fig. 8-3), so be careful when you go outside.

WRAP-UP

Broadcasters must be versatile, particularly newcomers trying to find that first job opportunity. Skill in announcing, equipment operation, or transmitter maintenance is not enough. Small-market broadcasters need to be well informed, prepared in advance, aware of potential trouble, and constantly verifying that their equipment and program materials are ready. This is not extra work; it is part of the job!

Broadcasters work with people, and good interpersonal relationships are important in building a successful career. Communication, openness, honesty, and a good attitude are all important ingredients in being a good employee.

Radio is an all-day, all-night, all-year service to the public. With so many hours of broadcasting available, each broadcaster needs to look for ways to stay

Fig. 8-3. Be ready for trouble. A local disaster can disrupt broadcast operations right when you want to cover big news!

fresh, interesting, and creative. Continuing education, innovation, and observation of other broadcasters are necessary parts of a broadcaster's life.

The best way to avoid trouble in broadcasting is to prepare for it and work to prevent it. Radio people need to develop good relationships with others, particularly the listeners. Broadcasters also need to know how to handle and maintain the studio equipment, write good trouble reports, keep the control room and studio in good order, practice good safety habits, and know how to handle studio and equipment fires.

Exercise 8-1.   Efficient Use of Studio Time

Listed below are the steps of audio production. Read each statement. Put an X by the steps that require you to use production studio equipment (console, tape decks, etc.). Leave the item blank if the step can be completed without the use of production studio equipment.

_____ 1. Discuss ideas for a commercial with a radio station time salesman and a sponsor.

_____ 2. Write a radio script.

_____ 3. Select possible jingles, sound effects, and music from radio station's record library.

_____ 4. Preview jingles, sound effects, and music to make final choices for what is appropriate to the spot being produced

_____ 5. Record a spot, including voices, music, and sound effects.

_____ 6. Evaluate the completed spot, listening for miscues, audio mixing problems, and timing overall production for correct length.

_____ 7. Return all production materials to correct storage locations.

Exercise 8-2.   Uncued Carts

Things are busy in the control room, and you must stop and remove a cart before it has completely recued itself. (Answer in short essay form.)

1. What must you do with that uncued cart to avoid trouble later?

2. How will you make sure you remember to do it, according to the procedure recommended in the text?

Exercise 8-3.   Fire Safety

1. What type of of fire extinguisher is the best for extinguishing fires in radio stations?

   A. Baking soda and water
   B. Dry chemical
   C. Carbon dioxide
   D. High-pressure air

2. What class of fire extinguisher is the best for extinguishing fires in radio stations?

   A. Class A
   B. Class B
   C. Class C
   D. Class D

3. If you notice that the room is filling with smoke, what should you do?

    A. Stay and fight the fire until firefighters come.

    B. Lie down on the floor and wait for help to arrive.

    C. Get down and crawl out of smoky areas.

    D. Throw water on the fire.

Exercise 8-4.   Electrical Safety

1. If you suspect someone is receiving an electrical shock, what is the first thing you should do?

    A. Pull the victim loose and then call a doctor.

    B. Don't touch the victim but turn off the source of power.

    C. Administer cardiopulmonary resuscitation (CPR).

    D. Loosen the victim's collar and give smelling salts.

2. What types of materials can be used to help you pull a shock victim loose? Check any that are safe to use.

    _____ A. Your hands in leather gloves

    _____ B. A loop of dry cloth

    _____ C. A metal chair

    _____ D. A dry stick

    _____ E. A rope

    _____ F. Bare wire

    _____ G. Bare hands

3. What basic safety precaution should you observe when you or someone else must work on transmitters or towers. (Check the best answer.)

    A. Never work alone.

    B. Be sure to ground yourself.

    C. Don't allow others nearby or they may distract you.

    D. Climb alone so that you don't overload the tower.

Vocabulary

contract	leader (on a tape)	studio time
covering a shift	overtime work	The Boss
cycling a cart	plug	uncued cart
format	production studio	union
job contract	pulling materials	union dues
job interview	remote broadcasts	union representative
labor union	setup	

Chapter 9

Emergency Broadcast Situations

Radio broadcasting is a versatile medium of mass communication. When an important news event occurs, reporters can provide on-the-spot reporting with portable tape recorders, live telephone reports, and small two-way radios. Handheld radio equipment has become more popular because of its light weight, excellent audio quality, and reliable range (Fig. 9-1). Reporting the news by radio link back to the studio is called *electronic news gathering* or *ENG*.

The go-anywhere-quickly ability of radio news has conditioned the listening public to trust it for information in any kind of an emergency. Broadcasters stand ready to serve the public in nearly every circumstance, and the widespread use of battery-powered portable radios has made this form of mass communication truly effective.

Emergency preparedness is important, both for the radio station and the audience. The station facilities and the individual listeners need to plan ahead for disasters. Broadcasters are equipped and trained to gather needed information quickly and accurately and to develop sound procedures for broadcasting this information. The broadcasters should tell the audience in advance when and how important information will be aired. The U.S. government sponsors the *Emergency Broadcast System,* established as a means of wide-area coordination of emergency information broadcasting.

PREPARING THE RADIO STATION

Radio stations prepare for all kinds of disaster and emergency broadcast situations. Yet, some kinds of emergencies are more likely than others (Fig. 9-2), depending on the weather, terrain, industry, and economy found in a particular station's coverage area. Large city radio stations often provide traffic spotters in airplanes, helicopters, or tall buildings to help motorists avoid traffic congestion. Stations along rivers get regular water level information, particularly in times of possible flooding. Seashore broadcasters are particularly strong on weather, water temperature, and surf conditions, while stations in the Midwest and Plains of North America offer effective coverage of thunderstorms and tornadoes. A radio station that has good farm news coverage is likely to broadcast livestock advisories

Fig. 9-1. Emergency preparedness. News reporters now use small, handheld radios to deliver on-the-spot coverage quickly.

GROWWRPH!

KONG

Fig. 9-2. Local emergencies. Your station's preparations depend *in part* on what is likely to happen in your area.

when weather conditions might have a bad effect on the health of farm animals.

The public turns to radio for quick information because most radio formats are easily interrupted for emergency broadcast situations. When you are on the air, you owe your listeners frequent reminders of when weather or emergency information will be broadcast.

Radio stations generally have the following equipment on hand as a part of their emergency preparedness procedures:

- ☐ News wire teletype
- ☐ Weather wire teletype
- ☐ Police and fire radio monitors
- ☐ Weather service radio receiver
- ☐ City, county, state, and regional maps

Some radio stations cover large metropolitan and rural areas. Many people depend on such regional stations for reliable information. The stations that are particularly committed to emergency broadcasting also have a number of special emergency items:

- ☐ Emergency power source (generator, batteries, solar power)
- ☐ Mobile or portable ENG equipment (remote-to-studio radios)
- ☐ Spare emergency antennas for the main transmitter
- ☐ Emergency food stored at the station and transmitter sites
- ☐ Storm-sheltered studio to protect the operators.

GATHERING EMERGENCY INFORMATION

Each radio station decides what kinds of news its particular audience needs and wants to hear. Local geography and weather conditions are important factors, although communities near potentially hazardous industrial sites expect local radio stations to be ready for emergencies of that sort.

In most areas of the country, a weather bulletin warning people of approaching storms is the most frequently broadcast emergency message. Few radio stations have staff meteorologists to predict the weather, so the information must come from outside sources.

Government Weather Service

Weather data, forecasting, and storm tracking are provided by the National Weather Service, an agency of the U.S. government. The radio station can install a teletype or weather radio receiver for constant weather information. The teletype is particularly good for quick access to weather information because the paper printout is intended for use as a radio script. The weather wire is tied into a network that provides local, state, and national weather information. Radio stations that subscribe to the AP (Associated Press) or UPI (United Press International) news wires also receive portions of the weather wire information.

The network of Weather Service radio stations, broadcasting on a special frequency, is growing and expanding in capability. It is useful as a warning device but lacks the printout needed by radio announcers. The weather radio can be used for direct broadcast, especially when severe storm warnings are issued. Some stations provide a tape recorder that starts automatically when the weather bulletin signal tone is transmitted. The audio quality of weather radios has often been fair to poor. Each station should make every effort to keep audio quality high so that the weather information will be understandable.

Private Weather Forecasting Services

Medium- and major-market radio stations often subscribe to commercially operated weather services. These private meteorologists use the government-collected weather data, but often do their own forecasting. This system has the advantage of using a qualified meteorologist who is also trained as a radio announcer. The listeners might be fooled into thinking that this weather forecaster actually works at their local radio station, when in truth, the meteorologist could be in another city a hundred miles away.

Commercial (nongovernment) weather services offer reliable information, and the announcers are able to answer questions or explain special weather situations. The fact that they might be some distance away is really not a barrier to accurately predicting the weather, plus the listeners benefit from an informative and understandable weather forecast, especially during severe storms. The local radio announcers often learn more about the weather this way, and so the station's overall weather reporting improves.

Police and Fire Monitors

Most radio news rooms include *VHF* (Very High Frequency) receivers that listen to radio messages transmitted by local police and fire departments. While it is illegal to directly rebroadcast police and fire department radio transmissions, these *police monitor receivers* can be used to gather *news tips*, which can be confirmed either by telephone or by dispatching a news reporter to the scene. Government radio secrecy laws prohibit you from mentioning anything on the air about something you heard on the police and fire monitors! These conversations are private.

Stringers and News Tips

Many radio stations have small news staffs, making it impossible to have a reporter available to cover all local news. Many stations, therefore, get news tips from people who are not station employees. These *informants* or *stringers* might be frequent callers because they live or work in an area where news often occurs. Or they might be members of the general public who just happen to see news in the making and call the radio station to tell about what they saw and heard.

Some radio stations encourage their listeners to provide news information, and might even pay for especially good or significant reporting. The news director needs to set down careful guidelines for the use of news tips because these informants are not trained in the ethics and skills of news reporting.

Audio News Services

Many radio stations are affiliated with national news networks that distribute hourly newscasts, plus features and special live coverage of national news. Some stations also participate in state or regional audio services that carry news and other information. Both of the national wire services provide audio services as well.

In addition to complete newscasts, these audio services provide *sound bites* and interviews, recordings of live-action sound or statements made by the newsmakers themselves. The local station writes the lead-in and tag announcements for the story or uses the wire service story from the teletype. As with wire service news and features, the audio material can be submitted to the network by a local station for regional or national distribution.

No radio station can provide all the information needed by all of the audience. Preparing for emergency broadcasting involves educating the station's audience to know what information will be available and when it will be broadcast.

TYPES OF EMERGENCY INFORMATION

Not all emergency information relates directly to an immediate emergency. Actually there are three types of emergency information, depending on the circumstances and the urgency of the information: routine information, health and welfare messages, and priority emergency messages.

Routine Information

Routine information is not urgent and usually does not need to be delivered to the listener at any particular time. The listener, however, learns about various kinds of emergencies and what procedures to take if an emergency occurs.

Routine information that prepares the audience for a future emergency is frequently delivered in the form of *public service announcements* (*PSAs*) that inform the listener about how to interpret storm information, poison control, boating or automobile safety tips, and similar situations. These PSAs are played many times so that eventually all of the listeners have had the opportunity to hear them.

Sometimes routine messages take the form of station *promos* that explain the station's readiness to report on the weather or other potential disasters. If some new development in public safety occurs, such as the installation of storm warning sirens, that information might be used as a regular news story first, then produced into a PSA later.

Health and Welfare Messages

Broadcasting is not normally used to carry messages intended for specific individuals. Normal telephone and mail service can be disrupted during a disaster, however. Under these circumstances, the local radio station can carry specific messages until normal communication lines are restored.

The health and welfare category also includes warnings about contaminated drinking water, damaged roads, and the availability of disaster relief supplies and assistance. Health and welfare messages can also appeal for public assistance in the search for a lost or missing person. Radio stations have occasionally been contacted by the police to broadcast a specific urgent message to a person known to be traveling in the area in the hope that they will be listening and receive the message.

Priority Emergency Messages

The most common example of priority messages is when a radio station transmits a severe weather bulletin. This type of information is timely in that it must be broadcast immediately and repeated frequently until the situation changes or returns to normal. Anytime a radio station is on the air during a true emergency, all on-duty staff members should be ready to help get priority information out to the audience quickly. This means being aware of bad weather conditions and knowing that the weather service is likely to be issuing weather bulletins. Similar alertness is required during summer heat waves, holiday traffic snarls, or at times when significant news events are taking place.

Remember, your audience can only hear what you put on the air. You need to think about the information needs of the audience and be ready to satisfy those needs.

WHEN TO BROADCAST EMERGENCY INFORMATION

The broadcaster has a responsibility to keep the audience informed but must also use judgment in not overloading the listener with too many unimportant facts. The news director, program director, and station manager must develop guidelines of when to interrupt regular programming to put special news, weather, or emergency information bulletins on the air.

Interrupting Regular Broadcasts. The public welfare dictates that regular programming should be interrupted to broadcast important information under the following circumstances:

- ☐ When asked to broadcast a severe weather warning message from the National Weather Service
- ☐ When an urgent news bulletin or weather advisory is received that the wire service or network describes as being *for immediate broadcast*
- ☐ When the station receives news or information that requires immediate broadcast to save or protect lives or property
- ☐ Any Emergency Broadcast System message from local or state civil defense authorities or from the national government
- ☐ In accordance with your station's established guidelines governing the interruption of regular programs for news bulletins

Delay and Broadcast Later. You should delay and broadcast at the first convenient opportunity the following kinds of news items:

- ☐ Weather information about possible storm activity that could occur later in the day
- ☐ News bulletins that are urgent but do not require immediate broadcast to protect life or property
- ☐ Health and welfare messages or public information, handled as requested by the originator of the message

Hold for Next Broadcast. You should hold for broadcast during the next newscast these kinds of news stories:

☐ Regular updated weather forecasts and data
☐ Routine news
☐ Notices of community event cancellations or postponements

THE EMERGENCY BROADCAST SYSTEM

The Emergency Broadcast System (EBS) uses existing broadcast networks and facilities as a quick and efficient way for local, state, and national authorities to transmit important information to the general public. The EBS was originally called *CONELRAD* (*CON*trol of *EL*ectromagnetic *RAD*iation), and its main purpose was for government-to-public communication during air raid warfare and national emergencies. In a few years it was obvious that air raids and national emergencies were rare, while the idea of broadcasters banding together for an emergency communications network seemed to have many uses.

The EBS was formed, still retaining the provisions for government takeover of the broadcast facilities when needed, but finding frequent use at the local level. The EBS's purpose and function is defined in this excerpt from the FCC Rules and Regulations, section 73.935(a):

> Examples of emergency situations (at the state or local level) which may warrant either an immediate or delayed response by the licensee are: tornadoes, hurricanes, floods, tidal waves, earthquakes, icing conditions, heavy snows, widespread fires, discharge of toxic gases, widespread power failures, industrial explosions and civil disorders.

Each radio station should post in the control room or newsroom a large folder clearly marked *EBS Checklist.* This list is a summary of the FCC rules concerning EBS and is written in a very understandable and clear way. All radio station employees should become familiar with the EBS Checklist and take the time to read through the entire FCC rules subpart on the subject, about twelve pages of material.

Simply stated, the EBS uses a network of monitor receivers so that radio and TV stations pass the information from one to another until everyone is notified. The relay procedures are clearly explained in the EBS information packet provided by the FCC.

Each station operates an EBS receiver that listens to some other specified radio station. EBS messages can be received either via the EBS receiver, the news wire, from local authorities, or the weather service radio or teletype. If an EBS message is to be broadcast, a special *EBS Attention Signal* is transmitted for about 23 seconds (Fig. 9-3). This two-tone combination trips alarms on other EBS monitor receivers and is distinctive enough (actually it is very annoying) to get the attention of regular listeners, notifying everyone that important information is about to be transmitted.

An EBS message usually includes the following information:

☐ Date and time of origination
☐ Agency or authority originating the message
☐ Intended geographic coverage area of the message
☐ Nature of the emergency
☐ Expected duration of the emergency
☐ Action to be taken by the public

Any time you hear an EBS message, listen carefully. This is important information for you as a broadcaster, and you will need to pass along accurate information to your listeners.

Each participating broadcast station and network sends periodic EBS test messages, which are clearly marked. These are for test purposes and should be logged to indicate that the test message was received. Many program or transmitter operating logs

Fig. 9-3. EBS attention signal. A loud two-tone signal is transmitted so that nobody misses an important announcement.

have special places to indicate reception of an EBS test message.

This discussion of the Emergency Broadcast System is far from complete. Be sure to check your station's latest EBS Checklist or a recent copy of the FCC Rules and Regulations, Part 73, for current information.

WRAP-UP

Radio news has become an important means of public communication, providing fast and reliable information to the public. This makes radio particularly useful in the distribution of emergency information of various types.

Just as radio stations prepare for emergencies, they can also inform and instruct the public into preparedness for future disasters through news stories and public service announcements. Radio stations are also ready to relay information from the weather service or government agencies for the protection of life and property.

The Emergency Broadcast System interconnects all radio and TV stations for coordinated emergency information broadcasts.

Exercise 9-1.   Emergency Preparedness

1. Radio stations have various means of gathering emergency information. Based on the text, list at least three such information gathering resources found in most radio stations.

2. List at least three special precautions, supplies, or equipment items that a station has ready for emergency situations.

3. List at least two different means by which a radio station gets weather information.

Exercise 9-2.   News Gathering Terminology

1. Define *ENG*.

2. Define *stringer*.

3. Define *EBS*.

4. Define *lead-in*.

Exercise 9-3.   Emergency Broadcast System

1. Under what circumstances must you interrupt regular programming immediately to broadcast news information?

    A. When doing so will protect lives or property

    B. When doing so will improve the station's ratings

    C. When a routine updated weather forecast is released

    D. When you hear a news tip on the police monitor

2. About how long does an EBS alert tone last?

    A. 5 seconds

    B. 12 seconds

    C. 23 seconds

    D. 32 seconds

Vocabulary

audio news service	news reporter	tag announcement
CONELRAD	news tips	timely information
direct broadcast	on-the-spot reporting	traffic spotters
EBS (Emergency Broadcast System)	police monitor receiver	weather bulletin
EBS Attention Signal	printout	weather radio
ENG (Electronic News Gathering)	priority information	weather service
health and welfare information	private weather service	weather wire
informants	routine information	
lead-in	sound bites	
news director	stringers	

102

Chapter 10

In the Public Interest: The FCC Rules

In the early days of radio broadcasting, the public was extremely interested in this strange new technology. These early broadcasting efforts were quite primitive, with poor-quality programming, unpredictable program schedules, wandering operating frequencies, and undependable equipment. It was chaotic.

THE BIRTH OF THE FCC

Commercial broadcasting had its infancy in the decade following 1920, yet broadcasters operated with little guidance or regulation until the United States Congress passed the Radio Act of 1927, followed by a more effective piece of legislation, *The Communications Act of 1934*. Regulatory efforts fared about the same in other countries of the world.

Finally, in 1934 the Communications Act established the *Federal Communications Commission (FCC)*, which was given jurisdiction over the use of the airwaves in the United States and its territories. The FCC controlled the use of radio transmitters, intending that they be used *in the public interest*.

Over the years the FCC Rules and Regulations have been established, modified, expanded, and deleted, but the goal of the broadcast service is to benefit the public interest in an orderly way.

The Communications Act of 1934 provides general guidelines describing what is expected of the various radio services. It is the foundation upon which the FCC's Rules are laid. The FCC Rules are far more thorough with specific instructions about the legalities of broadcasting. Beyond the specific rules is a less-formal set of guidelines called *good operating practice*. This is the "etiquette" of radio broadcasters.

Many books on the subject of broadcasting deal with the early years of radio as well as the establishment of the FCC. Check the bibliography for books that cover broadcast history.

GETTING ACQUAINTED WITH THE RULES

Each person operating a radio transmitter is obliged to do so in a lawful way. Proper transmitter operation avoids needless radio signal interference, and it also avoids expensive equipment trouble. When you apply for an FCC Restricted Radiotelephone Permit (the "disc jockey" license), you register your intent to comply with the rules.

Some operators never read the rules. They are either too busy to bother or are afraid they won't understand the legal language. Familiarity with the FCC rules is not such a big problem.

☐ Have your chief engineer show you where the rules are kept.

☐ Skim through Part 73, the rules for broadcasting.

☐ Notice how the rules are organized into specific subjects.

☐ Do not waste time on the overly technical information on your first read through.

☐ Feel free to look up anything that looks interesting to you.

☐ Pick up the rule book and read it again until you have read all of Part 73.

If you operate the station according to the policies and guidelines of that station, you will probably be in compliance with the rules. If your chief engineer doesn't want you to see the station copy of the FCC Rules, or if your employer repeatedly and deliberately violates the FCC's Rules, you should consider finding another place to work.

ORGANIZATION OF THE RULE BOOK

The FCC and the United States Congress are constantly revising the rules, so a discussion of specific rules runs the risk of being inaccurate. You will benefit from a general understanding of how the book is organized, however.

The FCC Rules for all radio services fill a large document many hundreds of pages in length. Because you are only concerned with Part 73 (the part for broadcasting), this makes the FCC Rules less overwhelming. Once you find Part 73, take some time to look over the index of subjects covered, found at the beginning.

Most radio stations subscribe to the FCC rules on a continuing basis so that corrections are received automatically. If you open the notebook containing the FCC rules, you might be confronted with an accumulation of transmittal sheets that came with each packet of updated rules. The transmittal sheets contain specific instructions about what rules were deleted or changed and what pages in the rule book should be removed and replaced. You can skip over these without reading them. You need to find *Part 73 Radio Broadcast Services.*

Part 73 of the FCC Rules is subdivided into over four thousand numbered sections, with each section also subdivided into numbered paragraphs. The sections are numbered consecutively, starting with 73.1, then 73.2, 73.3, and so on. The sections are grouped by general topic:

☐ Subpart A— AM Broadcast Stations
—73.1 through 73.190.

☐ Subpart B— FM Broadcast Stations
—73.201 through 73.346

☐ Subpart C— Noncommercial Educational FM Broadcast Stations
—73.501 through 73.599

☐ Subpart D— Reserved (for future rules)

☐ Subpart E— Television Broadcast
—73.601 through 73.699

☐ Subpart F— International Broadcast
—73.701 through 73.793

☐ Subpart G— Emergency Broadcast System
—73.901 through 73.962

☐ Subpart H— Rules Applicable in Common
(relevant to all stations)
73.1001 through 73.4280

There is nothing mysterious about the FCC rule book. It is written in a legal language style, but it is very specific and easy to understand.

In the beginning of Part 73 of the FCC's Rules, various definitions are given of terms used to describe the AM broadcast stations. Notice that each rule is very specific. Take special note of the cross-reference at 73.6 explaining where to look for the definition of *daytime.* You must turn several pages farther back into the rules because this definition logically belongs in Subpart H, the rules that apply to all radio and TV stations.

If you are ever unsure about whether or not some operating practice is legal, go straight to the FCC rule book and look it up. You can purchase your own copy of the rules. Ask your station manager or chief engineer for the address and price information or contact any field office of the Federal Communications Commission.

RULES OPERATORS TEND TO BREAK

Radio stations in small and medium markets often must train new or inexperienced announcers and operators. These newcomers are usually full of enthusiasm and good intentions but might not have developed good work habits fully. Sadly, some of the old timers can have poor work habits too.

FCC rules occasionally get broken, but in most cases this is not a serious problem if all station employees work to correct their errors and avoid repeating them. Some rules are broken quite frequently, usually because they involve often-used procedures that occasionally are overlooked in the rush of control room activity. Let's examine some common mistakes:

Missed Station I.D. Announcement

Forgetting to give the station ID is like forgetting to tell people your own name, but it happens often. Why? Because it occurs at the top of the hour, as required. The problem here is that many other things also happen at the top of the hour; getting out of a musical piece, playing spots, weather updates, news plugs, playing jingles, introducing the newscast, reading the news, buttons, knobs, log books . . .. OOPS! No ID announcement. The control room operator *forgot* in the rush of things. Here's what the rules say about that:

> **73.1201 STATION I.D. REQUIRE-
> MENTS.** (a) *When regularly required*:
> Broadcast station identification announce-
> ments shall be made: (1) at the beginning and
> ending of each time of operation, and (2)
> hourly, as close to the hour as feasible, at
> a natural break in program offerings.

If you miss the required ID at the top of the hour, make it as soon as you have a break in the programming. Often this ID announcement can be worked into the program content without causing a major disruption.

Make no apologies on the air! If you miss the ID announcement, just give the ID at a natural break in what you are doing. For instance, you could conclude a news story with a time and temperature check that includes the ID:

> . . . AND THE GOVERNOR SIGNED THE
> BILL LATE LAST NIGHT. *IT'S 73
> DEGREES AT 9:01 ON WXYZ, DETROIT.*
> IN OTHER STATE NEWS, IT'S BACK TO
> THE DRAWING BOARD FOR THE PRO-
> POSED FREEWAY INTERCHANGE . . .

Don't waste any time telling the audience that you missed the ID and are now making it up. The audience doesn't care!

Missing Operator Signatures on Logs

The rule about operators signatures is often broken by mere forgetfulness. The operator coming on duty might be busy or preoccupied and simply forgets to sign on the log book. Likewise, the operator going off duty might be in a hurry to leave, forgetting to sign off in the log book.

> **73.1800 LOGS, GENERAL REQUIRE-
> MENTS** . . . In the case of program and
> operating logs, the employee shall sign the
> appropriate log when starting on duty and
> again when going off duty, and setting forth
> the time of each.

Make it a part of your regular routine to look at the log immediately upon entering the studio for your air shift. Sign yourself into the log and make sure the other operator has signed off the log before he or she leaves the studio.

The chief engineer or assistant is required to perform a weekly inspection of the transmitter and the transmitter operating logs. You can save the chief engineer a lot of needless paperwork if you make sure the logs have been completely and correctly filled out. This is not pointless paperwork. You are accountable for the transmitter's operation while on duty.

Other Frequently Broken FCC Rules

Station managers and chief engineers see their employees make the same mistakes over and over. Listed below are some of the most common ones, along with the FCC rule number. If you don't understand exactly what is meant by something mentioned here, look up the rule and make sure you know what the FCC wants. Ask your station manager or chief engineer for further explanations if you need them.

Station ID

- ☐ Given at wrong time [see 73.1201(a)]
- ☐ Improper insertion of slogan [see 73.1201(b)]
- ☐ Improper location given [see 73.1201 (2)]

Operating Log

- ☐ Meter reading missed [see 73.1820]
- ☐ Transmitter not running licensed power [see 73.1560]
- ☐ Log corrections improperly made [see 73.1800(c)]
- ☐ Missing EBS test reports [see 73.962(4)]
- ☐ Meter readings not taken at sign-on or sign-off [see 73.1820(2) and (3)]

Program Log

- ☐ Missing signatures [see 73.1800(a)]
- ☐ ID announcement not logged [see 73.1201 and 73.1810(4)]
- ☐ Programs not signed on and off [see 73.1810]
- ☐ Length of spot not given [see 73.1810(2)ii]

Operating Practices

- ☐ Overmodulation and undermodulation [see 73.1570]
- ☐ Extra loud commercials [found in FCC policy statement referred to in 73.4075]

Many radio stations have a *discrepancy record* kept with the daily logs, in which operators note irregularities, problems, and errors. This gives the station management a good opportunity to note operational problems and provide station employees with further guidance on the subject. It is legal and acceptable to report an error you have made. Feel free to do it so that everyone can do better in the future.

One of the best ways to operate legally is to become familiar with the FCC Rules. Rules changes are noted and discussed in detail in various broadcast magazines, helping you stay informed of the additions, modifications, and deletions.

ABOUT RADIO STATION CALL SIGNS

The government of each country establishes laws that govern the use of all radio transmitters within that country. In the United States, the government has set up the Federal Communications Commission to regulate broadcasting and other radio services.

For stations licensed in the United States, the FCC must approve and register which call letters a station uses. This helps a listener know for sure what station is being heard. The hourly ID requirement also helps; the listeners know when to listen for the call letters. As it turns out, the stations want you to know who they are; therefore the ID announcements are plentiful, along with slogans and other types of identifying announcements (Fig. 10-1).

The FCC has observed a long-standing custom with broadcast station call signs: all United States radio and TV stations east of the Mississippi River have call letters beginning with the letter W, while stations west of the Mississippi begin with K (Fig. 10-2). There are a few exceptions to this rule among very old radio stations. Most radio stations have four letters in their call signs, although a few of the older ones were assigned only three letters. Eventually, all possible three-letter combinations ran out, then four-letter combinations were assigned.

WRAP-UP

Broadcasting was once a wide open, chaotic pur-

Fig. 10-1. Call signs that mean something. Some station call letters say a lot about a station's surroundings.

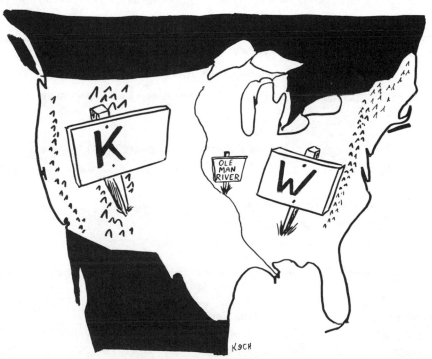

Fig. 10-2. How calls are assigned. Years ago the FCC adopted the idea that call signs for stations west of the Mississippi would begin with *K*, while those to the east would begin with *W*.

suit, with countless stations going on and off the air at random. Eventually the United States government created the Communications Act of 1934, which established the Federal Communications Commission. Regulation of all radio transmitters followed, bringing order and cooperation to the airwaves.

The FCC Rules commonly used by broadcasters is actually only a portion of the Communications Act of 1934, with Part 73 being specifically devoted to rules about radio and television broadcasting. The rules are grouped according to general subject matter, with an index referring the reader to specifically numbered paragraphs.

Operators do break the rules occasionally, but every effort must be made to avoid this. Corrections should be made as soon as possible by the person having actual knowledge of the error made.

The FCC assigns call signs, required by international law, so that each radio station can be positively identified. Most radio stations pick from unassigned calls to select call letters that have some significance.

Each operator should be familiar with the FCC rules by reading through them and referring to them as needed to answer any procedural questions. Copies of the FCC rules are available in any radio or TV station or can be purchased from the U.S. Government Printing Office in Washington DC.

Exercise 10-1.   Radio Station Call Letters

Goal: Discover why local radio stations have particular call letters.

Method:
1. List the call letters of several radio stations in your area.
2. Explain briefly why you think those letters were chosen by that station. (Hint: some stations are named after major local businesses or institutions.)
3. If you can't figure out why a given station has those call letters, try calling that station and asking.

Exercise 10-2.   Looking Into the Rules

Goal: Become familiar with the organization of the FCC Rules.

Method: Using the index found in the FCC Rules, look up each topic and write down the rule number that deals with that topic.

1. Requirements for tower lights
2. Different classes of FM broadcast transmitter power output
3. Definition of nighttime for AM broadcast stations
4. Allowable variations in transmitter power output
5. When directional antenna pattern changeover must occur
6. Pre-sunrise broadcast authorizations
7. Modulation level requirement for FM stereo pilot tone

Vocabulary

commercial broadcasting
Communications Act of 1934
discrepancy record
good operating practice

FCC, Federal Communications Commission
FCC Field Office
operating log

Part 73
program log
transmittal sheet

Unit III. Advanced skills. You'll be called upon to perform several duties at once. Here, the author stands transmitter watch at WHAS-AM and WAMZ-FM in Louisville, KY. The job also includes keeping the FM station's automation system computer and cart machines updated as well as helping with projection room and videotape duties at WHAS-TV—*all at the same time.*

UNIT III

Advanced Broadcast Skills

Unit III of *Skills for Radio Broadcasters* contains material that digs quite a bit deeper into the broadcaster's art. Once you've mastered the basics of cueing records and tapes and sounding reasonably confident as an announcer, you'll want to try more complex tasks.

As your exposure to radio broadcasting expands, you'll find yourself asking, ''How do they do that?'' You won't find all the answers to your questions here, but Unit III lays a firm foundation to help you ask ''Huh?'' intelligently.

Chapter 11

Advanced Scriptwriting

You've noticed it many times—the announcer says, "We'll be back, right after these messages." Producing all of those messages is a big part of a broadcaster's day. A lot of work is required to make good commercials, but it can be the most fun you'll have all day as a broadcaster. Radio advertising income is necessary for a commercial radio station to survive (Fig. 11-1). In this chapter, you'll learn more about how those messages are produced.

In Chapter 1 you learned about the many program events that are strung together to fill a radio station's broadcast day. Aside from the records played on a music station or the conversations heard on talk-format stations, the broadcast day is filled with hundreds of short program events called commercials, public service announcements (PSAs), and promotional announcements (promos). All of these short program events are collectively known as *spots*, generally lasting a minute or less. *Features* are slightly longer (up to five minutes) but use production methods very much like spots.

SOME SIMPLE DEFINITIONS

A *commercial,* short for "commercial message," is an announcement about someone's product or services. That someone, called the *sponsor,* pays the radio station for broadcasting the sponsor's message. Commercials pay to keep a station on the air. The sponsor is typically some commercial enterprise, a business that exists to make money for its owners. The commercial message is intended to generate profit for the sponsor.

A *PSA,* or *public service announcement,* is also a message telling about either products or services, but the sponsor does not pay for the air time. Furthermore, the sponsor is usually some kind of nonprofit agency that operates for the public benefit, such as charitable organizations and community service agencies. While PSAs serve to raise money for an agency, the intent is to collect money for public benefit rather than private profit.

The *promo* (promotional announcement) is aired by the radio station to tell about itself. In this case,

Fig. 11-1. Commercial broadcasting. Money is the lifeblood of most radio stations. Well-written commercials improve a station's earning power.

the product or service being "sold" is the radio station's own broadcast services. In some cases, a radio station will air promos for some other radio or TV station. Such promos are actually commercials. Promos tell about station-run contests, promote specific upcoming broadcasts, inform listeners about the station's format, or just serve to establish the station's image and style in the minds of the listeners.

Features are short, informative radio programs that are intended to educate the listener rather than sell a product or service. Even though their intent is quite different from commercials, PSAs, and promos, the production techniques are similar for all four types of program events. This chapter will look at the basics of scriptwriting and survey the process of producing commercials, PSAs, promos, and features.

SCRIPTWRITING

As you've probably guessed long ago, radio announcers have written material in front of them while they speak on the air. Even when they sound like they're making up spur-of-the-moment jokes, they're often actually reading from an ad-lib sheet. A good script is essential.

Creativity and individuality are important in commercial production. Standardization is important, however, when you're writing something that someone else must read. A well-written script appears on scriptwriting paper, as shown in Fig. 11-2.

Just as there are basic rules of the road for driving a car, there are rules for good scriptwriting. While styles and procedures vary from one station to another, most broadcasters would agree that a radio script for commercials, PSAs, promos, and short features includes several basic characteristics. A script should be:

☐ Easy to read
☐ Timed properly
☐ Properly identified
☐ Complete with all necessary production notes

Easily Read Scripts

Imagine yourself on the air, and you suddenly realize that in a few seconds you'll need to open the copy book and read a 30-second commercial live on the air. You hurriedly flip through the copy book, arranged alphabetically, and find the script you need.

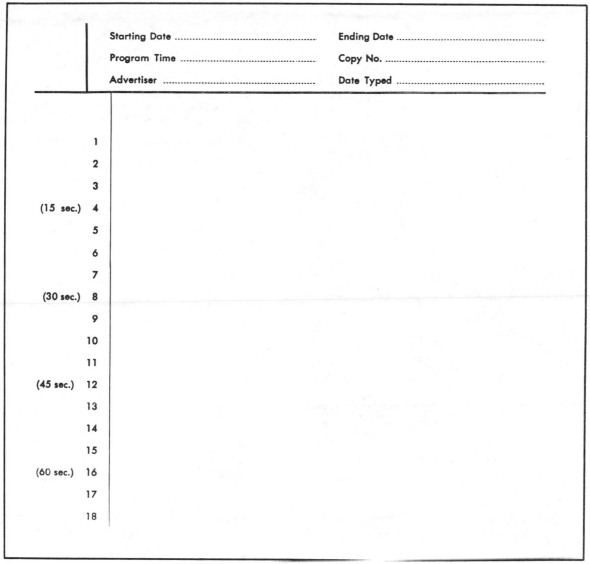

Fig. 11-2. Radio scripts. Script-writing paper has timing marks along the left margin and space at the top for other crucial information.

The script, to your horror, is handwritten by someone whose handwriting is awful—his pen skipped, words are crossed out, sentences are incomplete, and the numbers in the sponsor's prices are so sloppy that you can't tell a 1 from a 7 from a 9. If you try to read that mess, you're going to sound like a total fool (Fig. 11-3). Wouldn't you just hate to go through that?

Any radio station with some professional pride won't allow that to happen. One important motto for a good broadcaster is: "Make it easy on the other guy." The script should be typed neatly, making it easy to read. Broadcast scripts are typed in all-capital letters on standard scriptwriting paper in a double-spaced format.

If you don't know how to type yet, learn now! You'll thank yourself many times over throughout your broadcast career. Some radio stations now have

Fig. 11-3. Messy scripts are bad news. Nobody wants to get caught fumbling for words because of a sloppy script.

word processing equipment available to help make scriptwriting easier. Learn how to do that, too! It's a lot of fun and really helps translate your creative masterpieces to paper with a minimum of bother.

Properly Timed Scripts

The scriptwriter uses the timing marks on the left margin of script paper to judge how much time the announcers will need to read the script. One page of double-spaced script can be read in a minute, so it follows logically that a 30-second announcement requires a half-page script.

Timing will vary with the kind of spot as well as the personal style of the announcer. Some spots require a rapid-fire delivery, while others, because of the content of the message, go much more slowly and permit fewer words to be delivered within the allotted time.

Radio stations run on a strict schedule. If the sponsor bought a one-minute spot, the sponsor is entitled to that minute, not 45 seconds, not 70 seconds. In practice, spots are produced to run about a second short of their scheduled time. Spots must *never* run longer than the allotted time. A commercial or PSA might run during a network broadcast where precise timing is crucial for the broadcast to sound smooth. Spots cannot be too short or too long, or they will not mesh properly with the rigid network schedule.

Properly Identified Scripts

Standard radio scriptwriting paper for commercials has space at the top for certain standard information. Ideally, the following information is included at the top of each script:

- ☐ The sponsor's name
- ☐ The required total length of the message
- ☐ The dates the spot may begin airing
- ☐ The date the spot must stop being aired
- ☐ The sales person's name
- ☐ The scriptwriter's name
- ☐ The advertising agency's name (if any)

Some commercial scripts also include information identifying the tape machine used to record the master copy of the spot and the date the spot was produced, although this is less common.

Complete Production Notes

Production notes in a radio script indicate all the extra instructions for production of a spot beyond just the words being said. Such production notes include the names of the various voices in a multivoice spot, what music or sound effects are used, notes for audio mixing, and timing of elements of the spot. When using a cut from a record album or production library, be sure to include specific notes about where the music or sound effects came from.

In a small- or medium-market radio station, a particular announcer might write the script for a radio commercial and also have near-full creative control of any special effects, story lines, or humor created for use in that announcement. One announcer is likely to handle all of the audio control engineering for the production of the spot as well. In that situation, it is tempting to script out only the words to be spoken and just make mental notes about production.

It's a good idea to include full production notes, however, because commercial scripts are usually saved in a file cabinet. The spot might need to be produced again from scratch many months later. If a particular bit of music or a unique sound effect proved successful for one spot, complete production notes will later reveal where that information came from—a real benefit if you ever want to find that material again quickly for some other production effort.

You can incorporate complete production notes in your scripts in two ways: (1) simple production notes can be inserted as notes or remarks right in the sentences of the script or (2) the production notes can be written in a separate column to the left to indicate the approximate time when the special effects should occur.

Use whichever method makes the script easy to read and makes the production notes easy to follow.

Do what is necessary to write a clear script. The payoff comes in production sessions that will go much more smoothly—a time-saver in the long run. Taking the time to write a neat and orderly script might seem like a bother at first, especially because these things must usually be done in a hurry. After some practice, however, you'll have some very creative brainstorms and write beautiful 30-second radio drama commercials in less than half an hour.

The separate production notes in a script can include directions for *voice inflection*. These can give the announcer specific instructions about how the voice should sound. Such comments can be short, such as "breathless" or "frantic." The notes might also indicate what kind of accent the voice should have: "little girl—sounds like a spoiled brat" or "deep, spooky voice—sounds like its coming from a cave."

Scriptwriting doesn't need to follow the strict laws of grammar. Radio is for the ear, not the eye. Write in the normal conversational pauses with plenty of punctuation.

PRODUCTION RESOURCES

Think about the commercials, promos, PSAs, and features you've heard—and liked. Why were they interesting? Why did they stand out? Why didn't they sound just like the hundreds of other radio announcements that go by your ears every day?

If you work in a small- or medium-market radio station, it's likely that you'll get to write and produce spots in addition to your work as an on-air radio personality. In fact, it might be a required part of your job.

You don't have to be a world-class comedy writer to put some zing into your production work. Here are some ways to pep up your scripts.

It's no challenge to write a just-the-facts commercial script. An uninspiring script is full of standard, unexciting phrases. In fact, if you changed the name of the store and the product and just a few other words, you could use this script to sell auto parts or speed reading courses. Here's an example of an all-too-common approach to script writing.

****

FRANK'S DRESS SHOP 30 sec (Version 1)

	COME TO FRANK'S DRESS SHOP. FRANK'S, ON THE CORNER OF
	MAIN AND ELM, CAN SATISFY ALL OF YOUR WOMEN'S APPAREL
	NEEDS. THEY HAVE A WIDE SELECTION, FRIENDLY
10	CLERKS, AND LOW, LOW PRICES. FRANK'S IS OPEN MONDAY
	THROUGH THURSDAY, 10 TO 7, FRIDAY AND SATURDAY THEY'RE
	OPEN TILL 9. FRANK'S DRESS SHOP IS CONVENIENTLY LOCATED
20	IN THE HEART OF CLAYPOOL JUNCTION. FRANK'S HAS A
	CONVENIENT LAY-AWAY PLAN, SO DO YOUR HOLIDAY SEASON
	SHOPPING EARLY. LADIES, LET'S BE FRANK ABOUT THIS . . .
30	BUY YOUR DRESSES AT FRANK'S—YOU'LL BE GLAD YOU DID.

****

Didn't that spot for Frank's just thrill you? It didn't? No wonder! All of the essential facts were there, and there was even a little humor slipped in toward the end. Overall, though, it was a pretty boring spot. This kind of message will not make the sponsor's product stand out in the crowd.

A straightforward script like this one might be the best you can do if the sponsor has no plan to sell anything more than some dresses, but this ho-hum message does nothing to improve the sponsor's image. If you get handed one of these scripts already written, ask for permission to rewrite it to make it sparkle.

It's far more satisfying for you (and for the sponsor) to produce a standout piece of work—one that makes the sponsor call the station and say, "Hey! I just heard my spot on the air and it sounds great! Tell the guy that produced it that I want him to do all my spots!"

Take a listen to the top-rated radio stations in your area, and you'll hear a lot of things that are missing from that boring spot for Frank's Dress Shop. Good scriptwriters know that they have all kinds of resources available, and even the smallest radio station can usually find what it takes to produce some very creative stuff.

Here are some tricks of the trade used by many radio scriptwriters to add some zip to the straight facts spot. After each trade secret, you'll revisit "Frank's Dress Shop" to see how some creative ideas might be applied.

Use a Jingle Package

A *jingle* is music specially prepared for use in a commercial, PSA, or promo. It can be vocal or instrumental. Jingle packages might come from the radio station's own record library, which usually

116

includes a special record collection of jingles for all situations.

A production library has *musical beds* that come in 10-, 20-, 30-, and 60-second lengths. They also have singing jingles for nearly any product or service imaginable.

The jingle package for a particular spot might be supplied by the advertising agency or by the manufacturer of the product being advertised. In any vocal jingle, there is usually an instrumental musical bed for the local announcer's voice to give specific details and give the local dealer's name and address.

Let's see how the addition of a jingle can affect the spot. Because the script is already 30 seconds long, some rewriting will be needed to make time for the music. That's okay—the first script was pretty boring anyway!

****

FRANK'S DRESS SHOP   30 sec   (Version 2)

jingle source: Production Library Album 12, Side 1, Band 5

	(vocal jingle: "The shop that has more . . ." music bed under announcer) FRANK'S DRESS SHOP, ON THE CORNER OF MAIN AND ELM, HAS WHAT YOU WANT—LOW PRICES, FRIENDLY
10	CLERKS, AND THE LATEST STYLES. CASUAL, SPORT OR FORMAL, THE LADY LOOKS BEST WHEN THE DRESSES COME FROM FRANK'S. HOLIDAY SEASON SHOPPING IS EASIER WHEN YOU SHOP EARLY AT FRANK'S AND USE OUR CONVENIENT
20	LAY-AWAY PLAN. (jingle up ". . . there's more of what you're looking for . . ." music under announcer) FRANK'S IS OPEN WEEKDAYS TILL 7, FRIDAYS AND SATURDAYS TILL 9. COME TO FRANK'S DRESS SHOP AND SEE FOR YOURSELF.
30	FRANKLY—YOU'LL BE GLAD YOU DID. (music up to end)

****

Add an Instrumental Musical Bed

Unlike a prepared vocal or instrumental jingle package, the music bed is often just an excerpt from some popular music in the station's record library. Picking personal favorite musical selections and adding these to your commercial productions helps set the appropriate mood (Fig. 11-4). Make sure you pick music that fits the sponsor's company image. The music should also fit your station's format.

When you make your own musical beds, don't just use the first 30 seconds of a selection. You might find that the best portion for your needs is somewhere in the middle of the piece. The tune might have a very satisfactory conclusion, so you can edit the first 20 seconds and the last 10 seconds of the song together to make a dynamite 30-second bed.

Unlike the vocal jingle package used above, the musical bed is strictly instrumental. You have the full 30 seconds to deliver the message—no time is lost to singing voices. Don't forget to mention the source of your music on the script. You might need that particular piece of music again later.

Here's the Frank's Dress Shop script again, rewritten slightly from Version 2. This one fills the entire 30 seconds.

****

FRANK'S DRESS SHOP   30 sec   (Version 3)

music bed from "The Electric Ecclectics" side 2, band 1

	(music up to establish, then under) FRANK'S DRESS SHOP, ON THE CORNER OF MAIN AND ELM, HAS WHAT YOU WANT— LOW PRICES, FRIENDLY CLERKS, AND THE LATEST STYLES.
10	CASUAL, SPORT OR FORMAL, THE LADY LOOKS BEST WHEN THE DRESSES COME FROM FRANK'S. WE ALSO HAVE EVEN SIZES FOR THE MATURE WOMAN. HOLIDAY SEASON SHOPPING IS EASIER AND YOU'LL SAVE TIME, WHEN YOU SHOP EARLY AT FRANK'S.
20	USE OUR CONVENIENT LAY-AWAY PLAN. (music up for 1 second, then under) FRANK'S IS OPEN WEEKDAYS TILL 7, FRIDAYS AND SATURDAYS TILL 9. COME TO FRANK'S DRESS SHOP IN CLAYPOOL JUNCTION AND SEE FOR YOURSELF. FRANKLY—
30	YOU'LL BE GLAD YOU DID. (music up to end)

****

Use More Than One Voice

Sometimes you must deliver a lot of no-nonsense information in a spot because the sponsor demands it. If you can't include any sound effects, music, or other "frills," try alternating male and female voices with each sentence. Keep the pace snappy with no pauses between the end of one voice and the beginning of another. It also works to have 25 seconds of the spot delivered by one voice, and the *tag line* or final sentence delivered by a different voice.

Fig. 11-4. Musical bed. A piece of instrumental music under the voice announcement cushions the whole production and makes the listener more comfortable.

Try The Question-and-Answer Format

If you want to create some interest in your sponsor's product, a short dialog between two voices helps set the scene. Set up some tension in the opening couple of lines, then use the rest of the spot to resolve things. Then bring in an all-new voice for the tag line at the end.

Here is Frank's Dress Shop again. The script-writing in Version 4 gets a little trickier because it must show who says what. To make this absolutely clear to read, some space on the script gets wasted so that each announcer starts on a fresh line with some cue words describing the voice inflections. The timing marks on the left margin had to be moved to remain accurate. Also, take note that there are no jingles or music beds on this one.

****

FRANK'S DRESS SHOP   30 sec   (Version 4)

Note: Announcers #1 and #2 are female voices, #3 is male.

	#1 FRANK'S DRESS SHOP, AT MAIN AND ELM, HAS WHAT YOU WANT!
	#2 (skeptical) HOW DO *YOU* KNOW WHAT *I* WANT?
	#1 HOW ABOUT LOW PRICES AND FRIENDLY CLERKS?
	#2 (hopeful) YES . . .
	#1 CASUALS, SPORT AND FORMAL STYLES . . .
10	#2 (excited) REALLY?!
	#1 AND EVEN SIZES FOR MATURE FIGURES!
	#2 (thrilled) GREAT! SAY, DOES FRANK'S DRESS SHOP HAVE A LAY-AWAY PLAN FOR THE HOLIDAY SEASON?
20	#1 THEY SURE DO. AND FRANK'S IS OPEN WEEKDAYS TILL 7, FRIDAYS AND SATURDAYS TILL 9.
	#2 I'M GOING THERE RIGHT NOW—TELL ME WHERE IT IS.
	#3 (male voice) FRANK'S DRESS SHOP IS AT THE CORNER OF
30	MAIN AND ELM IN THE HEART OF CLAYPOOL JUNCTION.

****

Create a Mini-Drama with Sound Effects

Mini-dramas are fun to produce and can be a real ear-catcher for the listener as well. You're creating the illusion that the radio listener is eavesdropping on someone's conversation. Like the question-and-answer format, it involves verbal interaction between two or more voices. Appropriate sound effects are also mixed in to create the illusion that the voices are in a real-life setting instead of a studio (Fig. 11-5).

Add *sound effects,* abbreviated "SFX" in scripts, because it's a quick and easy way to write it. Many radio stations, big or small, have a production library containing many dozens of records. In addition to all kinds of musical jingles, they also contain every imaginable sound effect. Each production library comes with a large notebook indexing the descriptions of all available sound effects.

Back to beautiful downtown Claypool Junction and hear what the ladies are saying about Frank's Dress Shop.

****

FRANK'S DRESS SHOP 30 sec (Version 5)

Note: Announcers #1 and #2 are female voices, #3 is male

	(SFX: department store sounds, people murmuring, cash registers, background "store" music, security chime)
	#1 HI, CHRIS! IT LOOKS LIKE YOU BOUGHT OUT THE STORE! WHERE DID YOU GET THOSE CUTE DRESSES?
	#2 (excited, shuffling of packages) JULIE, YOU'LL LOVE THIS PLACE—I BOUGHT THESE CLOTHES AT
10	FRANK'S DRESS SHOP RIGHT HERE IN THE CENTER OF CLAYPOOL JUNCTION.
	#1 OH SURE, I'VE HEARD THEY HAVE FRIENDLY CLERKS . . .
	#2 (interrupting) . . . UH-HUH! AND THE PRICES ARE GREAT. SINCE I LOST WEIGHT I'VE NEEDED *ALL KINDS* OF
20	CLOTHES, AND THEY HAVE *EVERYTHING* AT FRANKS.
	#1 DO THEY HAVE A LAY-AWAY PLAN?
	#2 YES, AND THEY'RE OPEN NIGHTLY TILL 7, FRIDAY AND SATURDAY TILL 9.
	#3 (male voice) FRANK'S DRESS SHOP IS AT THE CORNER OF
30	MAIN AND ELM IN THE HEART OF CLAYPOOL JUNCTION.

****

Making Your Own Sound Effects

Even though a production library usually includes dozens of records full of sound effects and jingles, you can't always find exactly what you want for a particular spot. Version 5 of Frank's Dress Shop is a good example of a case where it might be easiest to make your own sound effects.

Take a portable cassette tape recorder downtown and get the natural sound right out of a department store. Another way is to record each of the sounds individually and mix them together. You can get "people and cash register" noises at a grocery store, mix in some very faint music typical of store background music, use a child's toy xylophone to make the "bong-bong" of the security chime, and shuffle your own packages to make the sound of Chris and Julie juggling their purchases and handbags.

I did a commercial for air conditioners for a sponsor whose goal was to make the listeners *want* to buy air conditioners. The sponsor said, "Try anything!" My broadcasting team used a multivoice spot with sound effects.

****

AIR CONDITIONERS 60 sec

Note: Announcers #1 and #2 are both male voices

	#1 DON'T YOU *HATE* THOSE HOT SUMMER NIGHTS WHEN IT'S TOO HOT TO SLEEP?
	#2 (SFX: interrupted snoring, yawn, etc.)
10	#1 DON'T YOU JUST *HATE* IT WHEN THE WEATHER IS STICKY AND MUGGY, AND WHEN YOU ROLL OVER, THE BED SHEETS ROLL OVER *WITH* YOU?
	(SFX: long peeling-away sound)
	#1 WELL GO TO GRANT'S IN BRYAN AND GET YOURSELF AN AIR CONDITIONER.
20	#2 (sounds groggy) HMMM, GOOD IDEA, I CAN'T SLEEP IN THIS WEATHER ANYWAY.
	#1 YOU KNOW, (SFX: birds chirping, under announcer) HAVING AN AIR CONDITIONER WILL KEEP YOUR HOME SPRING-LIKE AND COMFORTABLE ALL THROUGH THOSE
30	HOT SUMMER NIGHTS.
	#2 (getting interested) SOUNDS GOOD TO ME.
	#1 YOU'LL SLEEP WELL AND WAKE UP REFRESHED.
	#2 (enthused) GREAT!
	#1 GRANT'S HAS AIR CONDITIONERS FOR EVERY SITUATION,
40	FROM SMALL WINDOW UNITS TO LARGE AND ENERGY-EFFICIENT CENTRAL COOLING UNITS. THEY EVEN HAVE A WIDE VARIETY OF ELECTRIC FANS.
	#2 BOY, I SURE NEED *SOMETHING* TO COOL ME OFF.
	#1 SO GO TO GRANT'S IN BRYAN TODAY, AND YOU'LL
50	SLEEP BETTER TONIGHT.
	#2 HEY, WAIT! I CAN'T GO BUY AN AIR CONDITIONER RIGHT NOW!
	#1 WHY NOT?
60	#2 I'M STILL IN MY PAJAMAS.

****

Fig. 11-5. Mini-dramas. It's fun to produce interesting and entertaining commercials. Both the listeners and the staff enjoy it.

This spot starts out with a studio announcer (#1) sounding like he's going to do the usual straight facts, hard sell commercial. A surprise sneaks in when the sound effects from Announcer #2 turn the spot into a mini-drama; you're listening in on some poor guy trying to get some sleep! The sleeper doesn't seem aware of the announcer at first, but then starts interacting with him—and it all seems normal!

Some real creativity was needed about 12 seconds into the spot when the sleeper supposedly rolls over in bed. To make the listener feel the hot, soggy bed sheets peeling away from the sleeper's back, we needed some kind of "peeling away" noise. We finally tried ripping about a 2-foot piece of news teletype paper, holding the ripping paper close to the microphone. When we played the tape back, everybody in the radio station thought it

sounded just right and were astounded when they heard how we did it.

One other time, we needed the sound of a blimp motoring slowly overhead. The production library had all kinds of piston engine sounds, but they were tractors, cars, and bulldozers—nothing sounded like a blimp. Then the creative juices started flowing. We found the sound effect of a tractor that had a bad muffler. The album normally played at 33.3 rpm. We put the turntable in neutral and turned it by hand at something like 10 rpm. This gave the tractor noise a very deep and slow-going quality—you could practically see the blimp droning lazily overhead.

Try making your own sound effects. If your station doesn't have an echo chamber or reverb unit, and you need a reverberating voice, record that announcer's part in a bathroom or inside a large metal trash barrel. Use your imagination. You'll get just the effects you need if you approach the problem with an open mind.

If you put some creative effort into your production work, it will make your production sound better. It will keep your customers, and your boss, happier too!

Features

The scriptwriting techniques just discussed apply equally well to commercials, promos, and public service announcements, which usually last only a minute or less. These same techniques, however, also apply to feature productions. Features are often extended news stories that are informative or entertaining, and sometimes controversial.

If you want to produce a five-minute informative piece, you could crank out a dry script that sounds like a quote from the encyclopedia. Who would listen to that? It's better to make your feature live and breathe. Here are just a few ways to make a feature production more interesting:

1. Use background music to set the mood.
2. Interview the people involved in the event being featured.
3. Use sound effects from the record library or record actual sounds from an event like the one in the commercial.
4. Keep the script conversational, with short and snappy sentences.

If you produce a series of features, try to maintain some continuity from one piece to another.

1. Stick to the same theme music in all segments.
2. Use the same announcer to host the entire series.
3. Refer back to previous segments and forward to future ones.
4. Pick a topic that is of local interest to your audience.

Many small- and medium-market radio stations use features that are produced elsewhere. Some of these are excellent models for you to study if you ever have the chance to produce features yourself.

When to Play It Straight

Now and then you'll be just bursting with creative ideas for a particular spot. The only problem is, the sponsor insists on a straight delivery of facts with nothing fancy. You'll have no choice but to go along with it. At times like that, you'll be in deep trouble with the sponsor (and your boss) if you go against their instructions. Give them what they want and do your best job with a simple but accurate delivery of the message. Save your creative juice for the next opportunity. (They just don't know what they're missing!)

ON-AIR DELIVERY

Spots are prepared in a variety of ways, depending on the needs of the sponsor. There are four major methods of on-air delivery of a commercial message:

1. Prepackaged completed spots
2. Spots with live tags
3. Live spots read from prepared copy
4. Ad-libbed spots

Prepackaged Completed Spots

When a nationally-known product is being advertised and no special local support is needed, the national sponsor uses one standard commercial or series of commercials for the product. Such products include soft drinks, chewing gum, health care products, house paint, and so forth.

Commercials for nationally distributed products are often produced by a major advertising agency in New York or Hollywood, with copies mailed to radio stations all around the country. National spots run a full 10, 30, or 60 seconds. Indeed, some of these national radio spots are direct copies of the audio tracks from nationally distributed TV commercials.

Spots With Live Tags

Sometimes it is desirable to give a local dealer the chance to associate its name with a national product. In this case, the nationally distributed spot runs a few seconds short, typically 6, 25, and 52 seconds, with the remaining time left for the local announcer to give a *live tag*, an add-on announcement giving the local dealer's name and address. A live tag might sound something like this:

> . . . YOU'LL FIND THE POWER PICKLE PEELER AT BRISBANE'S DRUG STORES IN LUTHERVILLE, CLAYPOOL JUNCTION, AND PIERCETON.

Live Spots Read from Prepared Copy

Some radio stations like to feature their local announcers, rather than use jingles or fancy production. So the scripts are printed out on paper and/or computer screen for the announcer to read live. This allows the local announcer to keep contact with the listener without being fully interrupted by commercial messages, yet the script helps the announcer deliver the information requested by the sponsor.

Ad-Libbed Spots

A daring (and uncommon) practice among some radio stations is to have the announcers deliver the commercial messages from a page of notes and facts about the sponsor and product—*no script*! If the station's format is folksy, intimate, or very casual, the ad-libbed spot can work well, *if* the announcers are specially trained and prepared for the task.

WRAP-UP

Commercials, PSAs, promos, and features serve somewhat different purposes, but they are all produced using similar techniques. Radio stations have many resources for adding a creative spark to any spot production, including jingle packages, sound effects, and local creative scriptwriting.

Extremely elaborate and creative commercial production has been made possible by magnetic recording techniques. Tape recorders allow a variety of special effects, including echo, multiple and double voices, and remixing of the audio after the recording process is completed. Once they have been produced, spots are packaged in a variety of ways to meet the various needs of the sponsors and local radio stations.

Exercise 11-1.   Survey of Commercial Production Techniques

Goal: Listen to a radio station and make a simple program event log to note what kinds of production techniques are used in various spots. Compare production styles of radio stations having different formats.

Method: Using a copy of the chart in Table 11-1, check off each kind of production technique you hear in each spot. Listen to four different types of stations, for example:

☐ Small market AM station
☐ Major market AM station
☐ FM rock or country music station
☐ FM easy listening station

Listen to each station for 20 minutes during drive time on a weekday morning (6 to 9 A.M.) or afternoon (3 to 6 P.M.). You may tape record the station being observed if you wish.

In the TIME HEARD column, list the time in minutes and seconds that each spot is aired. Under SPOT TYPE write com, promo, or PSA to indicated commercial, promotional announcement or public service announcement.

Place a check mark in any of the remaining columns that describe a production technique used for each particular spot you hear. Some spots will use several different special production techniques, so check each box that applies.

Based on your observations of each station, answer the following questions:

1. Which station (give call letters) used a straight facts delivery most frequently?
2. What kind of format was used by the station that used the most production effects in the spots heard?
3. Compare the small market station observations with the major market station. What differences do you notice in the kind of production techniques used?

Table 11-1. Spot Production Techniques

Observer's Name:

Date of Observation:

Station Call Letters and Frequency:

Time Observation Began:

TIME HEARD	SPOT TYPE	MUSIC USED	JINGLE USED	MULTI-VOICE	QUESTION & ANSWER	MINI-DRAMA	SOUND EFFECTS	HUMOR USED

Exercise 11-2.   Scriptwriting

Goal: Try your hand at writing several different kinds of commercials similar to the examples in this chapter.

Method: Here's your chance to let your mind run loose creating a product and a store to sell it in. Unless your instructor directs you to do otherwise, create something that is humorous, even impossible. As with the commercial writing examples earlier in this chapter, start out simple and rewrite the spot using different production techniques.

Each spot must contain these basic, necessary elements:

☐ Describe the product.

☐ Name the store where it can be purchased.

☐ Tell where the store is.

☐ Make the listener *want* the product. Explain why it is necessary or desirable to have this product.

☐ The spot must be either 30 or 60 seconds long.

Write and rewrite the spots using these production elements:

- ☐ Spot #1—Use straight facts, no special effects.
- ☐ Spot #2—Devise a music bed that fits the spot. Including a good ending, not just a fade-out.
- ☐ Spot #3—Rewrite as needed to make it a multivoice spot using a simple question-and-answer format or alternating voices (no mini-dramas in this one).
- ☐ Spot #4—Give it all you've got. Using sound effects, mini-dramas, humor, whatever you can think up.

Vocabulary

ad-lib sheet

advertising agency

commercials

features

jingle package

live tag

master copy

mini-drama

multivoice spot

musical beds

natural sound

production library

production notes

promotional announcements, promos

public service announcement,

PSA

script

script files

sound effects, SFX

sponsor

spots

Chapter 12

Production Techniques

Correct engineering of a production is as important as the creative spark behind the scriptwriting. In fact, you'll probably use the production studio almost as much as the on-air studio. This chapter will look at the fundamentals of how a tape recorder works, building on the material already presented in Chapter 2. Then it will discuss the various methods of electronic editing and introduce you to studio cart machines. Don't expect to become an electronic engineer, but you'll get the most out of your tape machines if you understand a few things about how they operate.

TAPE HEADS

A magnetic tape head works something like a phonograph needle. In the playback mode, the magnetic patterns on the tape can be detected by the head and converted into electrical signals. Tape heads can also record signals onto the tape. Electrical signals fed to the head are recorded as magnetic patterns on the tape.

How does a tape head work? Figure 12-1 shows its basic structure. Internally, a tape head is simply a horseshoe-shaped piece of metal. The two ends of the horseshoe, called the *poles*, are very close together but do not touch. The space between the poles is called the *gap*. The other end of the horseshoe is wrapped with many turns of small wire. This coil of wire is connected to an audio amplifier.

The Record Head

To record sound onto a magnetic tape, an audio signal is fed into the *record amplifier*. From there, the audio signal is fed through wires to the coil of wire in the record head. Anytime an electrical current flows through a coil of wire, a magnetic field is developed through that coil. The horseshoe-shaped piece of metal in the coil focuses the magnetic field into a small and well-defined area in the gap.

The audio tape is pulled past the head at a steady speed, touching the head at the gap. Any magnetic

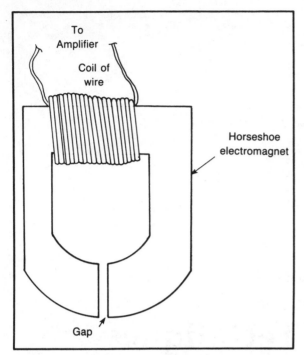

Fig. 12-1. Tape head. A magnetic tape head is basically a high-precision electromagnet. A coil of wire is wrapped around a U-shaped piece of metal. The opening of the U, called the *gap,* is the part that contacts the magnetic tape.

field that is created in the head gap area affects the magnetic pattern of the passing magnetic tape. This reproduces the electrical audio signal in the oxide coating of the magnetic tape.

The Playback Head

Listening to the information already recorded on magnetic tape is a simple process. As the tape is pulled past a head, the magnetic pattern on the tape sets up a magnetic field across the gap of the playback head. This magnetic field travels around the horseshoe to the coil of wire, causing an electrical current to flow. The tiny current from the playback head is fed through wires over to the *playback amplifier* of the tape machine and brought up to full volume.

Magnetic Tape

Magnetic tape has many millions of microscopic magnets glued onto a long ribbon of plastic. As the

tiny magnets on the tape move past the head gap, their magnetic patterns are moved around. The tape's magnetic pattern becomes a duplicate of the changes in electrical current fed originally from the audio amplifier. Some energy is required to change the magnetic pattern of a tape, so once it is recorded, it retains the new magnetic pattern until a large magnetic field comes near it again.

Erasing Magnetic Tape

Sometimes a recording is made on a tape that is totally blank. This is called *virgin* tape when it is new and has never been used. The magnetic pattern of virgin tape is totally random. Used tape can be returned to like-new condition by erasing it. A very large electric magnet, called a *bulk eraser,* scrambles the magnetic pattern on the tape. The previously recorded information is gone and the magnetic pattern is once again completely random and silent.

The tape machine is also able to erase tape as it records. Usually, a separate record head is provided, called the *erase head.* It records a very high-pitched and powerful tone on the tape. The effect is to wipe out all signals on the tape as they pass by the erase head (something like the scene in Fig. 12-2). The remainder of the tape is not affected. Sometimes the erase head is used to erase just a few seconds of information. This is called *spot erasing.*

Tape Biasing

Magnetic tapes resist being changed. It requires a certain amount of energy to put a new magnetic pattern on a tape. Therefore, the recording process sounds distorted, especially at low volume levels. This distortion problem is solved by adding a high-pitched signal to any information being recorded. The high-pitched tone (too high to be heard) is called *tape bias.* It's only purpose is to overcome the tape's reluctance to changing its magnetic pattern.

Each tape machine and each brand of tape requires a specific level of tape bias to give the best recorded sound. You might have seen a switch marked *bias* on home stereo cassette tape decks.

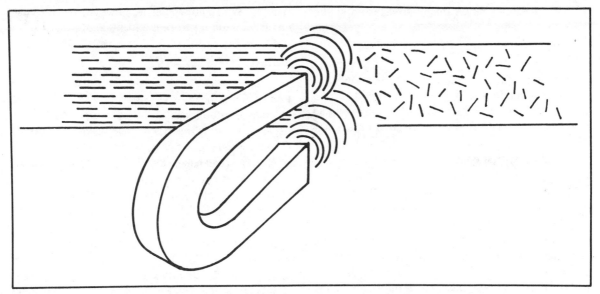

Fig. 12-2. Erasing a tape. A recording on a tape can be removed by passing the tape near a magnetic source. The eraser randomizes the magnetic pattern on the tape so that no audio signal can be heard when the tape is played.

The bias switch is a simple and convenient way to adjust the tape bias on home recording equipment. Studio equipment, however, requires a more complex process to set the tape bias. It is an adjustment that is best left to experienced audio engineers. It does not require frequent adjustment. The tape machine's service manual describes that machine's tape bias setup procedure, should that adjustment be necessary.

ELECTRONIC EDITING
AND POST-PRODUCTION

Electronic editing techniques permit elaborate productions to come from simple equipment and a small staff. Electronic editing also allows you to change your mind and redo the production until you're satisfied with the results. This "try-again" capability is the major advantage of magnetic recording tape.

A complex production can be brought together in several ways:

1. A recorded "live production"
2. Several segments edited together onto one tape
3. Many portions recorded onto a multitrack tape

Recorded "Live"

Sometimes you have no choice but to make everything happen at once and record the results. Sooner or later, you'll find yourself wanting to do an extremely elaborate commercial involving two voices, background music, sound effects, and a prerecorded jingle.

For instance, one cart machine can be used to record the spot. Three other tape decks and two turntables in the studio can be used to play back elements of the spot. They must be started with split-second timing so that all the elements come together properly. The problem is that three tape decks and two turntables must be started at the same time. This is impossible with just two hands. In this case, the task can be broken down into achievable pieces.

Deadrolling

The key to acting like you have six hands is a process called *deadrolling*. This is the process of backing up a turntable or tape deck several seconds before first audio so that you can start it early, giving you time to do something else before the audio begins. The three tape decks, two turntables, and the cart machine are given different deadroll times so that only one or two things are started at the same time.

Measuring Time

Studio production depends on split-second timing. Oddly enough, the highly accurate digital clocks now available are not the best tool for timing audio productions. You don't really care what time it is—you just want to measure intervals of time. For this, a large clock with a continuously sweeping second hand is the best.

When your hands are full with operating the studio equipment, you don't want to mess with a stopwatch. Instead, just keep an eye on the clock's sweep second hand. When it reaches the top of the clock face (at 12), begin the spot. Keep an eye on the second hand and be sure to conclude the spot at around 29 seconds, just before the second hand reaches the bottom of the clock.

Electronic Splices

Most studio-quality, reel-to-reel tape decks permit you to place them into the record mode while they're already rolling in the play mode. This is very handy if you want to add on to something already recorded. The technique is called *electronic splicing*.

For instance, you recorded a 30 second spot, and upon playing it back, you found that it lasts only 26 seconds. Don't record the whole thing over! Just look through the production library for a short, three-note tune called a *musical sting*. These vary from one to ten seconds long. You might find one that is three seconds long—just what you need to make your 26-second spot stretch to 29 seconds.

Cue the musical sting for a one-second deadroll, about half a turn back from first audio. Then play back the spot but be ready to start the turntable *and* punch the tape machine into the record mode immediately after last audio at the 26-second point. The three second musical sting will then be recorded onto the end of the spot, making it a perfect 29 seconds long.

Electronic editing takes some practice, and you run the risk of turning on the record mode too soon and spoil the recording you're trying to add some-

thing to. With a little practice, however, you can use electronic editing to real advantage.

Multitrack Recorders

Some studio reel-to-reel tape machines have two audio tracks. We know these as *stereo* machines. Studio quality stereo tape decks can usually record on one track while playing the other. Elaborate radio production studios use wide recording tape and can handle 8 or 16 separate audio tracks. Each track on the the tape can be recorded and played back independently of the other.

In the early 1970s, a brother-sister singing group called *The Carpenters* recorded beautiful, lush tunes that sounded as if they were sung by a 20-voice choir. Yet there were only two of them, and they didn't use other singers to help them out. (Backup singers were used for live concerts, however).

Making two voices sound like many voices works something like this. Karen and Richard Carpenter recorded themselves singing two-part harmony on one track. Then they played back their two combined voices and listened to themselves while singing two additional parts onto another track. They listened to those four parts while recording themselves yet again on another track. This procedure was repeated until The Carpenters had the huge choir-like sound they wanted.

The multitrack recording process, shown graphically in Fig. 12-3, shows four audio segments recorded separately on four tracks. When played back, the audio levels can be fed into four separate channels of a mixer, and the sound mix can be adjusted until it sounds just right.

Some disc jockeys who do multivoice comedy routines use multitrack tape machines so that one person can do all of the voices. First, one half of the conversation is recorded on Track 1, leaving appropriate pauses for other persons who speak. Then the announcer plays back Track 1 on headphones, while recording another voice on Track 2. Yet a third voice can be recorded later on Track 3. On a fourth go-around, sound effects can be recorded on the remaining tracks.

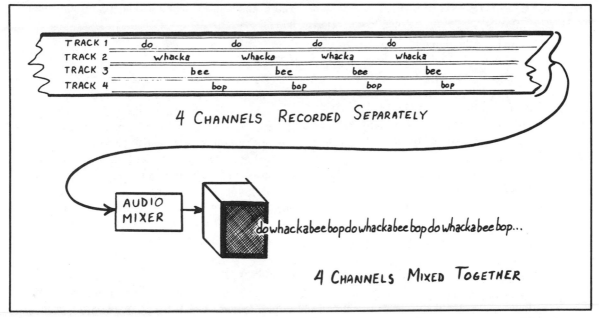

Fig. 12-3. Multitrack recording. Four different sounds can be recorded separately on four different tracks. When they are played back together, they can be combined into a single sound.

If you look at the face of a multitrack recording head, you will see several tape head gaps. A two-track head has two gaps, an eight-track head has eight gaps, and so on.

Synchronizing Multitrack Recordings

The first time you try to do a multitrack recording, you might get frustrated. Even though things sound fine in your headphones while recording, when you play the whole thing back, the tracks won't be together. If this involves music, some tracks might be a beat or two ahead of others. This will, as they say, have you talking to yourself! How does this out-of-step recording happen, and how can you avoid the problem?

Tape machines are time machines. The concept of the word "now" moves around a bit, depending on what you're doing with the tape machine. Take a look at Figure 12-4. (It might look familiar because you saw it in Chapter 2.) The tape moves from left to right. As the tape travels through the tape path, it passes the erase head, then the record head, and finally the playback head. This setup is called a *three-*

head tape machine because it uses three separate tape heads.

In most radio stations, the tape in a reel-to-reel machine moves at 7.5 inches per second. Think about it—a given point on the tape passes the record head and needs nearly a quarter of a second to travel along over to the playback head. If you reduce the tape speed to 3.75 inches per second, the tape will need nearly half a second to travel from the record head to the playback head. In either case, this is a noticeable delay.

Studio-quality multitrack tape decks allow you to listen through the record head while doing multitrack recording. This ensures that all of your recorded audio tracks will be synchronized—they'll all be in step. Some multitrack tape machines have a playback function knob marked PLAY and SYNC to allow you to play through either the regular playback head or to play back through the record head.

Why play through the record head? Why not use just one head for both functions? There are times when you want to record and play back on the same track at the same time.

SPECIAL EFFECTS WITH TAPES

A tape machine is a time machine. "Now" at the record head isn't the same place on the tape as "now" at the playback head. Something recorded onto a tape can be picked up a fraction of a second later by the playback head, which is farther "downstream" on the tape path (Fig. 12-4). This ability to play something shortly after it has been recorded is very useful in radio production and other broadcast station functions.

Tape Monitoring

When a tape recording is being made, the engineer sets the record volume level so that peaks are between 85-100%, and the tape deck is placed in the record mode. Once you have begun the recording process, use the cue channel or some headphones connected to the output of the machine. Now switch the the tape deck's output control to TAPE, and you'll be listening to the tape through the playback head a split-second after it is recorded.

You'll know immediately if the recording sounds good.

Tape Echo

The idea of monitoring the tape while recording it permits you to make a reverberating echo effect. Assuming the audio being fed to the tape recorder is routed through an audio console, then the tape output audio is also fed into another mixing channel of that same console. Figure 12-5 diagrams how this hookup is done. Depending on the tape playback volume, the echo can be faint and subtle, or it can make a thunderous crashing sound. Experiment with it. Just remember that too much of it can be annoying.

Double-Voice Effect

If you have ever listened to a rock music radio station, sooner or later you have heard a promo or commercial in which the announcer's voice sounds odd, almost as if there were two people reading the

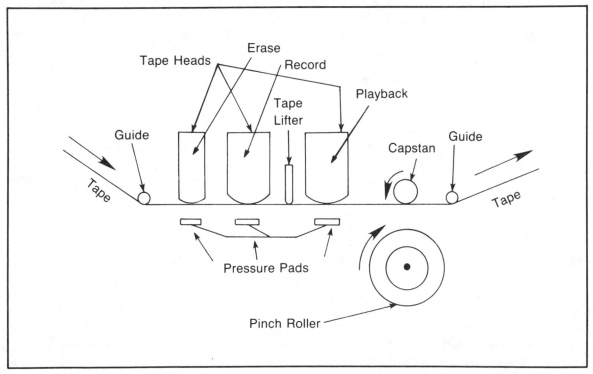

Fig. 12-4. Reel-to-reel tape path. This is the standard layout of the tape path of nearly all tape machines.

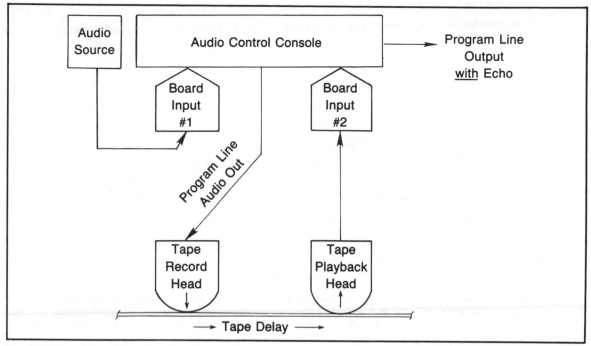

Fig. 12-5. Tape echo. A reverberating (repeating echo) effect is made when a combination of tape delay and feedback is used. The sound goes from the source, through the board, to the record head, and onto the tape. A fraction of a second later, the playback head picks up the sound and plays it back through the board to the record head again.

script in exactly the same way at almost the same time. This is a variation on the tape echo effect that takes advantage of the synchronization problem of multi-track recording. Figure 12-6 shows how to make the double-voice effect.

Although there are several ways to set up for double-voice recording, one of the easier ways is to use both the program channel and audition channel of the audio console. The original audio source is fed through the program channel to tape recorder's left-track record head. The left-track playback head picks up the recorded audio a split second later and feeds it to the audio console's audition channel (completely isolated from the program channel).

The audition channel then feeds the tape recorder's right track record head. The tape-delayed right track audio should be recorded slightly softer than the leading left track, unless you want to hear a truly other-worldly sound. The result is that the audio from the left track is dubbed over to the right track with about a quarter of a second delay, giving the audio equivalent of a double image.

Tape Delay Loops

Radio talk shows have been popular for a long time. The audience's ability to phone in and get on the air heightens listener interest. Now and then, some sick mind phones in and makes an obscene remark, however. How do radio stations prevent unwanted callers from getting on the air? Tape delay loops have fulfilled the job for a long time.

The tape itself is a standard audio cart, usually just a few seconds long. Remember, carts use a continuous loop of tape. Figure 12-7 shows the special tape path used in a tape delay machine. Take a close look at the layout of the heads—the order of the heads is different from normal tape decks. The playback head is positioned to the left of the erase head and record head instead of to the right of the record head.

Assume the tape loop is completely erased. Audio is fed to the record head and is recorded onto the tape. The continuous tape loop travels clockwise. Ten seconds after the audio is recorded onto the tape, that point on the tape winds around the

133

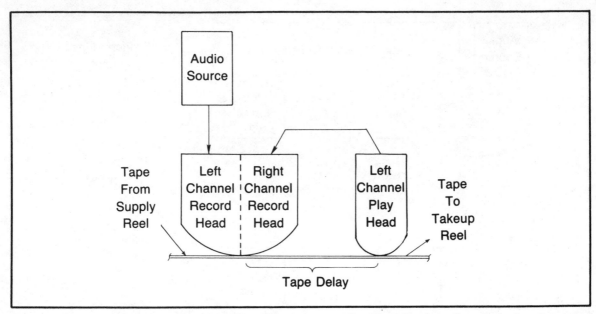

Fig. 12-6. Double-voice effect. A single echo effect is made by recording the audio source through the board and onto the left channel of a stereo tape machine. The left playback head picks up the sound, then routes it to the right channel record head.

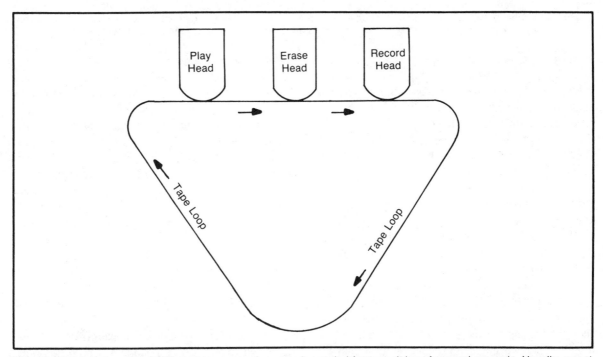

Fig. 12-7. Tape delay path. A different tape recorder setup is needed for tape delay of several seconds. Usually, a cart machine with a unique head arrangement is used. The tape passes the play head, followed by the erase head, and then the record head. The tape delay itself is handled by the audio cycling physically around the tape spiral of a standard broadcast tape cart. The length of the cart determines the length of the delay.

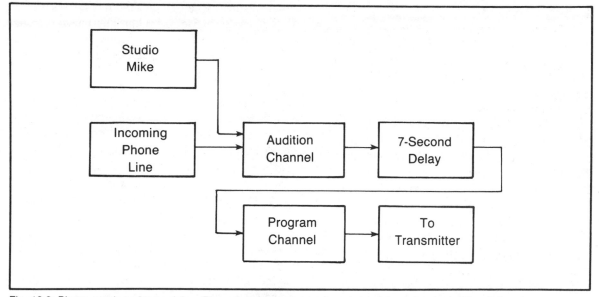

Fig. 12-8. Phone patch and tape delay. Phone-in talk shows require a tape delay setup to avoid unfortunate comments from getting on the air. The studio microphone and phone line are connected to the console's audition channel. The output of the audition channel is fed through the tape delay machine to an input of the program channel, and then on to the transmitter.

spiral and is picked up by the playback head. The tape moves on to the erase head and the tape is then erased and made ready for recording again.

The purpose of a tape loop is not to tape record a program for preservation. The tape loop is used strictly to provide a time delay. When the unwanted caller gets on the radio station's telephone talk show, the tape delay loop is placed between the phone patch and the program line feeding the transmitter. The DJ has a few seconds of grace to kill the program audio before the unwanted language is broadcast.

Figure 12-8 shows how the tape delay works. The DJ's studio mike and the phone patch are connected to the audio console's audition channel. The output of the audition line feeds the record head of the tape delay machine. The delayed audio from the playback head is fed to the console's program line and from there to the transmitter.

Using Different Tape Speeds

Most broadcast reel-to-reel tape recorders pull the tape at 7.5 inches per second. This speed is standard all over the country, and nearly all radio shows distributed by tape are recorded at this speed.

Most studio tape machines are capable of operating at two different tape speeds. In addition to 7.5 i.p.s., the other standard tape speeds are twice that fast (15 i.p.s.) and half as fast (3.75 i.p.s.). Some tape decks can change speeds with the simple flip of a front panel control. On others, however, you much reach inside the back of the tape deck and manually move a belt from one set of pulleys to another.

Have you ever heard a commercial or children's cartoon show using a high-pitched voice that sounds like a chipmunk talking? That effect uses different speeds on a tape recorder. The normal voices are recorded at 7.5 i.p.s. and the "chipmunk" voices are recorded at 3.75 i.p.s., then played back at 7.5 i.p.s. If you try to record chipmunk voices, remember to talk more slowly while recording so that the playback will be understandable.

Like any other interesting audio effects, the chipmunk voice technique is cute if used now and then. Don't overuse it, though, or it will become tiresome.

Digital Recording

The reel-to-reel tape recorder has been in use since the late 1940s. While advancing technology has made improvements in tape recorders, the basic mechanisms have not changed much in four decades. Some major changes are coming down the road to change that situation.

Since 1980, inexpensive videocassette recorders have become commonplace. These machines were intended to record television pictures, but they have excellent sound quality as well. Some people use just the audio portion to record long-playing tapes that are six to eight hours long.

Some professional recording studios have modified the video-recording portion of the machine to record incredibly accurate sound recordings. This technique converts audio signals into computer-readable strings of data and records it on the video track of the videocassette. When the tape is played back, the computer data is converted back to an audio signal. This process is a form of *digital recording*.

Digital recording and digital audio processing techniques are quickly finding their way into broadcast use. The main advantages of digital recordings include:

- ☐ Extremely good-sounding recordings
- ☐ Virtually no tape hiss or background noise
- ☐ No loss of quality when the audio signal is recorded onto tape or copied from tape to tape

There's More!

The subject of tape production techniques is complex enough to fill a whole book all by itself. Now you are aware that tape recorders are incredibly versatile machines. Once you use them enough to be comfortable with them, you'll have a lot of fun producing top-notch spots and features.

AUDIO MIXING

Have you ever been in a crowded room trying to talk to a very soft-spoken person? It's annoying to the listener when the desired message is drowning under the noise of background music or room noise. The same thing can happen if your special audio effects make too much noise, covering the message you're trying to deliver. Don't kill the sponsor's message with fancy production.

Background music that is behind an announcer's voice, for instance, is loud enough if it kicks up the VU meter to the -10 db mark—that's about 25% modulation. Depending on the music and the announcer's voice, the background music might need to be even softer, like -15 db. Likewise, other sound effects don't need to be full volume. They seldom are in real life.

Remember, you're trying to set a mood, not overwhelm the listener. Once you have completed your production, be sure to have a co-worker listen to the audio mixing. Ask your friend if the sound balance is comfortable. It's better to redo a spot and get it right *before* the boss or sponsor hears it. Almost any boss will respect you when you recheck your work to make sure it is perfect.

DUBBING TO TAPE CARTS

In today's broadcast world, many recorded program events are aired from a tape cartridge. Carts are versatile, easy to handle, self-cueing, and can withstand repeated playing without noticeable loss of quality. Once an audio production session is complete, the next task usually is to dub the completed work over to a cart.

Erasing a Cart

As with any audio tape, carts can be used and reused. Because of their construction, however, carts are a bit tougher to erase compared to open reels of tape. Bulk erasing a cart involves slow and thorough movement of the cart across the bulk eraser several times. Be sure to erase the edges, particularly the open edge where the playback heads enter the cart.

After bulk erasing a cart, play it for a few seconds to shift the tape around in the cart. Then repeat the whole bulk erasing process, again moving the cart slowly across the bulk eraser several times.

Always pick up the cart and move it away from the eraser to arm's length before you turn off the eraser.

If you didn't erase the cart properly, you'll know by playing it. A bad job of erasing either leaves brief bursts of audio on the cart, or the bulk eraser itself will record a "woop-woop-woop-woop" sound on the tape. You can prevent these problems by moving the cart slowly and continuously, erasing the cart twice, and by keeping the cart completely away from the bulk eraser while turning the eraser on and off.

Finding Cart Splices

All carts are made of continuous loops of audio recording tape. Well, they're almost continuous loops because they do have a splice in them somewhere. No matter how carefully the splice was made, the tape usually has some *audio dropouts* around the splice, making a second or two of the tape poor for recording and playback.

After you have bulk-erased a cart, your next task is to find the splice and cue the tape a few seconds past that point. Most carts have clear plastic tops, so the "cheap and dirty" method of finding the splice is to play the cart and watch it closely. As the tape is pulled up at the hub and travels across the top of the cart, the backside of the tape is clearly visible, making the inch or so of white splicing tape easy to see. Watching for a splice is tedious work, but you can usually do it without too much agony on a cart that is less than 90 seconds long.

Some radio stations have special cart machines called *splice finders* that erase carts, then automatically find the splice for you. Splice finders are a real lifesaver when you're in a hurry, and especially when you must find the splice in longer carts. (You can turn into a blithering idiot looking for splices, especially when you watch a 40-second cart for two minutes and you still haven't seen a splice!)

Playing the tape before recording on it also allows you to check the cart's physical condition. If it rattles, sticks, or doesn't turn at all, tag it with a trouble report so that the station's engineer can repair it. If you hear an audio dropout after you record on a cart, dub your production work onto a different cart and tag the bad cart so that the engineer will have the worn-out tape replaced.

Cart Cue Tones

A tape cart cues itself automatically to the beginning of the recording. The program audio is recorded on one track (two tracks if it's a stereo machine), and a completely separate track contains a special signal called a *primary cue tone* that tells the machine where to stop. The cart machine automatically records the cue tone, lasting about one second, when the cart is recorded.

When carts are recorded for use in broadcast automation systems, a *secondary cue tone* can be recorded on the program audio track of the cart. The secondary cue tone occurs right at the end of the recording, telling the radio station's computer that the cart's program content has ended. Another set of tones that can be used is called an *account code*. Computer data can be encoded on the cart so that the station's automatic program logger knows what cart is playing.

WRAP-UP

Broadcast production techniques rely heavily on the use of recording tape. While combo operators can do good work without knowing anything about how tape machines work, the more you know about tape machines, the more performance you'll be able to wring out of your equipment.

Some reel-to-reel tape machines are capable of recording many separate audio tracks on the same tape. These can be recorded at the same time or individually at different times. Multitrack recording allows one performer to record several different voices, instruments, or other sounds on the tape. Post-production then allows the studio engineer to mix all the tracks together to achieve the desired results. Electronic splicing also permits various elements of a production to be edited together in a desired sequence without the tedium and cost of cutting up reels of tape.

Once a production session is completed for spots, PSAs, and promos, the finished product is often dubbed from reel tape to cart. A good bit of production work can be destroyed if the cart is not prepared properly. A cart should be erased thoroughly, and the recording should begin a few seconds after the splice in the tape loop.

Exercies 12-1.   Audio Production Terms

Demonstrate your knowledge of basic audio production terms by defining the following words.

1. Bulk eraser
2. Audio dropouts
3. Deadrolling
4. Stereo
5. Capstan
6. Spot erasing
7. Multitrack recording

Exercise 12-2.   Tape Machines

1. Name the three heads in a three-head tape machine, listing them in the order they are arranged in the tape path.
2. Which head has the job of recording a very strong, high-pitched tone to remove earlier recordings from used tape?
3. A tape's reluctance to changes in its magnetic pattern is overcome by the use of what kind of signal added to the recording audio?
4. List the three common audio tape speeds.

Exercise 12-3.   Cart Machines

1. How many tape hubs are used in a cart?
2. Where should the recording start on a cart, just before a splice or just after? Why?
3. What does the primary cue tone tell the cart machine to do?
4. What does the secondary cue tone tell the automation?

Vocabulary

account codes	erase head	tape echo
audio dropouts	gap	tape monitoring
bulk eraser	multitrack recording	three-head tape machine
cue tone, primary	playback amplifier	tape delay loops
cue tone, secondary	playback head	splice
deadrolling	poles	splice finder
digital recording	record amplifier	spot erasing
double-voice effect	record head	stereo
electronic splicing	tape bias	virgin tape

Chapter 13

Remote Broadcasts

Radio has been called "the go anywhere medium." The listener can go anywhere, tuning in stations with portable radios ranging from nearly invisible radios-in-headsets to suitcase-sized boom boxes that make enough noise to fill an airplane hangar. The combo operator is portable, too. The radio studio goes anywhere to originate a radio program, bringing unique listening experiences to the audience.

A *remote broadcast*, sometimes just called a *remote*, occurs when a radio program originates from a temporary studio at a location away from the radio station's home-base studio facilities. Figure 13-1 is only half ridiculous—remotes have operated from moving roller coasters, elevators and race cars! Remote broadcasts are tremendously appealing to the audience. Thus, they are a worthwhile part of a radio station's efforts to deliver what the listeners want to hear and increase the station's visibility in its community.

TYPES OF REMOTES

Probably the most often-used remote broadcast occurs in news gathering. For instance, a radio sta-tion's news reporter might hear about a large fire taking place. The reporter rushes to the scene, gathers the facts, and then makes a live, on-the-scene report using a telephone or a two-way radio.

Another very common remote broadcast is coverage of a local or regional sports team. Many radio stations send their own announcing staff out to broadcast live from local high school and college football and basketball games. Likewise, a major-market radio station might serve as the point of origination for a regional network of stations that carry professional sports events.

Radio stations using all types of music formats set up remote broadcasts of concerts. Because of the many microphones and high-quality stereo mixing involved, concert remotes are probably the most demanding of flawless broadcast engineering. Some stations set up remotes at businesses to promote a special sales campaign, such as a grand opening sale or a year-end warehouse clearance. Similarly, marathon radio broadcasts from a remote site are useful in fund-raising for charity.

A remote broadcast implies a temporary studio

Fig. 13-1. Unusual remote sites. Getting out of the studio and into community events can make a station a real local leader. It is not necessary to go over Niagara Falls in a rowboat to attract the audience's favor!

setup in an unusual location. Remotes are similar to regular network programming that comes via phone line or satellite to the radio station. Both originate outside a radio station's established facilities.

Some radio stations do little or nothing involving remote broadcasts and network programming. Other stations have formats that take full advantage of broadcasts that originate outside of the main studio.

CONNECTING THE REMOTE SITE TO THE STUDIO

Broadcast remotes have existed since the first years of commercial broadcasting. Remote audio comes to the station through a variety of means (Fig. 13-2). Since the early days of broadcasting, the remote site has been linked with the main studio using either of two methods: telephone lines, or two-way radio.

Remotes by Telephone Line

Many radio stations have discovered that the audience responds well to phone-in talk shows.

Listeners also enjoy the chance to chat with the on-air personality and to request songs. Telephones are used for station-promoting contests. Getting the listener's voice on the air can liven up a radio show.

Connecting the telephone to the radio station equipment requires a device called a *phone patch*. This electronic circuit brings the telephone conversation into the control room console and sends the control room audio onto the phone line. The phone patch prevents damage or problems for either the studio equipment or the phone company's equipment, and legal standards must be met. Always comply with phone company regulations when installing a phone patch!

Dedicated Broadcast Telephone Lines or "Loops"

Circumstances dictate when a long-term telephone line connection is required by a radio station, making it impractical to tie up one of the dial-phone lines. This permanent or semipermanent phone line is called a *dedicated line* or *loop* because it is re-

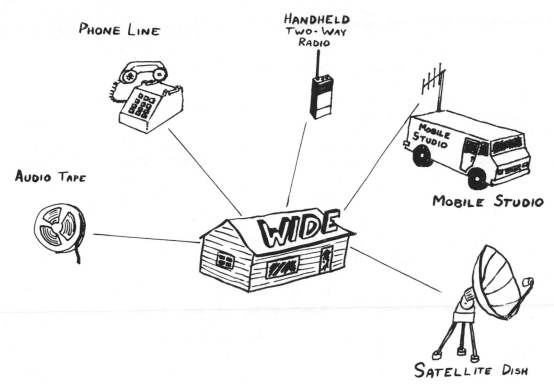

PHONE LINE

HANDHELD TWO-WAY RADIO

AUDIO TAPE

MOBILE STUDIO

WIDE

SATELLITE DISH

Fig. 13-2. Programming from all over. Even a small-town station can have a "big" sound if it taps into program material from a variety of sources.

served or dedicated to a specific purpose. These might include:

- ☐ Sporting events with local schools
- ☐ Professional sports networks
- ☐ News networks and teletype services
- ☐ Open lines to traffic spotters, stock brokers, or a weather forecasting service
- ☐ Permanent remote studios in another building or town
- ☐ Weekly church broadcasts

Most radio stations have many dedicated lines, but the typical studio audio consoles can't handle more than two or three remote lines at a time. Therefore, remote lines are brought to a routing switcher, which then selects which remote lines need to be fed to the control room console. (Routing switchers were discussed in Chapter 3.) Dedi-

cated phone lines are also referred to as *telco*, which is short for telephone company.

Some dedicated lines allow audio to pass in both directions between the remote site and the studio. Such phone lines are called *loops* or *broadcast loops*.

While loops are by far the most convenient means of establishing a wire connection from a remote site to the studio, they are also the most expensive to set up. Many radio stations therefore utilize a business telephone arrangement for broadcasts, and the audio comes in as a long-distance or a local phone call to the station, getting on the air through the phone patch.

Radio Links and Satellites

Radio links between a remote broadcast origination point and the station have been used since the early days of broadcasting. These radio links have been cumbersome and used infrequently, however, until the mid-1970s. Now, compact and high-quality handheld radios have made electronic news gathering (ENG) common in many radio stations. The mobile radio links are two-way units, so reporters can be dispatched by radio to the site of fast-breaking news while away from the station.

Other remote broadcasts, such as sports events, also use radio equipment for all or part of the link back to the studio. Some *short-hop remote links* are small handheld or tripod-mounted transmitters and receivers connecting the audio across a mile or less from the event site to a telephone line. Other remote broadcast transmitters can relay program audio many miles.

Satellites have become popular in the last few years as well. At one time, radio stations subscribing to a network had no choice but to receive live programs via telephone line. Now many stations have a dish antenna set up on the roof or in the yard. They pick up programs directly from network headquarters via a communications satellite 22,000 miles up in space. *Satellite feeds* (network programming transmitted through satellites in space) are dependable and have excellent audio quality when compared to telephone lines. The long-term costs to the station and network are much lower than telco connections.

In the early days of radio, the term ''wireless'' was used to describe radio equipment because messages could be sent and received without connecting telegraph or telephone wires. Then broadcasting advanced to such an elaborate state that the term wireless became hilariously inaccurate. The advent of radio and satellite links is once again liberating communications from the limits of the copper cable.

JOINING NETWORKS ON TIME

Live, scheduled network feeds are commonplace in local radio station formats. The most common is the network newscast, usually occurring at the top of the hour. Another common network feed is a sports broadcast, either originating locally (down at the town high school) or from a regional professional sports team network.

Whatever the program content, a scheduled network broadcast must get on the air on schedule (Fig. 13-3). That means you must be on schedule.

If the noon news feed from network starts at 12:00 and *zero* seconds, you cannot be even one second late in wrapping up your local programming before putting network on the air.

Network Time-Check Tones

Meeting network schedules on time involves two major procedures. First, make sure your studio clock is accurately set. Second, listen to the time checks provided on the network line during *closed circuit* (not for broadcast) feeds.

Most network newscasts on the hour begin with some kind of beep or bong sound signifying an accurate top-of-the-hour time check. You can use this to set the studio clock's sweep second hand or to reset a digital clock's seconds counter to zero. Some radio stations have a shortwave receiver to listen to the National Bureau of Standards time standard broadcasts from radio station WWV. Your station's chief engineer will usually be responsible to set the clocks with WWV, but you can use the network bong at the top of the hour to check the clocks anytime.

If the studio clock is a couple of seconds off compared to the network's time-check tones, you might not want to reset the studio clock. Instead, just make a note of how far off the clock is. The clock's accuracy depends on the accuracy of the electricity generated by the local power company. Some towns' generators allow enough fluctuation to cause electric clocks to run several seconds fast or slow in a given day, although the clocks remain generally accurate over a period of many days.

Network Time Check Announcements

Most sports networks offer special closed circuit announcements that tell local stations of the upcoming broadcasting schedule. These closed circuit feeds are not intended for broadcast, but the combo operator listens to them on the cue speaker to find out exactly when a network program will begin.

Network time check announcements might be a simple announcement of what time the network thinks is correct. You then check that against your clock and note any difference. This kind of network time check might sound like this:

OKAY STATIONS, ACCORDING TO OUR CLOCK, WE'RE COMING UP ON TEN MINUTES BEFORE THE HOUR . . . IT'LL BE TEN-TILL WHEN I SAY 'MARK' . . . IN FIVE . . . FOUR . . . THREE . . . TWO . . . ONE . . . *MARK*! EXACTLY TEN MINUTES BEFORE THE HOUR.

Some network announcers say *woof* instead of *mark* when giving time checks, so don't let that throw you. It sounds a little strange, but it's hard to miss! A network time check might also sound like this:

HELLO, STATIONS, WE'LL BEGIN THE BROADCAST IN ABOUT FIFTEEN MINUTES. COMING UP ON FIFTEEN MINUTES TO AIR ON MY MARK . . . FIVE . . . FOUR . . . THREE . . . TWO . . . ONE . . . MARK! FIFTEEN MINUTES TO AIR.

The Final Countdown

A countdown to air must end sometime. This is not like a countdown to a space launch; there is not a verbal countdown all the way to air time. The combo operator needs a silent network line just before air to allow the network line to be turned up a few seconds before the network starts.

Typically, the last verbal countdown begins ten seconds before air but goes silent five seconds before air, like this:

HERE WE GO STATIONS, FIFTEEN SECONDS TO AIR . . . AND, TEN . . . NINE . . . EIGHT . . . SEVEN . . . SIX . . . FIVE . . . (silence)

The silence after "five . . ." gives the stations a chance to join the network or remote line on the air without catching the last second or two of countdown.

Fig. 13-3. Meeting network. Whatever you do, be sure to get to the network *on time!*

Cutaways

During a network or live remote broadcast, the network announcers will usually pause for local stations to insert local commercials and station ID announcements. These local interruptions or network broadcasts are called *cutaways, local availabilities*, or *station breaks*. Commercial breaks are typically 60 seconds long, while ID breaks usually last ten seconds. The network announcers should allow one or two extra seconds per break, permitting the local stations a little *slop time* to start the spots and then rejoin network. This ensures that none of the network broadcast gets missed.

Announcers at the remote site should be careful what they say during a scheduled local cutaway. Occasionally the local combo operator misses the cutaway, and the network stays on the air. The network announcers should assume that they are on the air at all times.

Covering a Spot

Sometimes a sports or news network will air its own spots and PSAs during a broadcast. Some of these spots might be intended for broadcast only at the originating station, and other stations on the network are not to carry them. When a local station inserts its own spot in place of a network spot, this is called *covering a spot*.

Stations around the network must be alert for network broadcasts that include spots intended only for the originating station. Such network feeds are called *dirty feeds* because they include material not intended for broadcast by all stations and must, therefore, be "cleaned up" by the local station.

Cueing the Remote Site

If your station is tied to a remote announcer through a two-way broadcast loop, you might be able to talk to the announcers. Some studio consoles provide for connecting the remote line to either the audition channel or program line. You can then put the studio mike on audition and feed time checks and other information out to the remote announcers.

You can also hook the remote line to the program line and let the remote announcers hear what

you're doing on the air. You can communicate to the remote site by telling your listeners something like this:

WELL, WE'LL BE GOING LIVE TO THE COUNTY FIELDHOUSE FOR THE TENTH ANNUAL HIGH SCHOOL BASKETBALL TOURNEY. THAT'S COMING UP IN EXACTLY TEN MINUTES, HERE ON FM-103.

The announcers at the remote site should be alert to this kind of message, and one of them will probably respond to the studio announcer by saying something like this:

OKAY, HARRY, I UNDERSTAND THAT WE'RE GOING ON THE AIR IN TEN MINUTES.

Be careful about listening to the remote announcers on your headphones while you're live on the air. If they start telling jokes while setting up for a remote, it could make you laugh or say something on the air that shouldn't be broadcasted.

REMOTE BROADCAST FACILITIES

Radio stations use all kinds of setups at remote sites. The equipment depends on what kind of program material is being originated at the remote site.

Remote Studios

A typical remote DJ-and-record show might originate in a specially built trailer or van that houses a complete portable radio studio. Some stations also have smaller, fully equipped portable consoles that can be set up in a closet, a storefront window, or on the bar of a nightclub.

If your remote involves a live music concert, the remote audio console will probably have many mixing channels to handle up to several dozen microphones. A typical sportscast remote, however, has a simple mixer that handles two microphones and one or two cart machines.

Securing Cables

Whenever you run microphone or audio cables in a public place, you must be careful to route them safely so that nobody trips over them or gets tangled up in them. Personal injury liability lawsuits can be very troublesome. Also, you don't want someone to trip over your cable and take you off the air!

Whenever you go out on a remote, be sure to take lots of tape for holding down cables. Three-inch wide gray tape is probably the most useful tape in a broadcaster's bag of tricks. This tape is sometimes called *duct tape*, although stage and TV personnel often call it *gaffer's tape*. Gray tape has a cloth backing, is fairly waterproof, and is incredibly strong. It is perfect for nearly any situation on a remote setup.

Other kinds of tape are less useful. For instance, adhesive tape has a paper backing and can be torn or broken easily. Black plastic electrical tape rarely sticks well to floors or greasy surfaces, so it isn't much good for sticking cables down in areas where they'll be walked on.

If cables must be run overhead or through the air, be sure they are suspended high enough so that people can walk under them without any problems (Fig. 13-4). Likewise, overhead cables should be suspended high enough that pranksters can't easily grab them and pull them down. Be careful not to put too much mechanical strain on cables—you don't want them to break or develop intermittent connections.

WRAP-UP

Remote broadcasts occur for all kinds of reasons. Virtually any radio station format can benefit from the excitement and audience appeal generated by a live, remotely originated program.

Audio signals from a remote site come to local radio stations through a variety of means. Telephone lines have long been used, but radio stations with

Fig. 13-4. Safety first. Be sure to keep remote site cables out of harm's way—or Mr. Harms might get hung up in them.

the latest facilities also use radio links and even satellite hookups.

Coordination is essential between the remote site or network broadcasters and the local station's combo announcers. Time tones, verbal time-check announcements, and countdowns all help keep everyone on schedule to mesh the local programming smoothly with the remote program material.

Remote facilities exist in several forms. Small, portable audio consoles incorporate mixers, turntables, and cart machines. Some stations use fully equipped trailers or vans for a truly mobile studio operation.

Use caution when stringing cables in public. Route cables carefully and tape them down securely to prevent someone from tripping or falling. Likewise, route cables to be the least possible temptation for someone to tamper with them, or broadcast operations maybe disrupted.

Exercise 13-1. Remote Broadcast Possibilities

Some radio stations use remote broadcasts to enhance the station's image, promote community events, or to air program-length commercials such as all-day sales events. Use your imagination and the following questions to describe a remote broadcast (other than the usual high school sports event) that would arouse interest and entertain or inform the station's audience.

1. Describe briefly a community event that would make an interesting remote broadcast program—tell what will happen at the event.

2. Describe the format for the remote broadcast.Is it a series of short reports, a two-hour program, all day event, etc.?

3. What kind of equipment will be needed to get the event on the air? How many microphones; how many of feet of mike cable; how many engineers, announcers, audio console, cart machines, etc.?

Vocabulary

broadcast loops	gaffer's tape	short-hop remote links
closed circuit feeds	local availabilities	telco
covering a spot	loop	telephone company
cutaways	mark	time check announcements
dedicated line	phone patch	slop time
dirty feeds	remote	station breaks
duct tape	remote broadcast	woof
electronic news gathering (ENG)	satellite feeds	

Chapter 14

Automated Radio Stations

Computers never fail (click!) . . . never fail (click!) . . . never fail (click!) . . .

In spite of that old joke, computer control of radio stations has been around for decades. It is a useful part of many broadcast operations (Fig. 14-1). *Broadcast automation* applies to a wide variety of devices that start and stop equipment and route the proper audio sources to the transmitter at the right time. Some automation equipment is very simple and can store information for only a few program events before a human must take control again. Other automation systems can run for days, handling all of a radio station's studio and transmitter control functions, including turning on the coffee pot for the chief engineer!

Why automate? Simple. Broadcasting is a business, and any business needs to be cost effective. Broadcasting is also repetitious at times. It makes good sense to let a machine handle the predictable, repetitive situations to free the humans on the staff for more creative work.

HOW AUTOMATED CAN YOU GET?

Many radio stations use live combo operators all day because the personal touch of a living human on the air is important to their formats. Some automation has crept into these stations, however, where it can help the DJ do a better job. For instance, some audio consoles link the audio control and start/stop functions together for cart machines. When a cart has been played on the air once, the machine *can't* get on the air again until the cart has been removed and another has been inserted. Many radio stations that tape-delay network broadcasts use a simple timing device to start a tape recorder connected to the network line in the production studio.

Automated Assist

A radio station that makes heavy use of live remotes might have the announcer at the shopping center, while all the commercials and songs are loaded into automated cart machines back at the station. The remote announcer uses a couple of simple remote controls to start and stop the automation. Depending on how sophisticated the automation is, the remote announcer might be able to randomly access any spot or song, or he might need to follow

Fig. 14-1. Broadcast automation. A full-time automated radio station can keep running with only an occasional visit from a human being.

a rigid program log with a preplanned order of events.

Full Automation With Live Breaks

Yet another level of automation has all music and spots on tape controlled by a computer. The live announcer must show up at the control room only occasionally for a *live break-in*, a program event in which the automation turns on a studio mike for the newscast at the top of the hour (Fig. 14-2). In this case, the automation waits for the live announcer to pull a *next event* lever, sometimes called the *go button* when the live break-in is over. This signals the computer that the automated programming should resume.

Full Automation

Automation systems can even eliminate the live break-in. Newscasts can be prerecorded on cart. Either a live announcer handles that function, or the automation system uses a time clock to catch a network newscast on schedule, taping it for broadcast

several minutes later when the automation system's program log calls for it. Automations are also able to join a network feed live and on schedule.

One broadcast automation manufacturer had a clever ad years ago. It was a photograph showing all who came to an automated radio station's staff Christmas party. Stretched across the room were several racks of tape machines, cart machines, and a computer, all decked out in holiday decorations. Nearby was one lonely janitor who was sweeping up. The point was, the station could operate with practically no human help.

SEQUENCERS AND CONTROLLERS

How does an automation system store the program events? All sorts of methods have been devised. Some early automation systems were very much like jukeboxes that you've seen in pizza restaurants. Someone had to load a hundred records into the thing, and it played whatever was next, starting with slot number one, then number two, and so on.

Fig. 14-2. Hazards of automation. One occupational hazard in an automated station is that the operator might forget to do anything at all, even if it's just giving the 10 o'clock station ID announcement.

In the 1960's, automation systems commonly used a mechanical *sequencer* made of a few dozen numbered wheels, called *thumbwheels*. Each wheel could be turned to select one of ten possible audio sources, such as "reel #1," "cart 4," or "studio." A mechanical scanner worked its way down the row of numbered wheels, starting with the first one. As each program event concluded, the scanner moved to the next thumbwheel, starting whatever audio source was indicated.

As small computers became practical and relatively inexpensive in the early 1970s, much more sophisticated automation systems were devised. Because computer control is no longer limited to just ten audio sources, more elaborate cart machines holding a hundred or more carts are commonplace. The computer relies on an accurate digital clock and listens to special cue tones on the network line to ensure that network newscasts and programs are met on schedule.

COMPUTERIZED AUDIO MIXING

Computer-controlled automation systems also permit more flexibility in audio control, handling smooth audio crossfades, voice-overs, and other kinds of audio mixing. Major audio production studios now have automated audio consoles linked to computers. The computer can be programmed to mix together multitrack audio recordings in whatever way the studio engineer wants. The programming is either done by typing in codes on a computer keyboard or by having the computer actually learn from how a human handles the mixing by hand. With a little time spent in programming the production studio's computer, one studio engineer and computer can do the work of many studio engineers, and the results are consistent and accurate, time after time. Because a good studio engineer can command a large salary, computer-assisted mixing can really help keep production costs down.

Automated production involves recording the computer's instructions onto a blank track of the tape machine as well as storing information in the computer itself. This ensures that everything happens exactly when it should.

CUE TONES

Automation systems still aren't as smart as humans. They don't know when a song or commercial is over just by listening to the program content. Therefore, all program events must end with a special *cue tone*. The industry standard for the primary cue tone is to use a very low note, 25 Hertz, which is lower than most people can hear. The automation system is always listening for the cue tone. When a cue tone is detected, the automation system takes the present audio source off the air and switches to the next one.

Cue tones also control the stopping of tape machines. Cart machines use several cue tones. The 25-Hertz tone tells the automation system to move on to the next event, while a differently pitched cue tone tells the cart machine when to stop the cart, leaving it re-cued for the next time it is needed. Reel-to-reel machines use two 25-Hertz tones, working in pairs. The first cue tone comes at the end of a musical selection to tell the automation system to move on to the next event. The tape continues to roll until a second cue tone is detected. The tape stops at the second cue tone, leaving that tape cued up to the next musical selection on that reel.

Networks use a variety of tones to signal cues to their stations. Different frequencies mean different things. An automation system can put a network newscast on the air, use the cue tones to cut away from network for a local 60-second commercial, and rejoin network for the rest of the newscast. The network cue tone signifying the end of the newscast tells the local automation system to resume local programming. Network cue tones can also be used to interrupt local broadcasts, putting the network on the air immediately for special news bulletins. When you listen to network programs, listen for little high-pitched chirps or pairs of tones (sounds like someone saying "bee-doop"). These are the network cue tones.

As satellite broadcasting becomes more commonplace, separate audio channels for cue tones are becoming available. Eventually the chirps and bee-doops of network cue tones will disappear from the program audio.

REEL TAPES FOR AUTOMATION

When an automated radio station relies on recorded music for much of its program content, that music is recorded onto large 10-inch reels of tape. Some stations make up their own tapes, but most buy or rent them from a music syndication service.

Warning—Tails Out!

If the radio programs are received on reels of tape, take a moment to check the reel or container for a label that tells you how the tape is loaded. A common practice is to send tape *tails out*, meaning that the loose end of the tape is at the end, not the beginning of the program. You must rewind the tape before you play it on the air. A backwards-playing tape is no joking matter if you put it on the air that way.

Headers

Many syndicated tapes come with a *header*, a brief voice announcement at the head of the tape, followed by a test tone. The announcement tells you about the program content of the tape, but the header announcement itself is not for broadcast. Likewise, the test tone is there to help the operators set levels—it is also not for broadcast.

A sure sign of a sloppy operator is when the listeners hear an automated music station suddenly transmit: "Smith Tape Services, oldies reel number 14-A, beeeeeeeeeeeeeeeeee . . ." (Fig. 14-3). Don't you get caught cueing up a tape that way! Always listen to the beginning of any taped program material to be sure it is properly cued up.

Most syndicated music tapes follow the header with several seconds of silence, a 100% volume test tone, and then a cue tone preceding the first musical selection. If time permits, you can thread up a tape (remembering to rewind it if it's tails out), then just hit the play button. It might take five minutes, but eventually the tape will play through the header and test tone and cue itself up automatically. It's still best to listen to the tape to make sure it's really cued-up to what you want. You never know if someone inserted a stray cue tone in the header.

MIXES OF MUSIC TAPES

Chapter 4 discussed formats, pie charts, and music mixes. Many automation systems and music syndication services permit the local stations to determine the music mix. Typically, the automation system has four or more reel-to-reel tape decks, and different types of music are loaded onto each deck.

Reel #1 might be a tape of all vocal groups; reel #2 is all male and female vocalists; reel #3 is oldies; and reel #4 contains all instrumentals. Other tape services provide a thorough mixture on each tape, and the automation system needs only two or three reel-to-reel decks to play the tapes.

Some automated stations have major changes in format during the course of the day. An easy listening station might have faster-paced music during the day but switch to slower, more mellow tunes at night. That requires changing all the reels of tape at some specified point.

Pay attention to the automation's sequencer at reel change time. If you're rewinding reel #2, and it's due up next on the air, you'll get caught broadcasting the "monkey chatter" sound of a rewinding tape. Take a moment to figure out which tape deck will be idle the longest; rewind and re-cue that one first.

FILLING THE GAPS

Some station formats require that no music be faded out in midsong in order to meet the network on schedule. It is never acceptable to fade out of a vocal selection that is not completed. How do automated stations meet the schedule?

Instrumental Fill Music

Some automation systems have a reel of instrumental-only music that is used to fill in the time to keep things on schedule. This is called *fill music*. All of the cuts are exactly the same length, such as two minutes. The automation's computer knows that if a song ends less than two minutes before the scheduled network program event block, the automation can fill the time precisely by deadrolling the two-minute instrumental and fading it up when the

Fig. 14-3. Cue tapes properly. Syndicated radio programs delivered on tape can include nonbroadcast material at the beginning. Be sure to cue the tape to the start of the program material—not just first audio on the tape.

previous song ends. The instrumental will play along, ending precisely when needed to give the station ID and join network. It sounds all nice and tidy, as if some person were sitting there making everything come out just right.

Timed Jingles and Fill Music

Some more-sophisticated automation systems have a variety of fill music and jingles on many different carts. The automation system calculates how much time is needed to fill between the last selection and the top of the hour and selects the cart that

will fill the time the best. A lot of fill music must be available, or the fill music carts must be replaced frequently. Otherwise, your listeners will get used to hearing the same song leading into the 2 P.M. news every day, and that sounds bad!

Silence Sensors

Most automation systems have built-in circuits that signal for human help under certain circumstances. The most common is a simple *silence sensor*, a circuit that rings an alarm if no audio comes down the program line for a while. A Top-40 rock station might have a silence sensor that waits only two or three seconds before signaling for help because silence is not part of a rock format. An automated classical station, however, might have a much slower silence sensor delay, waiting up to a minute before signaling for help.

The silence sensor's alarms often include a shrill whistle and bright light mounted on the automation system itself (Fig. 14-4), plus additional lights and whistles elsewhere in the radio station, such as the AM control room, newsroom, or by the receptionist's desk in the lobby. When the alarm sounds, someone better come running to fix the problem right away!

Fail-Safe Systems

Most computerized automation systems have build-in fail-safe systems that can help the automation system get itself out of trouble. The computer has designed-in methods of dealing with common problems. For instance, if the silence sensor activates, the computer assumes something is wrong with the audio source now on the air. It moves on to the next program event. If several sources in a row are dead, the computer assumes a major failure and plays fill music from a specially dedicated cart machine. If a reel-to-reel machine fails to provide audio after two tries, the computer assumes that the tape has broken or the machine has failed,

Fig. 14-4. Silence sensors. Most automation systems will let you know when they get in trouble.

and it skips over that machine every time the program log calls for it to be used.

In all cases, however, if the automation system determines that there is a fault in the system, it signals for human help, even while it does its best to keep things going. Listeners are quickly lost from a radio station that sounds like it is having problems. Lost listeners mean lost advertising dollars and a poor reputation. No radio station can afford that.

Emergency Fill Music

Most automation systems have some kind of "last resort" program material to put on the air when all else fails. This usually takes the form of a large cart or reel of tape specially reserved to be aired only when the automation system can't find any other valid audio sources. Emergency fill music can be triggered if the computer determines that no tape or cart machines are making any sound (indicating a failure in the audio system or a power outage in an equipment rack). Emergency fill music can also be started if some fail-safe circuit determines that the computer itself has gotten confused. This happens occasionally, resulting in either no audio sources getting on the air or everything getting on the air at once!

Emergency fill music is recorded with occasional jingles and station IDs. Some stations use special jingles that are not heard at any other time. That way the station's staff knows that the automation system is secretly signaling for help, although the listeners probably won't notice the difference.

AUTOMATION CART MACHINES

Automated radio stations were possible before cart machines were commonplace, but doing everything with reel-to-reel machines was a very tough way to go. A lot of work was required to make a daily *spot reel*, a large reel of tape containing all commercials, PSAs, promos, and even ID announcements.

Cart machines have made automation systems much more versatile, and several different kinds of cart machines are commonly used. Most stations now have some kind of multiple-play cart machine that holds from 12 to 48 carts. Some of these multicart machines have the carts loaded in a round

carousel. When a specific cart is needed for air play, the carousel spins around until the proper cart is in position by the playback heads.

The 48-cart machines have one shared capstan for each vertical stack of 12 carts, but each cart has its own playback head. Several of these large cart machines can be run in combination, permitting hundreds of carts to be instantly available for airplay in any order required.

In addition, automation systems can be set up to use a record/playback cart machine. The automation system's computer uses a time clock to automatically record a network newscast for rebroadcast at a more convenient time. Other play-only cart machines are used for ID announcements. Two cart machines can be used together to provide time-check announcements. One cart holds announcements for even-numbered minutes, while the other cart holds announcements for odd-numbered minutes. The automation's computer keeps cycling the carts each minute without putting them on the air. Then, when the computerized program log calls for a time check, the appropriate cart is instantly ready to play the correct time announcement.

MONITORING AN AUTOMATION SYSTEM

Automation systems are very reliable, but now and then things can go wrong. A tape can break, a tape machine can fail, or the computer's programming can be defective, causing all kinds of strange problems. Some kind of safeguard is required to make sure the automation system keeps running correctly. Three main methods are used to make sure a broadcast automation system is working properly:

☐ Human monitoring
☐ Silence sensor alarm, and
☐ Fail-safe system

In some stations, a member of the radio station's staff is required to listen to the automation constantly. If anything sounds like it's going wrong, that staff person is required to check the automation system and get it straightened out quickly. Usually, the staff person has other duties, such as serving as the station's receptionist or working in the station's transmitter room.

Some AM/FM stations have a live DJ who must do his or her own show live on AM while checking the FM automation frequently to make sure it is working smoothly. This setup can be a real pain to the combo operator who is already pretty busy conducting the live show. Because failures are rare, it is easy for the operator to fall into the habit of not listening to the automation at all. If the automation system fails, no one at the station might know about it until a listener calls in to complain.

AUTOMATED LOGGING

Although the FCC relaxed logging requirements several years ago, most radio stations continue to need an accurate record of what was played and when it was on the air. Requiring a human to sit there and log the program events as they are aired can be a tiresome business. Therefore, automatic logging systems exist that are accurate and reliable.

Printer Logging

Most automation systems provide means of printing out the actual start time of each program event and a description of what that event was. The automation system can keep track of what audio source is being used and just log that information. More sophisticated systems use specially encoded carts to tell the computer exactly what spot, PSA, promo, or ID was played.

Tape Loggers

Many radio stations, automated or not, keep a complete recording of their broadcast days. Special tape recorders are used, permitting a full 24-hour day to be recorded on one reel of tape, along with continuous time information on a separate track. The tape logger has an advantage over printer loggers because the tape also records exactly what was said by the announcers and newscasters.

WRAP-UP

In today's broadcast business climate, many radio stations are using some type of automation system to air the program events. This replaces the combo operator partially or completely. Older automation systems used mechanical sequencers and required frequent updating by a human operator. Many radio stations now use versatile computerized automation systems, allowing a mechanical system to sound much more like one being run by a live DJ.

Automation systems can keep accurate records of when each program event was aired. They can also record network newscasts and play them back later. Automation systems can be set up to fit any musical format, even providing the correct mix of certain types of music.

Complex and highly reliable tape cart machines have been developed to make automation systems extremely flexible. Even so, most automations systems monitor themselves to make sure everything is performing properly. If anything goes wrong, the automation system is programmed with instructions for keeping the station on the air and signaling for a human to check the system immediately.

People no longer need to handwrite the time each program event goes on the air. Automated logging systems record the station's on-air activities moment by moment, using both a computer-driven printer as well as a continuous tape recording.

Exercise 14-1.   Automation Terminology

Demonstrate your knowledge of the basic concepts of broadcast automation systems by defining the terms listed below.

1. Fail-safe system
2. Fill music
3. Live break-in

4. Next event button
5. Sequencer
6. Silence sensor

Exercise 14-2. Common Automation Practices

1. If you are about to play a reel tape of music and notice that it is marked ''tails out,'' what should you do to the tape before playing it?

2. If an automation system senses a 25-Hz cue tone, what will the system's computer do with the next scheduled program event?

3. If the automation system turns on a studio mike, and the silence sensor doesn't detect any audio, what will probably happen?

4. If all normal audio sources fail, what will the fail-safe system do?

Vocabulary

automation

cue tone

fail-safe system

fill music

''go'' button

header

live break-in

''next event'' button

sequencer

silence sensor

spot reel

tails out

thumbwheels

Chapter 15

Broadcast Transmitters and Antennas

Broadcast engineering is a subject beyond the scope of this book. Many nontechnical combo operators, however, like to know a bit more about the transmitter and antenna systems at a radio station (Fig. 15-1). Very little has been written to help the non-engineer make sense out of the engineer's domain. In this chapter, you'll be given a layman's guided tour of AM and FM transmitting systems, with a bit more inside information on what makes transmitters and antennas tick.

THE AUDIO INPUT

The process of combining the control room's audio signals with the transmitter's radio frequency signals is called *modulation*, defined as the process of change. When no audio signals are being sent to the transmitter, the radio frequency signals are steady or unchanged and only silence or *dead air* is being transmitted. When the transmitter is on the air transmitting dead air, it is called an *unmodulated carrier*.

If the audio being fed from the control room has peaks at the 100% level on the audio console meter, and all other program line audio levels are correct, the transmitter will receive audio signals that cause *100% modulation*. When the transmitter is fully modulated, it means that the transmitted signal has the least distortion, is the loudest possible, and travels the farthest while causing the least interference with other radio stations.

The 100% modulation level is a standardized level easily checked by the chief engineer. Modulation percentage can also be read in the control room on a special meter in the modulation monitor (described later in this chapter).

It is possible to transmit audio signals that are too loud (more than 100% modulation). When this happens the transmitter is *overmodulated*. Overmodulation causes distortion, interference with other radio stations, and actually decreases the useful range of a radio station. The audio processor and the combo operator are both responsible for making sure that the transmitter is not overmodulated.

Fig. 15-1. Transmitter site. Many radio stations have studios in a central location, while the transmitter building and tower are out in the country. The satellite receiving dish (lower right) picks up network broadcasts that are relayed back to the studio. (WPOP-AM, Hartford, CT)

Stereo transmitters have two audio inputs: one each for left channel audio and right channel audio. In the case of stereo transmission, the modulation must be controlled on each channel so that neither channel is overmodulated.

It is important to maintain full modulation of the transmitter to get maximum performance out of the station's transmitter. It is also important, however, for all program material to be transmitted with the same modulation level in general. Drastic changes in volume are annoying to the listeners.

Each transmitter licensed for broadcasting operates at a specifically assigned power level. This is similar to renting an apartment where the landlord requires you to use 60-watt light bulbs in all lamps. If you decide to use either a 45-watt bulb or a 75-watt bulb, you would have to get permission from the landlord. Likewise, broadcast transmitters are assigned power levels so that each transmitter covers a specific geographical area without causing interference to stations many miles away.

A 1000-watt transmitter may legally drift down to 900 watts or up to 1050 watts. If the transmitter is found to be operating at any other power level besides the assigned output power level, it must be adjusted at once! It is not legal to routinely operate a 1000-watt transmitter at 900 watts just to save on electricity. It is also not legal to push a 1000-watt transmitter up to the 1050-watt limit just to get a little more coverage area. (It won't make a noticeable difference anyway.) You must maintain the licensed transmitter output power level.

TRANSMITTER OPERATING LOG SHEET

When taking the regular meter readings, you must check several crucial points in the transmitter. Quite possibly you might also check the performance of the antenna system. A sample log page is shown in Fig. 15-2. Each log entry is explained in some detail below.

☐ *Feedline*—The feedline is pressurized with nitrogen gas. The typical reading is usually a few pounds per square inch. Any reading greater than zero is acceptable. The gas keeps water out of the feedline, which takes the power from the transmitter to the antenna.

☐ *IPA*—Intermediate Power Amplifier. An amplifier that raises the radio signal to about 5% of the output power. This reading should remain steady in most cases.

☐ *PA FIL*—Power Amplifier Filaments. Found only in tube-type transmitters. Indicates one of the voltages applied to the power amplifier. This reading will vary during the day because commercial power varies a little.

WGCS - FM 91.1 MHz
Goshen College Broadcasting Corporation
Goshen, Indiana

Transmitter Operating Log

Time On Duty	Operator's Signature	Time Off Duty

Day: _____

Date: _____

All Times Are In EST / EDT

EBS Messages
Received Via _____
Time Received _____
Time Sent _____

Time	Feed Line psi	IPA K amps	PA Fil volts	PA Current amps	PA Voltage kV	Power Out kW	SWR	Remarks	Opr Initials

Remarks:

Fig. 15-2. Transmitter logs. Although many transmitter operations have been taken over by automatic transmitter control, handwritten logs are still used in some stations.

□ *PA Current*—Power Amplifier Current. Shows how many amps of electricity are flowing through the power amplifier.

□ *PA Voltage*—Power Amplifier Voltage. Indicates the main voltage applied to the tube. Note: Both PA CURRENT and PA VOLTAGE can vary if you raise or lower the output power of the transmitter.

□ *Power Out*—Indicates how many watts of radio energy are being produced by the transmitter. Some transmitters have output meters marked in percentage, with normal licensed output power being a 100% reading.

□ *SWR*—Standing Wave Ratio. A very technical term that indicates if the antenna and feedline are handling the transmitter power output correctly. The meter scale of an SWR meter is shown in Fig. 15-3. Notice that the scale begins at 1 rather than zero. A low reading is desirable; a reading of 1 is ideal. If the reading rises above 1.5, trouble might be developing.

You should become well acquainted with the normal readings so you will notice any unusual variations instantly. These terms might be confusing to you, but unless you intend to become a transmitter engineer, you really don't need to understand the meaning of these readings. Additional information about reading meters comes later in this chapter.

Many radio stations post a list of normal readings, along with a range of allowable variations. *Memorize it!*

VARIATIONS AMONG TRANSMITTERS

Most broadcast transmitters operate in about the same way. There are, however, some significant variations in the operation of transmitters. AM transmitters are arranged differently from FM transmitters, and the meter readings are also different. Likewise, the meter readings differ between a tube-type transmitter and one that is all-transistorized. Broadcast transmitters can have power output levels as low as 100 watts and as high as 50,000 watts. Naturally, the meter readings on the high-powered transmitters will be different from those of the smaller ones. Of all these variations, the differences between AM and FM transmitters are probably the most important.

AM—Amplitude Modulation

Earlier in this chapter, a transmitter's function was defined as the combination of audio signals with radio signals. This process is called modulation or "change."

An *AM transmitter* has a modulated signal that changes in intensity or loudness, the definition of amplitude modulation (Fig. 15-4). The radio signal becomes stronger and weaker in step with the audio signals being fed into the transmitter.

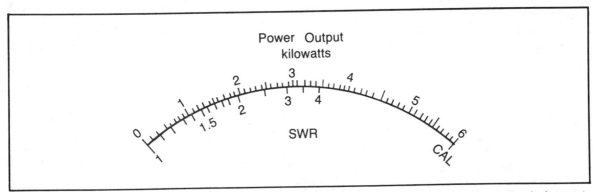

Fig. 15-3. SWR meter. Some say that SWR stands for "see what returns." An antenna system that is developing problems won't radiate the transmitter's output power efficiently, causing the SWR meter's reading to climb. Ideally, the SWR reading will be less than 1.5:1.

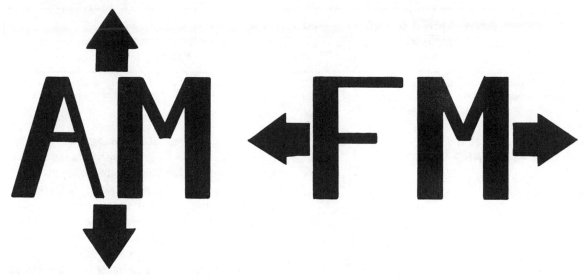

Fig. 15-4. AM versus FM. To put it (too) simply, AM signals stay in one spot on the dial but get bigger and smaller. FM signals stay the same size but slide back and forth along the dial.

Because the signal levels are changing in the output of the transmitter, the power amplifier meter readings will waver back and forth with modulation. This wavering of the meters is normal for AM transmitters. The most accurate meter reading is taken with no modulation.

FM—Frequency Modulation

Another method of combining the audio and radio signals involves holding the amplitude of the transmitter signal constant and changing the transmitter's operating frequency. The transmitter is putting out a modulated signal that moves slightly back and forth on the dial; frequency modulation means changing the frequency.

In an AM transmitter, the *amplitude* of the signal varies while the frequency is held constant; but in an FM transmitter, the *frequency* varies while the amplitude is held constant. AM signals get bigger and smaller while FM signals stay the same size but move back and forth.

Therefore, in a properly functioning FM transmitter, the meters do not wiggle with modulation. If an FM transmitter's meters do move around, even a little bit, it could be a sign of trouble, and you should notify the station's chief engineer immediately.

OPERATING FREQUENCY

As a radio listener, you have noticed that there are two groups of radio stations: the AM broadcast band stations and the FM broadcast band stations. The AM broadcast band was well established by the year 1935, with some of the oldest broadcast radio stations already on the air as far back as 1920. The FM broadcast band wasn't finally established until the late 1940s.

Figure 15-5 is a simplified frequency spectrum chart. The AM broadcast band is centered around the frequency of 1 megahertz, which means that the radio waves vibrate about one million times per second. The AM broadcast band extends from 0.540 megahertz to 1.600 megahertz. The FM broadcast band is centered around 100 megahertz, a much higher operating frequency than the AM band. The FM band extends from 88 to 108 megahertz. Each radio station is assigned a specific operating frequency within the band. Naturally, all stations assigned to the AM broadcast band use amplitude modulation and all FM band stations use frequency modulation. There are no exceptions.

The FCC requires that a transmitter be operated on a *specifically assigned frequency*. Only small variations are allowed so that stations do not overlap and interfere with each other.

161

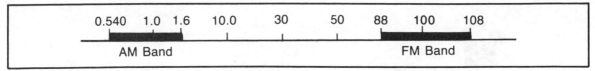

Fig. 15-5. Radio frequency spectrum chart. The AM broadcast band is centered around 1 megahertz, while the FM broadcast band is centered around a frequency that is 100 times higher. Each band has its own advantages, making both types useful for providing maximum coverage and high quality.

DIFFERENCES BETWEEN THE AM BAND AND FM BAND

The most obvious difference between the AM band and the FM band is the huge difference in operating frequency. The center frequency of the AM band is 1 megahertz while the FM band is centered at 100 megahertz. (A *megahertz* is one million electrical vibrations per second.)

The huge difference in the operating frequencies of the AM and FM bands cause some major differences in how the radio waves behave as they travel through space. These differences in radio wave *propagation* (the movement of radio waves through space) are important when assigning radio stations to specific operating frequencies. This is because propagation affects a station's coverage area and potential interference between stations.

AM Band Radio Waves

The AM band has a low frequency, only *one* megahertz, which means that the radio signals vibrate relatively slowly. This causes the individual radio waves themselves to be about a thousand feet long. Long radio waves travel along the earth's surface and easily go through buildings, trees, and into all but the steepest valleys. During the daytime, long radio waves travel out through the atmosphere in all directions (including straight up) and gradually get weaker until no receiver can pick them up.

A 250-watt AM station radiates usable signals out no more than 15 miles under ideal conditions and often provides dependable coverage to listeners only up to 10 miles away. A large 50,000-watt metropolitan station, however, radiates a much stronger signal. It can easily have a daytime coverage area out to 150 miles or more from the transmitter, depending on the terrain between the transmitter and the listener's receiver.

Things change drastically at night for AM band propagation. Those same 1 megahertz radio waves that faded out in the daytime are suddenly able to travel all over the world after dark. If there were no other stations around to interfere, the little 250-watt station could be heard for a thousand miles or more at night and, under favorable conditions, might be heard on the other side of the earth. The 50,000-watt stations regularly put signals out for several thousand miles at night. Some of these stations are protected from interference after dark and are called *clear-channel stations.*

The reason for the AM band's increase in coverage area is that the sunlight causes changes in a layer of the atmosphere called the *ionosphere* (see Fig. 15-6). In the daytime, the lower ionosphere absorbs some radio waves, including those from the AM broadcast band. At night, the lower ionosphere loses that characteristic of absorbing radio waves. The radio waves then reach the upper ionosphere, which acts like a mirror and reflects the radio waves back to earth many miles from the transmitter.

FM Band Radio Waves

FM band radio waves, centered around the frequency of 100 megahertz, are only about 10 feet long compared to the 1000-foot wavelength of the AM band waves. The FM band radio signals behave much like visible light. They travel in straight lines; they have trouble passing through buildings, trees, and hills; and they are nearly unaffected by the ionospheric changes between day and night.

The area covered by an FM station's signals is primarily dependent on the height of the antenna above ground. A higher antenna can "see over" more obstacles and reach out to a more distant horizon. An FM station with a 100-foot tower operating a 250-watt transmitter might cover an area out

162

Fig. 15-6. AM band at night. At night, even a flea-powered AM band station can be heard around the world because its signals bounce off a layer of the upper atmosphere. Interference from other stations limits the station's useful range at night.

to about 12 miles from the transmitter. That same 250-watt transmitter, when feeding an antenna at 500 feet, will easily be heard 30 miles away. FM stations have power levels up to 100,000 watts.

Regardless of tower height, operating power, or the time of day, FM radio stations are seldom heard more than 100 miles away. A listener with an exceptionally good FM receiver and antenna, however, can regularly pick up stations 150 miles away. Occasionally, weather conditions help FM band radio signals travel out several hundred miles.

FM transmitters modulate (or change) the transmitter's operating frequency to transmit sound. FM has a significant advantage: near immunity to static from electrical storms and electrical equipment. Because static is an AM-type signal, AM receivers pick it up easily while FM receivers virtually ignore it—a great help during thunderstorms.

These explanations are quite simplified and might be too brief to explain the subject of wave propagation adequately. If you have further interests in this field, the hobby of Amateur Radio is an excellent means of learning more about electronics and radio signals. To learn more about Amateur Radio (also called ham radio), write to the worldwide headquarters for Hams, the American Radio Relay League, 226 Main Street, Newington, CT, 06111. The League's phone number is (203) 666-1541.

FEEDLINES AND ANTENNAS

Routine operation of a transmitter requires very little attention to the electrical cable or *feedline* that carries the radio signal from the transmitter out to the antenna. This feedline is a very expensive and important part of the station, however. You need to follow a few simple guidelines to maintain a proper feedline and to ensure your personal safety:

- [ ] Never disconnect a feedline unless you are personally sure that the transmitter is not operating.
- [ ] Never nick, puncture, or sharply bend a feedline.
- [ ] Never walk on a feedline.
- [ ] Never touch a feedline that is on or near a radio tower.
- [ ] Never look directly into the end of a broadcast transmitter feedline or metal pipe waveguide.

If you pursue a career in broadcast engineering, you will learn much more about the proper way to handle feedlines.

Once the feedline has delivered the power to the antenna, the radio waves begin vibrating back and forth in the antenna structure itself. If the feedline and antenna are functioning properly, all the power from the feedline goes through the antenna and into space. The antenna must be constructed to specific dimensions for the radio frequency used by the transmitter. The lower-frequency radio stations have physically larger antennas when compared to higher-frequency radio stations.

STANDING WAVE RATIO

Standing Wave Ratio (abbreviated *SWR* or *VSWR*) is a technical term too complicated to explain in this book. For now, you need to know that SWR is a measure of how well the antenna system is performing. The lower SWR meter readings are better than higher ones. An SWR meter reading of 1 is ideal, but a reading of 1.5 or more can indicate problems. Many transmitters will experience serious damage if the SWR meter reads higher than 3 for any length of time.

High SWR readings indicate that something has gone wrong with the antenna system or the feedline from the transmitter to the antenna. SWR readings normally climb in the winter when ice builds up on the antenna (Fig. 15-7). The ice changes the antenna's electrical characteristics and makes it work

Fig. 15-7. Effects of weather. Beware of ice on the tower, although it seldom gets this bad!

less efficiently. Not all of the power is radiated; some of it is rejected by the antenna and returns down the feedline back to the transmitter. Therefore, some engineers jokingly say that the term SWR means "see what returns." You don't want any power to return at all—you want it all to leave the antenna and go out to the listeners.

In most transmitters, the SWR meter is combined with the *Power Output Meter*, and a three-position switch controls the Output/SWR meter functions. Here is how to read SWR (see Fig. 15-8).

1. Set the selector switch to CAL (this means *calibrate*, a step necessary for accurate SWR meter readings).

2. Adjust the knob marked SWR CAL ADJ (sometimes called the *sensitivity* knob) until the meter's needle rests directly over the CAL mark on the right side of the meter.

3. Set the selector switch to the SWR position and get the SWR reading. This is typically a number somewhere between 1.1 and 1.17.

4. Return the selector switch to POWER OUT.

Read the SWR meter often when the weather is changing. It could help you head off trouble that might take your radio station off of the air.

DIRECTIONAL ANTENNAS FOR AM STATIONS

The simplest AM broadcast antenna is a single vertical tower that radiates signals out to the horizon in all directions. This type of radiation pattern is called *nondirectional*. Antenna patterns are often drawn as if the viewer were floating in space directly above the tower or towers. Figure 15-9 shows the radiation pattern for a nondirectional antenna.

Many small-town AM radio stations must go off the air at night to avoid interfering with other regional or clear-channel stations on the same frequency. Many medium-market AM stations stay on the air at night, however, by using *directional antennas*. These radiate the transmitted power in certain specific directions while not radiating power in certain other directions.

A two-tower directional antenna can radiate a signal pattern like the illustration in Fig. 15-10. The

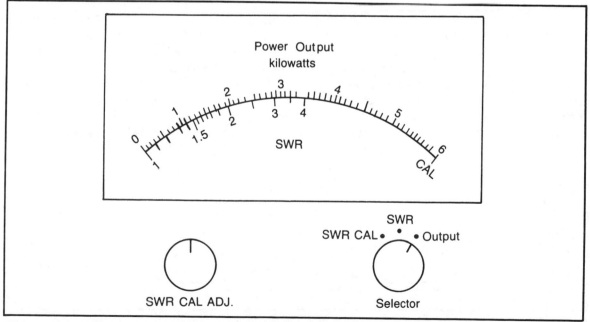

Fig. 15-8. SWR meter and controls. During bad weather, particularly in icy conditions, frequent checks of the SWR meter might be needed.

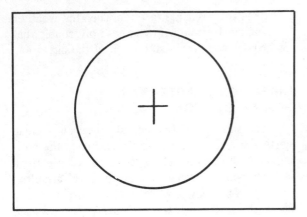

Fig. 15-9. AM band nondirectional one-tower antenna pattern. As viewed from above, a one-tower AM band antenna radiates equally well to all points on the horizon.

transmitter power is fed to both towers that are usually just a few hundred feet apart from each other. The transmitter radio waves from the two towers interact with each other; they add together in some directions while canceling each other in other directions.

Many different radiation patterns can be achieved by varying the distance between the towers, varying the amount of power fed to each tower, or varying the *phase* (inserting a time delay) in the signal being fed to one tower.

Directional AM antenna systems require additional meter readings to ensure proper operation. These meters indicate the amount of power being fed to each tower and the phase of the signals in each tower. This monitoring equipment is fairly simple to use. Your chief engineer will instruct you on how

to take meter readings from the directional antenna monitoring system. As with any other meter readings, be careful to take accurate readings. Notice any readings that are out of normal limits.

Sudden weather changes will often cause noticeable variations in directional antenna meter readings. This can be anything as subtle as the dew falling around sunrise, although sudden temperature changes and storms will have an effect as well.

FM ANTENNAS
AND EFFECTIVE RADIATED POWER

The FM antenna is relatively small and often resembles a ring or hoop about 2 or 3 feet in diameter. While an AM antenna uses the large metal tower itself, the FM antenna is usually several small metal hoops mounted at the top of a tall tower. The tower serves only to hold the FM antenna high enough to provide line-of-sight coverage to distant horizons.

The simplest FM antenna has one hoop (Fig. 15-11). This is called a *single-bay antenna*. When power is fed to such an antenna, the radio waves radiate out in all directions, including up and down. The power that goes out to the horizon, however, is the only power that does the listeners any good; the power going up or down is wasted.

Therefore, most FM stations stack several antenna *bays* (or several identical antennas) on a tower (Fig. 15-12). Like the AM directional antennas, the multiple FM antennas interact with each other. The signals radiating out to the horizon are reinforced, while the power going straight up and down is can-

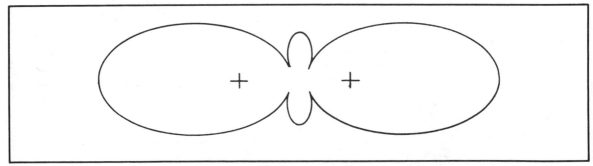

Fig. 15-10. AM band directional two-tower antenna pattern. Power from the transmitter can be directed in specific directions by using two towers. This arrangement also reduces power radiation in other directions, protecting distant stations from interference.

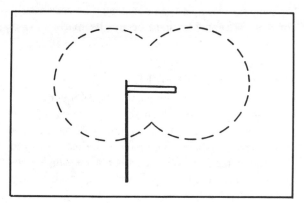

Fig. 15-11. FM band single-bay antenna pattern. This antenna radiates in all directions equally well. Only the power radiating straight out to the horizon is useful to the listeners. Everything else is wasted.

celed. This concentrates the transmitted power out where it is most useful.

Effective Radiated Power

An FM station's power output is rated in watts of *effective radiated power*, also called *ERP*. This is based on what effect a given power output has at the receiving point.

Assume, for the moment, that an FM station has a 1000-watt transmitter feeding a single-bay antenna. The power is radiated in a spherical pattern equally in all directions including straight up and straight down. A multibay antenna focuses the radiated power by taking away power radiated up and

down and adding it to the power that radiates straight out. Because the listeners are *out*, not up or down, a multibay antenna radiates the power more effectively, concentrating the power into a flattened doughnut pattern.

Many small-town FM stations use three-bay antennas, but major-market stations often use four, six, or eight bays. Such large antennas (up to 80 feet tall) must be mounted on very tall towers to work effectively.

Transmitter Meters

When you take the meter readings on a transmitter, you measure the voltage, current, and watts at various points in the transmitter circuits. These meters are marked in such a way that the needle is usually in the middle third or upper half of the meter face because this is the range at which the meter is most accurate.

When reading a volt meter you should follow these steps:

1. Observe the major meter scale markings with numbers. Use the major dial markings to get a general idea of the value being represented by the needle position on the meter face.

2. Look for the intermediate marks. Count how many divisions there are between the numbers, and decide how much each inter-

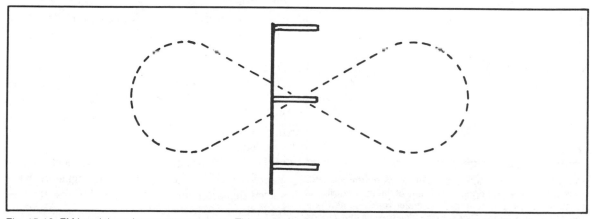

Fig. 15-12. FM band three-bay antenna pattern. This type of antenna can focus all available power into a flattened doughnut pattern, increasing its effective strength out to where the listeners are.

mediate mark represents as a fraction (decimal).

Look at the volt meter in fig. 15-13. How many volts are indicated? Here's how to tell:

1. The needle is between the 2 and the 3, so the reading will be more than 2 and less than 3.

2. The meter has marks for every tenth of a volt.

3. The needle points halfway between the marks representing 2.4 volts and 2.5 volts.

4. The meter indicates 2.45 volts. If the needle had been between 2.4 and 2.5, but was much closer to 2.4, you might have guessed the reading to be 2.43, but you could not have reasonably said that it was 2.425—that's trying too hard.

Don't try to wring more accuracy out of a meter reading than what is reasonable. The transmitter meter readings are a way of making sure that everything is going well. Extreme accuracy is not important, but consistency in meter readings is important.

Some engineers ask the operators to read the meters to the accuracy of the marks. If the needle lands anywhere in between the marks, consider it

halfway between. If the needle is on or very nearly on a mark, consider it to be on the mark.

DECIMAL MULTIPLIERS AND METRIC PREFIXES

Sometimes a meter must indicate a very large voltage or a very small current. There isn't room on the meter to put all of the numbers on the face in a readable fashion. The meter is therefore marked in a simple fashion, and you must make a simple conversion to get the true reading. (Hang on, this really won't hurt much if you pay attention.)

Many high-powered transmitters have very high voltages inside. It would be difficult to mark the meter face clearly if the meter typically read around 4000 volts. The major meter markings would be 1000, 2000, 3000, 4000, 5000 and 6000. All those zeroes take up space.

Kilovolts

There is another way. The major marks would be numbered 1, 2, 3, 4, 5, 6. Then the meter would read out in *kilovolts* or *thousands of volts*. A kilovolt meter is simple to read. If the meter indicates 4.6 kilovolts, you can write "4.6" in the log. But what you are really saying is that the meter is measuring 4.6 thousand volts, which is the same as saying 4600 volts. The Greek word *kilo* means "thousand," so a kilovolt is 1000 volts.

Milliamperes

Very small electrical currents flow in some parts of a transmitter. The electrical unit of current is the *ampere*, often shortened to *amp*. Often, the current flowing in a transmitter circuit amounts to less than one amp. A meter can be marked so that the full-scale reading is one amp. You could then interpret the meter reading to show an indicated current of 0.15 amps.

Such a reading puts the needle in the lower third of the meter's range of movement, where the accuracy isn't very good. Electrical engineers have solved this problem with a couple of tricks. If a meter indicates 0.15 amps, or something near to that, the meter can be devised so that the full-scale mark

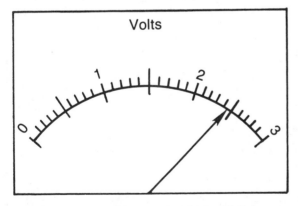

Fig. 15-13. Reading meters correctly. Look for the major divisions first. Then determine the value of the minor divisions to get an accurate reading. This meter reads somewhere between 2 and 3 volts. Closer inspection reveals that it reads between 2.4 and 2.5 volts. The correct reading is 2.45 volts.

is only 0.3 amps. This would put the needle about midscale to indicate 0.15 amps, where the accuracy is good. It is no problem to manufacture meters with various markings, or *calibrations*, to suit specific needs.

The decimal figure of 0.15 amps is a bit awkward and can be misunderstood. Electronic engineers therefore use another metric word to simplify things: *milli*, which means "one thousandth of" or the fraction 1/1000.

So the number *0.15 amps* could be called *150 milliamps*, which is *150 thousandths of an ampere*. By the way, nobody ever talks about tenths or hundredths of an amp. Broadcast engineers often abbreviate milliamperes to simply *mils*, so 0.15 amps would be called 150 mils.

Kilowatts

There is also the case of the wattmeter on the transmitter; sometimes the numbers can get awkwardly large. If a transmitter normally has an output power of 5000 watts, the wattmeter (or power output meter) is likely to be marked in *kilowatts*, or thousands of watts. A 5000-watt transmitter has an output power of 5 kilowatts.

"Arbitrary" Meter Scales

There is one other kind of meter that might confuse you. It has no particular units and is just divided off into a scale reading 1 to 10, or 1 to 100. Sometimes the power output meter is marked so that the normal licensed output power level is indicated at the 100 mark, indicating 100% of normal power. Other meters might be labeled something like DRIVE LEVEL, and a typical reading could be some arbitrary number, like 72. Nobody knows if it is 72 volts, 72 amps, or 72 flying chickens! It's just 72. If the chart of normal meter readings says that the DRIVE LEVEL meter is usually around 72, you're okay. If the drive level strays very far from 72, possibly below 65 or above 80, then you need to contact the chief engineer and find out if this is a problem.

Don't feel too bad if transmitter meter readings are somewhat meaningless to you. It will take time before you begin to get a feel for what normal meter readings look like. After you have logged about 10 hours of transmitter operation, you will start to feel at home. If you work part-time, especially if you work just a few hours a week, it will take somewhat longer for you to feel comfortable.

If you ever feel insecure or uncertain about your meter readings, be sure to consult the posted typical meter readings and look back at previous log pages to see what normal readings should be. Don't copy someone else's log entries! It is illegal and a waste of time.

Directional Antenna Monitors

If you work for a station that includes a directional AM antenna system, you will be required to read two meters for every tower being used. One meter tells how much power is going to that tower, and the other meter tells of the electrical phase relationship between one tower and another.

Usually, one tower is designated as the #1 reference tower, and the other towers' meter readings are compared with the #1 tower. When reading AM transmitter and directional antenna meters, the most accurate reading is obtained when there is no modulation of the AM transmitter.

WRAP-UP

The process of combining audio signals with radio signals is called modulation. Amplitude modulation is the process of varying the loudness or intensity of the transmitted signal, and frequency modulation involves shifting the transmitted frequency itself.

The AM broadcast band operates on a relatively low frequency. This means that the radio waves are physically very long. The waves are affected by the presence or absence of daylight, and at night, the AM band signals travel greater distances. AM stations avoid interfering with each other by restricting transmitter power, going off the air at night, or by using directional antenna systems.

The FM broadcast band operates on a much higher range of frequencies, with shorter radio waves that behave somewhat like light. Signals in the FM broadcast band are not affected by daylight or night but can travel great distances during certain weather conditions. FM stations use very tall towers and multibay antenna systems to focus strong signals to the largest possible population density.

Exercise 15-1.   Modulation Fundamentals

Check your comprehension of transmitter modulation by answering the following questions.

1. List at least two consequences of overmodulation.
2. List at least two consequences of undermodulation.
3. Which will sound louder, a transmitter modulated at 50% or a transmitter modulated at 90%?
4. Which will probably sound distorted, a transmitter modulated at 85% or a transmitter modulated at 135%?

Exercise 15-2.   Transmitter Fundamentals

Check your comprehension of basic broadcast transmitter facts by answering the following questions.

1. According to the FCC, the transmitter's output power may deviate how many percent greater than the licensed power? How many percent less than licensed power?
2. A radio station's FCC license states that its transmitter should put out 2000 watts. If the transmitter's power output drifts upward from the normal output level of 2000 watts, what is the maximum legal power output allowed?
3. A radio station's FCC license states that its transmitter should put out 500 watts. If the transmitter's power output drifts downward from the normal output level of 2000 watts, what is the minimum legal power output allowed?
4. Is it normal for the power output meter to move with modulation on an AM transmitter?
5. Is it normal for the power output meter to move with modulation on an FM transmitter?
6. What kind of transmitter is modulated by varying the transmitted signal's *strength*? (amplitude modulation or frequency modulation)
7. When a transmitter's output power is held constant, but its output frequency varies with modulation, is it *AM* or *FM*?
8. Is an SWR meter reading of 4.0 normally acceptable?
9. Is an SWR meter reading of 1.2 normally acceptable?
10. If the weather changes suddenly from clear and dry to foggy with freezing rain, would you expect the SWR meter reading to increase or decrease?

Exercise 15-3.   Radio Wave Propagation

Check your comprehension of how radio waves travel through space by answering the following questions.

1. Which broadcast service has radio waves that travel mostly line-of-sight? (AM band or FM band)
2. Which broadcast service is not affected much by thunderstorm and automobile static? (AM band or FM band)
3. Which broadcast service has relatively short range in the daytime and much longer range at night? (AM band or FM band)
4. Which broadcast service has radio waves that are bent back to earth by the ionosphere? (AM band or FM band)
5. The AM broadcast band is centered around what frequency in the radio spectrum?
6. The FM broadcast band is centered around what frequency in the radio spectrum?

7. Which broadcast service has radio wave propagation that is relatively unaffected by the time of day? (AM band or FM band)

8. Which radio service has radio waves that follow the earth's curved surface, making reception possible many hundreds of miles away at night? (AM band or FM band)

9. Which radio service has radio waves that go straight out from the antenna, through the ionosphere, and out into space? (AM band or FM band)

Exercise 15-4.   Broadcast Antenna Basics

Check your comprehension of basic broadcast antenna characteristics by answering the following questions.

1. Which broadcast service uses antennas with the power radiating from one or more small metal hoops mounted near the top of a tower? (AM band or FM band)

2. Which broadcast service uses antennas with the power radiating from one or more tall metal towers using the full tower(s) as radiators? (AM band or FM band)

3. Does an AM directional antenna radiate equally well to all points of the horizon?

4. Does an FM multibay antenna radiate equally well to all points of the horizon?

Exercise 15-5.   Principles of Meter Reading

Check your comprehension of broadcast transmitter meter reading skills by answering the following questions.

1. Which is greater, a volt or a kilovolt?

2. Which is greater, 2 amps or 150 milliamps?

3. Which is greater, 250 watts or 0.5 kilowatts?

Vocabulary

ampere	Frequency Modulation	radio wave propagation
Amplitude Modulation	interference	SWR, Standing Wave Ratio
AM broadcast band	ionosphere	saturation
antenna de-icer	kilovolts	sign-off
calibration	kilowatts	sign-on
carrier	log book	single-bay antenna
chief engineer	megahertz	solid-state transmitter
clear channel	meter	stacked bays
current	milliamps	transistorized transmitter
de-tuned antenna	modulation	tube-type transmitter
directional antenna	modulation monitor	vertical tower
distortion	multibay antenna	volt
effective radiated power	nondirectional antenna	warm-up
feedline	PA, Power Amplifier	watt
filaments	phase	
FM broadcast band	plates	

Chapter 16

Stereo Broadcasting

Sounds come from all directions. You use your two ears plus some mental processing in your brain to identify those sounds. You can accurately state a sound's position in three-dimensional space and about how far away it might be. *Stereo broadcasting* also has the lifelike quality of sound coming from several directions.

Stereo broadcasting began in earnest in 1961 when the FCC permitted FM broadcast stations to transmit two channels of program audio (Fig. 16-1). Stereo broadcasting on the AM band did not begin until about 1980, twenty years later. AM stereo was followed in the mid-1980s by stereo television broadcasting. Four-channel FM service was tried during the 1970s but never became very popular because of its complexity, high cost, and the variety of incompatible methods being used. Similar problems have also limited the appeal of stereo broadcasting on AM and TV, causing a weak consumer market for AM and TV stereo compared to strong acceptance of FM stereo.

HOW DOES STEREO WORK?

Stereo audio usually involves two audio channels, called the *left channel* and the *right channel*. Stereo audio consoles must therefore contain two of everything; the program amplifier is actually two separate amplifiers (one each for left and right audio), cart machines have two outputs, tape recorders have two inputs, and so on. In other parts of a radio station's equipment, a variety of methods are used to keep the two channels of audio separated.

Even though only two channels of audio are used, stereo audio can give the listener the sensation of a panorama of audio positions; full left, full right, dead center, or any point in between. If an audio source is fully modulated in the left channel, but not at all in the right channel, the listener perceives that the sounds comes from the left. Likewise, 100% modulation of the right channel with nothing in the left gives the full-right sensation to the listener. If the audio source is fully modulated in both channels, the listener hears the sound com-

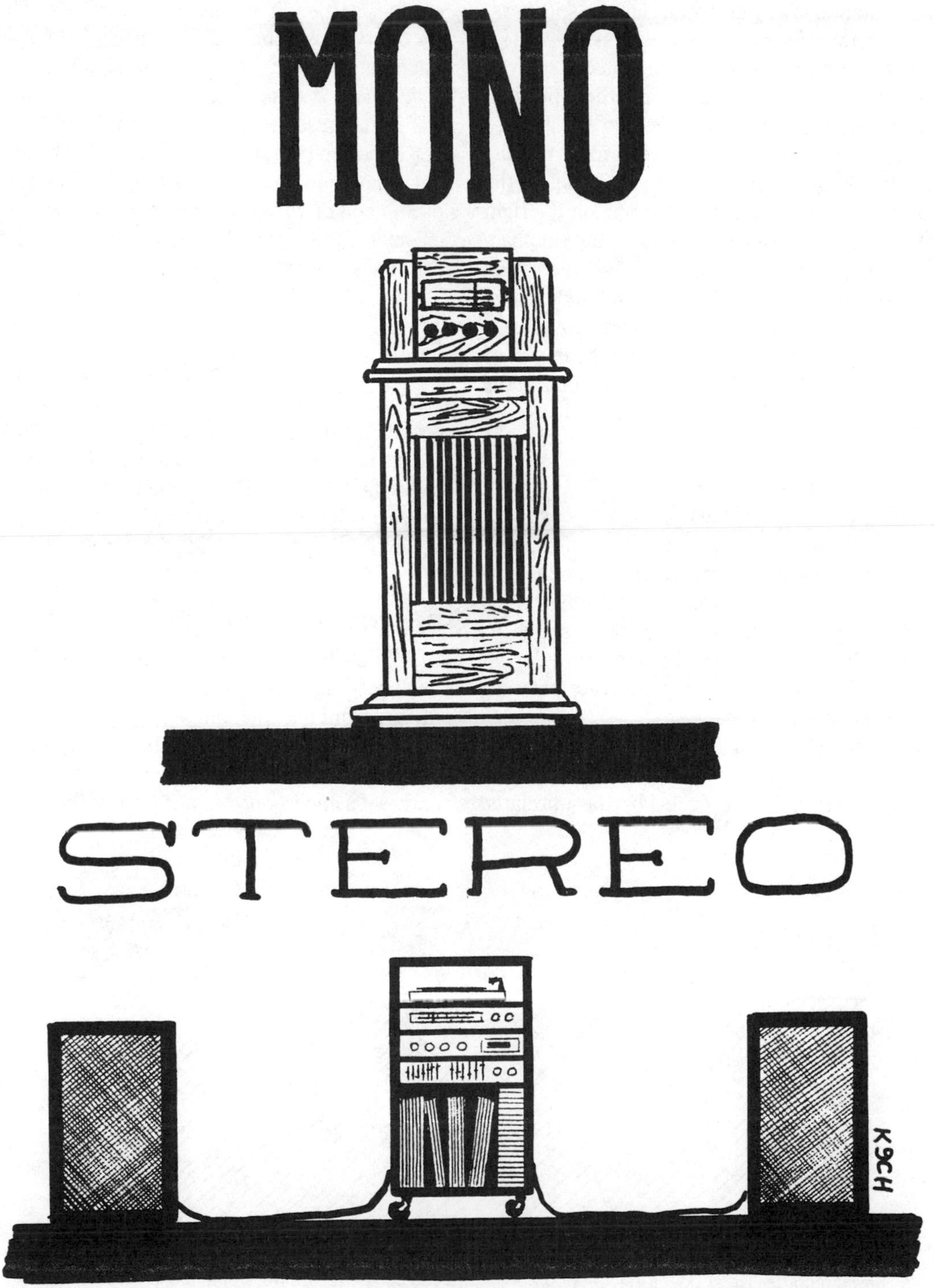

MONO

STEREO

Fig. 16-1. Mono versus stereo. The old Gothic receiver sure looked impressive, but the breadth and depth of stereo broadcasting gives wider frequency response and better quality sound reproduction.

ing from a point halfway between the two speakers, even though there is no third speaker in the center.

In real-life cases, many different audio sources are recorded at the same time, and their physical position relationships are preserved for the listener in a stereo recording. For instance, a male vocalist on the left side of the stage is recorded only on the left channel. A female vocalist standing on the right side of the stage is recorded only on the right channel. A single guitar player standing in between them is mixed equally onto both left and right audio channels. The listener equipped with a stereo sound system with only two speakers will then hear a male on the left, a female on the right, and a guitar in the middle, even without a center speaker.

Stereo Phonograph Records

Phonograph records have a spiral groove that winds from the outer edge to the catch groove near the center of the record. Records store sound patterns in the form of wiggles and irregularities on the walls of the spiral groove. The groove itself is V-shaped (see Fig. 16-2). Stereo records store the left and right audio tracks by having separate patterns on each wall of the groove.

The stereo phonograph tone arm is constructed to detect the movements of the needle so that separate audio signals are produced by the unrelated changes in the left and right groove walls. The needle or stylus is connected to a pair of tiny magnets. Each magnet is near a tiny coil of wire, called the *pickup coil*. If sound patterns occur only on the left wall of the groove, the needle wiggles the left magnet while the right magnet holds still. The left magnet's movement causes a current to flow in the left pickup coil of wire, and a signal appears in the left channel of the turntable's audio output while no signal appears in the right channel.

Stereo Tapes

Two or more separate tracks can be recorded side by side on the same audio tape. Stereo tape recordings therefore have fully *discrete audio*, which means having complete separation between the left and right channels. This is true for reel-to-reel tapes as well as broadcast carts, audio cassettes, 8-track automobile carts, and video cassettes.

BALANCE AND PHASING

When listening to two sound sources, you must be able to hear both about equally well or some of the program information will be lost. Stereo broadcast equipment ensures that both channels are fully modulated. Likewise, stereo receivers and players have a *balance control*, permitting the listener to

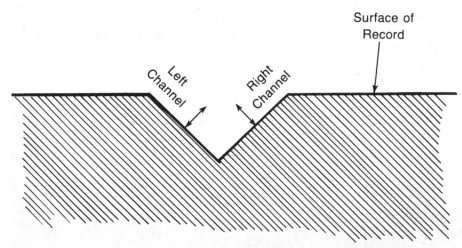

Fig. 16-2. Stereo records. The grooves in a phonograph record can carry two channels of audio information; one channel on one side of the groove and the other channel on the other side. New compact disc recordings use strings of computer data, an entirely different method.

adjust the left and right audio volume until both are clearly audible. Stereo audio is not always heard through stereo equipment. Inexpensive radios, record players, and tape machines might have only one audio channel; they're *monaural*, producing one sound source. Combining the left and right channels into one audio signal is called *mono*, short for monaural.

When the same audio information occurs in both left and right channels, they must be delivered at exactly the same time, then they are said to be *in phase* with each other. If the right channel's audio is transmitted slightly sooner or later than the left channel, the two channels are said to be *out of phase*. In-phase audio signals reinforce each other. If they are completely out of phase, however, the audio signals cancel each other. You might have heard this now and then when listening to a stereo station on a mono receiver; out-of-phase audio problems will cause the lead singer's voice to sound hollow, distorted, or even missing completely.

Broadcast engineers for stereo stations must work hard to keep the left and right audio channels in proper phase and balance, or the station will sound like mud. The combo operator, however, has little or no control over balance and phase—it's not your problem.

STEREO BROADCASTING

A stereo transmission is also called a *multiplex transmission* because it includes multiple components in the audio signals being applied to the trans-

mitter's audio input (Fig. 16-3). First of all, the left and right channels are mixed together to form a mono signal, called *left-plus-right* (or $L + R$). This allows inexpensive mono receivers to pick up stereo broadcasts without missing any program information. Because stereo receivers need some information to separate the mono information back into stereo, some additional signals are transmitted in a way that mono receivers can't hear them but stereo receivers can.

In addition to the mono (or *main channel*) audio, a multiplex transmission includes a *pilot tone*. This is a special signal that turns on the stereo decoding circuitry in stereo radio receivers. It also is used to light up the stereo light on your radio, telling you that the broadcast is in stereo.

The third channel of information in a multiplex transmission is the *left-minus-right* information (or L-R). The stereo receiver uses the L-R signal in combination with the $L + R$ signal to separate the two audio channels back into discrete left and right audio signals.

The stereo decoder's electronic circuits are too involved to explain in this book, but the stereo decoding process is something like the simple arithmetic problem in Figs. 16-4 and 16-5. One section of the receiver *adds* the $L + R$ and L-R signals together to get just the left channel audio (Fig. 16-4).

Another section of the stereo receiver *subtracts* the $L + R$ and L-R signals to get the just the right channel audio (Fig. 16-5A). Because the negative sign reverses the sign of both the positive L and the

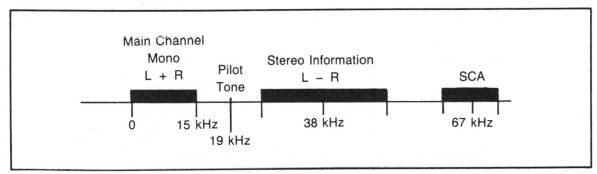

Fig. 16-3. FM multiplex transmission. The transmitted audio channel of an FM stereo transmission includes many components. The basic mono information can be decoded by any FM receiver. Above the range of human hearing, however, are additional components, including the 19 kilohertz stereo pilot tone, the left-minus-right stereo information, and unrelated SCA program material.

```
   L + R
 + L - R
 ─────────
 = 2L + OR or LEFT audio only
```

Fig. 16-4. Decoding the left channel.

negative R of the L-R signal, the math problem can be restated as shown in Fig. 16-5B.

Stereo transmission and receiving methods vary between AM, FM, and TV multiplex broadcasting. Through one means or another in all broadcast services, however, the left and right channels are always transmitted in a way that ensures that existing mono receivers can recover all of the program information found in the L + R component of the signal.

SCAs

Many FM radio stations can transmit one or more additional mono audio channels not related to the program channel. The additional audio channel is transmitted on a *subcarrier*, which is engineering hocus-pocus for piggybacking one signal onto another without the two interfering with each other. The rules that allow FM broadcasters to use subcarriers were originally called *subsidiary communications authorizations*, abbreviated *SCA*. The term SCA also refers to the *S*ubcarrier *A*udio channel.

SCAs are used for all kinds of information. Typically, an FM station's SCA is background music with no commercials or announcements of any sort. Restaurants and public buildings have special FM receivers with decoders designed to ignore the main channel audio and deliver the SCA audio instead. Besides carrying "elevator music," SCAs are used to deliver reading services for the blind, current stock market information, paging signals to businessmen, slow-scan television signals and high-resolution photographs, and even telemetry data to bring remote-site transmitter meter readings back to the studio.

SCAs are not available on AM stereo broadcasts because of the interference they would cause to other AM broadcast stations—the AM band is too crowded. FM and TV stations are spaced far enough apart in the frequency spectrum, however, that SCAs can be used.

WRAP-UP

Stereo broadcasting allows listeners to hear multiple audio sources in such a way as to perceive their placement in three-dimensional space. FM stereo broadcasting began in 1961 but did not happen on AM and television until about 1980.

Stereo audio consists of two separate signals, the left channel and the right channel. These must be mixed, processed, and transmitted in parallel. Sometimes the left and right channels are kept completely separate, while at other times they are mixed together. The left-plus-right signal is essential so that simpler and less expensive mono receivers can recover both left- and right-channel program information.

FM and TV stereo audio includes several components, including the left-plus-right and left-minus-right audio mixtures, the pilot tone for controlling stereo decoders, and sometimes additional non-related audio programming transmitted on SCAs.

```
A        L     +   R                    B        L     + R
      - (+L)     - (-R)                       -  L      + R
      ───────    ───────                      ─────────────
                                              = 0L      2R
                                              or RIGHT audio only
```

Fig. 16-5. Decoding the right channel.

176

Exercise 16-1.   Stereo Broadcasting Practices

Demonstrate your knowledge of basic concepts of stereo broadcasting by answering the following questions.

1. In a stereo broadcast, is the "main channel" left-plus-right or left-minus-right?
2. A mono receiver picks up what component of a stereo broadcast, left-plus-right or left-minus-right?
3. What will cause unwanted cancellation of some of a stereo broadcast's program in a mono receiver, in-phase audio or out-of-phase audio?
4. Can the listener normally hear the pilot tone?

Vocabulary

balance

discrete audio

in-phase audio

left channel

left-minus-right, L-R

left-plus-right, L + R

main channel audio

monaural, mono

multiplex transmission

out-of-phase audio

pilot tone

right channel

stereo

subcarrier audio channel

subsidiary communications authorization, SCA

Chapter 17

Taking The Next Step

You don't know all about broadcasting yet. This book is only a beginning. You will never know everything there is to know about broadcasting. The field is too broad and changes too quickly. This makes the broadcasting profession a very interesting, even captivating, field of work.

In Chapter 1, you were warned that stagnation is death for a broadcaster (Fig. 17-1). Stagnation occurs when you find yourself saying, "Now I have arrived." Stagnation settles in when you stop trying new equipment and methods. The good news is this: stagnation is not necessary and is easy to avoid.

Here are three good ways to keep your broadcast skills fresh and growing:

☐ Continue your education.
☐ Read broadcast trade magazines.
☐ Read books related to broadcasting.

EDUCATE YOURSELF

Regardless of the route you used to enter the broadcast profession, your training must not stop once you secure your first job. The equipment and operating practices are changing constantly, and you need to expose yourself to this information. The continuing education process can be carried on in an informal way, or you can enroll in organized classes. Become fully familiar with the equipment you use daily at your radio station. You can do this yourself as a part of your job when you have a spare moment.

Read the Equipment Manuals. Each piece of studio equipment has a complete instruction manual explaining the operation, circuit features, and maintenance. Ask your chief engineer where these manuals are kept and explain your interest in understanding the studio equipment better. Take very good care of the equipment manuals and never take them out of the station.

Study Each Piece of Equipment. Take the time to draw the front and back of the equipment you are studying. This will force you to notice each control and connector, and will make the instruction manual easier to understand.

Ask Questions About the Equipment. Talk to your chief engineer, station manager, or other

Fig. 17-1. Staying alive as a DJ. The tombstone says it all.

more experienced staff members if you have trouble understanding something. (Be sure to ask first if they have the time to talk about it now or should it wait until later.)

Listen to Other Radio Stations. Don't restrict yourself to your favorite style of radio entertainment. Listen to all kinds of formats, especially when you are traveling away from home. This will broaden your base of experience.

Visit Other Radio and TV Stations. Compare equipment in other stations to that used at your station. Also compare the arrangement and use of equipment. Ask your chief engineer or radio station sales staff for contacts with other stations. You'll get in the door much more quickly if you are the guest of someone that already works there.

Study Network Radio and TV Announcers. Listen to major market announcer styles. Notice the smoothness of the operating. Notice how fast (or how slowly) they talk. Notice what they do when ad-libbing. (Watch for the mistakes, too!)

Make "Air Check Tapes" of Yourself. Record yourself under various announcing situations. Play the tape back and write down specific problems you have. Also note specific things you do well. Affirm what you do well; improve any way you can.

Informal education has a major positive effect on your broadcasting talents. Take advantage of every opportunity to expand your knowledge in the field. Keep an archive tape of your work from the beginning. As in Fig. 17-2, keep the *bloopers* (mistakes), funny or well-done spots, history-making newscasts—whatever you do that you might find interesting later.

FORMAL EDUCATION

Self-teaching is inexpensive and readily available, but you should also seek out ways to be taught by experts. You need accurate information to communicate effectively with other broadcasters. Opportunities are everywhere.

Factory Representatives. Be alert for new equipment arriving at the station. Major equipment purchases often include installation and training by a representative from the factory. Ask your boss for permission to be present during the phases of the installation process, as your work schedule allows. Remember to stay out of the way, though. Listen to the conversations surrounding the installation work and take notes if you want to ask a question later. If you appear interested and available, you might be invited to help.

Correspondence Courses. Your chief engineer can help you select mail-order instruction in electronics and broadcast engineering. Some of these courses are very well structured. You should discuss this with the station manager and see if the station is willing to help pay for the course. Local college or high school instructors might also know of home-study courses in speech and journalism.

179

Fig. 17-2. Remember your mistakes. Many broadcasters record everything they do and edit together a "Great Moments in Radio" tape. It can include your best moments, and your worst! Both are useful.

Adult Continuing Education Classes.
These are classes taught by high school or college professors or nonprofessional teachers who are experts in particular fields. These courses are not formal college or trade school classes but do offer excellent and inexpensive means of receiving additional training. Contact area colleges and the city board of education for the availability of classes.

College Classes. Whether you have any previous college experience or not, most colleges and universities will allow you to enroll in a class that interests you. Discuss your interests with the college's registrar or admissions counselor, then take that information to your station manager. A full-time broadcaster has a busy schedule, but your station manager might be willing to arrange your work load around your class schedule.

Keep written records of what formal training you have received. This information looks very attractive on your job record and will help you advance in the broadcast profession.

READ BROADCAST TRADE MAGAZINES

Several good magazines are published that are intended for broadcasters. Each seeks to inform the reader of the latest in equipment, techniques, and current issues in broadcasting. Here is a brief description of several popular ones, although inclusion or exclusion of a specific magazine is not intended to reflect on the worth of that particular publication.

Broadcasting magazine is published weekly, with a subscription price similar to any other weekly news magazine. It covers all facets of radio, television, and cable, current FCC rules and proceedings developments. It is often subscribed to by the station manager but not always left out where the staff can see it, due to the excellent classified "help wanted" ads in the back!

Broadcast Engineering and *Broadcast Management & Engineering* are two entirely separate monthly magazines with somewhat similar formats. Both are supported heavily by the equipment advertising money. These ads are very instructional and are often supported by articles that explain the latest developments in broadcast equipment and techniques. FCC news, industry news, and classified ads are also included. Both of these magazines are available without charge to radio station staff members who have any kind of influence in equipment purchases. If you have a title such as program director, news director, assistant chief engineer, music director, production manager, etc., you can fill out the subscription card in the back of any of these magazines and will probably receive a free subscription. Anyone can receive the magazines with a paid subscription as well.

TV Guide is intended for home television viewers, but it often contains articles that deal with major ethical issues faced by broadcasters. The primary focus is on television, but radio broadcasters also find this magazine useful.

Many other excellent magazines and newsletters are available. If you are employed at a TV or radio station, even as an intern or volunteer, ask the chief engineer or station manager to show you this literature.

BOOKS ABOUT BROADCASTING

Skills for Radio Broadcasters is designed to be an introductory work on broadcasting. Many books have been published that pick up from here and cover the material in greater depth and detail. Some books specialize in certain aspects of broadcasting, while others provide very broad coverage. It is not possible to recommend specific books because new ones are being written all the time and current ones are updated in new editions.

Look at the Bibliography in this book for the names and addresses of some publishers that offer other books about broadcasting. Inclusion of specific publishers is not intended as an endorsement of their products. The author has found that all of the available texts of the subject are helpful to some degree. You should ask other radio station staff members for specific recommendations on books that they found particularly helpful. One source of good used books at low cost is a college or university that offers broadcasting courses.

THE AUDITION TAPE

Many new broadcasters make the mistake of spending painful hour upon hour producing a tape that shows their talents in perfect form. These tapes are often too long.

The audition tape gives a prospective employer a taste of your announcing and operating ability. If you make a good impression in the first 30 seconds, the employer will probably keep listening. The first five minutes of the tape usually are enough for a decision to be made.

Probably the most effective format for an audition tape is to provide an actual air check of your work. Edit out the majority of the music and avoid long commercials unless your voice is being included in the spot.

Many different audition tape formats are possible, but it is recommended that the air check include the following program events:

1. Begin the tape with a very brief leader announcement like this one: "Audition tape for Curt Holsopple from an air check recorded on June 10, 1970."
2. Two-second pause.
3. End of a song with your tag-out.
4. Plug upcoming news, sports, and weather.
5. Station slogan, legal station I.D., and time.
6. News intro.
7. One local story.
8. One state story.
9. One national or international story.
10. One sports story and a few sports scores.
11. Weather forecast including current conditions, such as temperature, wind, and barometer.
12. Another spot produced by yourself, either 30 or 60 seconds long.
13. Lead-in to a song, music up full for 10 seconds, then fade to silence.

Try to keep the whole thing about five minutes long, recorded on a new 5-inch or 7-inch tape (or cassette) with your name on it.

THE RESUME

When you are seeking employment, provide a written description of yourself. You should devote your best writing techniques to this. Remember, you are actually *selling yourself* as a desirable product. Use your best advertising skills in making an honest but inviting presentation. Type out your resume and correct any errors. Have someone else read it over slowly and carefully to double-check it for you.

When you write to a prospective employer, make every effort to get the name of the station manager or program director. If you are sending your resume in as a response to a job ad in a magazine, the ad will supply you with address information. Otherwise, consult the most recent edition of *The Broadcasting and Cablecasting Yearbook*. It is available in practically all radio stations.

When composing your resume and job application letter, include the following information:

The Cover Letter (page 1)

- ☐ Your name, address, and phone number
- ☐ Prospective employer's name, title, station address
- ☐ The date
- ☐ A short opening paragraph explaining your interest in working for that particular radio station
- ☐ A second paragraph explaining that you have enclosed a resume and that you have an audition tape that is either enclosed, being mailed separately, or available upon request
- ☐ A short third paragraph mentioning your availability for an interview in person or by telephone and when you will be available to start work.

Keep the letter very brief—short enough to fit comfortably on one page.

The Resume (page 2)

- ☐ Your name, address, and phone number
- ☐ Position being applied for
- ☐ List of broadcast-related experience
- ☐ List of other applicable training, hobbies, or skills

THE FOLLOW-UP

After you have mailed your resume, wait until you think the letter has arrived before calling. Try to time your mailing so that it arrives on Monday or Tuesday of the week. Time your first call to the station early in the day, around 8:30 or 9 A.M. (local time for that station) to catch the manager before he leaves his office.

Regardless of who you talk to, be sure to ask, "When can I call back to find out if the job has been filled?" Be polite but ask that you be kept informed of progress on filling the job opening.

Call back at least once a week unless you are asked to do otherwise. Don't let them forget that you are interested but also don't make a pest of yourself. When you call about the job and think you will need to call again, be sure to get the name of the person to whom you should direct your calls next time.

If at all possible, develop an inside contact with someone who already works at the station. Ask that person about typical working conditions, pay scales, progress on filling the job opening you are seeking, etc. Your success rate in securing a job will be much higher if you have already developed an acquaintance in that station.

THE NEXT STEP

All of the education, magazines, and books in the world will not make you a broadcaster. The only way to fully reach that position is experience. You must get out there and actually operate the equipment, make the announcements, read the meters, write the scripts, and deal with the people. When these things have become automatic and second nature, then you can call yourself a broadcaster.

At this point, you have reached the beginning of your broadcast career. You've read the book. Now go into the studio and get to work!

Fig. 17-3. Ready? Now it's your turn to please the audience.

EXERCISE 17-1.   THE AUDITION TAPE

Using the format listed in this chapter, make an audition tape on an audio cassette. Have someone listen to it and give you an honest critique of its good and bad points.

Glossary

The beginning broadcasting student must absorb a large number of new words and expressions. This is the language or jargon of other broadcasters. Over 350 such terms are listed here in alphabetical order. Each term is followed by a brief definition. If the term has more than one common meaning, additional definitions are given.

The numbers in brackets {} give the chapter where the term is mentioned in the text. If no number in brackets is given, the term was included in the glossary because it is useful information to the reader, but it has not been covered in the text.

account codes—Special computer data recorded on carts. When the cart is played, the account code data is read into the station's computer, automatically logging the exact name and length of the spot {12, 14}.

ad-lib—"Without script." A remark made by an announcer or performer that is not part of the planned program script or is intended to sound as if it were not part of the planned program script {6, 11}.

ad-lib sheet—A list of remarks, usually humorous, prepared by the announcer for use during a radio show. These are actually scripted remarks, but they are intended to sound like true ad-libs {6}.

advertising agency—A business that works to bring potential advertisers in contact with radio stations that can broadcast the advertiser's commercials. An ad agency might also produce the commercials {11}.

AGC amp, automatic gain control amplifier—An amplifier found in the program audio line of a radio station that delivers a compressed audio signal. An AGC amp raises the average modulation level of an audio signal {3}.

air monitor—The special receiver used to monitor the radio station in the studio speaker system. The air monitor includes metering and test functions and feeds received audio to the control room speakers {3, 5, 15}.

all-caps—"All capital letters." This style of typing is used on news wire teletypes and typewriters when writing scripts for news or commercial copy {7}.

AM, amplitude modulation—A method of combining an audio signal with a powerful radio frequency signal. Modulation varies the output power of an AM transmitter while the frequency of the transmitter is constant {5, 15}.

AM broadcasting—Transmitting radio signals intended for reception by the public by using the amplitude modulation system {1, 15}.

AM broadcast band—The band of radio frequencies extending from 535 kilohertz to 1605 kilohertz (or 0.535

to 1.605 megahertz). All transmissions in this band of frequencies use the amplitude modulation system {15}.

Amateur Radio—See *Ham Radio*.

amp, ampere—The unit of electrical current. Indicates how many electrons flow past a given point in an electrical circuit during one second of time {15}.

amp, amplifier—An electronic device used to increase signal strength of audio or radio signals {3}.

announcer—The person who speaks on the radio, either in a live broadcast, over network circuits, or in a recording session {1, 6}.

antenna—A metal structure used to radiate radio waves created by a transmitter. An AM broadcast antenna is a tall metal tower several hundred feet high; an FM antenna has one or more metal hoops, a few feet across, held up in the air by a tall tower {5, 15}.

antenna de-icer—A heating device that melts ice and snow off radio antennas, to preserve their electrical performance during severe winter weather {15}.

audio console—A piece of studio equipment that selects between several audio sources, controls audio signal levels, routes audio signals to the desired destination, provides audio monitoring and VU metering, and can include other optional features {3}.

audio dropout—A momentary loss of audio, particularly because of a flaw in a recording tape, or loss of signal through a wire or radio link from a remote site {12}.

audio news service—A network that provides news and feature materials intended for broadcast by radio stations. Distribution can be made by telephone line, satellite, microwave radio link, or through the mail via magnetic tape {7, 9, 13}.

audio processor—A special amplifier that responds automatically to variations in audio signals. It holds the level of its output signals within a specific range of levels regardless of the input signal level {3}.

audio production—The recording of program material intended for broadcast at some later time, usually involving editing or complex operations, music, sound effects, or more than one announcer {6}.

audio signals—Varying electrical currents that represent sound patterns. Audio signals are produced by any audio source equipment and can be carried by electrical conductors {1}.

audition—(1) To listen to an audio source via the cue or audition channel or in a studio that is not on the air {3}; (2) to preview program material or a performer to determine whether they should be used on the air {4}.

audition channel—That portion of the audio console that duplicates the functions of the program channel but is used to route audio signals not to be broadcast {3}.

automation—A computer-controlled radio station playing program events in a prescribed sequence without real-time human control. The automation might be capable of handling only one to two program events, or it might operate the station all day with only occasionally updated program log information {14}.

balance—The proper adjustment of left- and right-channel audio so that both are equally audible {16}.

block diagram—A simple drawing of an electronic device using labeled squares to represent each functional group of circuits. The blocks are connected by lines and arrows to show their relationship to each other {3}.

board—Another name for audio console {3}.

boom—Mike boom; a metal arm that holds a microphone in front of an announcer without taking up table space. It can be adjusted for varying height, length, and angle {2}.

broadcast loop—A dedicated telephone line that carries audio between a remote location and the studio or between any two points needed for broadcast operations {2, 12, 13}.

broadcasting—The transmission of radio signals and programs intended for the general public.

bulk eraser—An electromagnet that puts a random and silent magnetic pattern on an audio tape. All recorded material on the tape disappears completely and the tape can be reused for a new recording {2, 12}.

bulletin—An important announcement; a news bulletin or weather bulletin contains information that is very important to the public and is usually broadcast immediately by interrupting normal ongoing programming {7}.

calibration—The process of adjusting a meter or metering circuit so that it provides accurate measurements. The marks and numbers on the face of a meter are called calibrations {15}.

call letters—The unique group of 3 or 4 letters assigned to each broadcasting station by the government that is used to identify that radio station {1, 4, 10}.

capstan—The rotating metal shaft in a tape machine that pulls the tape past the heads at a specific speed {2, 12}.

cardioid pattern—Heart-shaped pattern; refers to broadcast microphones, indicates the directions to which the mike is most sensitive for sound pickup {2}.

carrier—A radio station's transmitted signal, minus any modulating audio signals {15}.

cart—Audio tape cartridge; a tape wound in a continuous loop around a single hub encased in a plastic box or cartridge. Broadcasters use carts to hold recordings of frequently used spots, jingles, announcements, and music {2, 5}.

cart machine—A tape machine designed to play and/or record tape carts {2}.

cassette—Audio tape cassette; a reel-to-reel tape, including the reel hubs, encased in a plastic box or cassette. They are most often used for broadcast news gathering in small portable tape machines {2}.

cassette machine—A tape machine designed to play and/or record audio tape cassettes {2}.

chief engineer—The radio station employee responsible for the technical quality of the radio station. The chief engineer is in charge of equipment maintenance and technical training of all operators, and must be knowledgeable of the FCC rules {15}.

clear channel—An AM broadcast band frequency assigned to only one radio station in a large geographic area {15}.

clear channel station—A radio station in the AM broadcast band that is protected from interference from other radio stations. The primary station on a clear channel broadcasts to areas more than a thousand miles away at night. Any secondary stations operating on the same frequency must either sign off the air at night, reduce power, or use directional antennas to avoid interfering with the primary station's service area {1, 15}.

closed circuit—A direct or private connection not intended for direct broadcast to the public. The connection from network headquarters to the stations is considered closed circuit and not intended for direct public listening {13}.

combo, combo operator—The combination of the announcing and operating jobs performed by one person. Combo control rooms are arranged to allow the control operator to also speak into the microphone {1}.

commercial—A radio announcement that advertises a product or service. The radio station receives money for each commercial broadcast, which is paid for by the sponsor {1, 2, 11}.

commercial broadcasting—A radio or TV station whose operating costs are paid for by selling time on that station to advertisers {11}.

commercial saturation—The number of commercial minutes broadcast during an hour, compared to the number of noncommercial minutes of programming during that same hour. The Federal Communications Commission and the National Association of Broadcasters have guidelines limiting the commercial saturation of a radio station {1}.

Communications Act of 1934—The law enacted by the U.S. Congress in 1934 that established the Federal Communications Commission as the government agency designed to regulate most radio services in the United States, its territories, and possessions. The Communications Act is amended as needed to keep up with current technology and practice.

compression—Reduction of the dynamic range of an audio signal, reducing the difference between the loudest and softest portions {3}.

CONELRAD—**CON**trol of **EL**ectronic **RAD**iation; the name given to an early form of the present Emergency Broadcasting System, which required most radio stations to go off the air during an emergency {9}.

console—(1) The audio console; (2) the entire operating desk, including the audio console and associated equipment racks {2, 3}.

contract—A business agreement between two parties, such as a labor contract between a radio station and its employees, or between a radio station and its commercial sponsors {8}.

copy—A written script for news, spots, or announcements {11}.

copy book—A notebook in the control room that contains copy being used on the air {4}.

covering a shift—Working hours not normally assigned to you in times of emergency, illness, or vacation {8}.

covering a spot—During a network broadcast, a station does not use a network's spot, but it plays a local spot during that same time period instead; sometimes called a *cutaway* {13}.

cross-fade—The transition between two program events, accomplished by fading down one pot while fading up another; sometimes called a *segue* {3}.

cue—(1) To position a record or tape so that first audio begins less than one second after the machine starts; (2) to signal an announcer or performer to begin talking.

cue cards—Another name for script; cue cards for radio containing brief notes rather than a fully-written script.

cue channel—An audio path in the console provided for listening to an audio source without putting it on the air {3}.

cue sheet—A written format or a listing of program contents on a tape. The cue sheet also contains technical information about tape speed and format as well as timings and end cue information.

cue tone—A tone used to signal that a program event

has begun or ended or will soon begin or end. Sometimes found on audio tapes and carts and used by networks to signal local stations. Used to tell a station's automation to move on to the next program event {14}.

current—See *ampere* {15}.

cutaway—A pause in a network broadcast for local stations to play their spots. During a cutaway, the network may or may not send any audio to the local stations. See *covering a spot* {13}.

day book—See *copy book*.

dead air—Complete silence on the air; unmodulated carrier. This is a very undesirable situation because a listener who hears nothing is likely to turn up the radio and be annoyed by the blast of sound when modulation resumes {5}.

decibel, dB—A tenth of a bel. A decibel is the unit of loudness used when comparing the loudness of two signals. A change in loudness of one decibel is typically the minimum loudness change that can be detected by the human ear. The VU meter has a reference point of zero VU at the 100% level point, with all other volume levels marked in dB above or below that point. See *dynamic range* {3}.

dedicated line—A telephone line specifically assigned to a particular remote audio source. Also called a *broadcast loop* {13}.

de-tuned antenna—A radio antenna that is out of adjustment, either due to mechanical problems or electrical loading due to a covering of ice or snow {15}.

direct broadcast—(1) A live broadcast that goes from the point of origin, through the studio, and directly onto the air without delay. (2) In television, direct broadcast TV signals go from network headquarters to an orbiting satellite, then the signals are retransmitted from the satellite directly to the homes of the viewers {2, 9}.

directional antenna—An antenna that has a specially shaped radiation pattern that concentrates radio signals in specific directions while radiating little or no power in other directions {15}.

directional mike—A microphone that is sensitive to sounds approaching from certain specific directions yet is not sensitive to sounds coming from other directions. The directional mikes used in combo operations are designed to pick up the announcer's voice while not picking up the sounds of the nearby studio equipment {2}.

dirty feed—A network feed containing spots and other program events that are not being used by the local station, forcing the local station to cover spots. A local combo operator cannot leave a dirty feed on the air while airing local spots because unwanted network spots or other program events will also be heard on the air {13}.

disc jockey, DJ—Another name for the combo operator who talks and plays records during a radio program {1}.

discrepancy record—An addition to a station's program log that describes any deviations from the predetermined broadcast schedule, any mistakes made that affect the accuracy of the program log, or any problems that arose worthy of permanent recording in the station's legal records {10}.

discrete audio—Multichannel audio; two or more audio channels found in separate tracks on tape or in separate cables {16}.

dish antenna—A microwave radio antenna placed in the focus of a large metal dish. When used for reception, the dish collects radio wave energy and concentrates it on the antenna itself—when transmitting, the dish focuses the transmitted radio energy into a well-defined beam aimed in a specific direction. Dish antennas are used in microwave radio links on earth plus are used to communicate to and from satellites {2}.

distortion—Poor sound or signal reproduction; the introduction of unwanted noise into a signal {3, 15}.

distribution amp, DA—Distribution amplifier; an amplifier having several outputs so that one signal source can feed several inputs without undesired interaction between those inputs {3}.

drive time—The morning and evening hours when many radio listeners are playing their car radios while driving to or from work. Morning drive time is radio's most popular time {4}.

dropouts—Momentary loss of audio signals because of flaws or damage to magnetic tape recordings or signal fades in a microwave radio system {4}.

dub, dubbed—Duplicate, duplicated; a copy of a recording.

duct tape—A gray, cloth-backed, adhesive tape commonly used by broadcasters for bundling and securing cables; also called gray tape or *gaffer's tape* (theatrical and TV usage) {13}.

dynamic range—The difference in signal levels between the loudest and softest portions of program material. The unit measurement of dynamic range figures is the decibel (dB). The dynamic range of the human ear is approximately 100 dB, which is the difference between a barely audible sound and a noise so loud that it causes pain.

EBS Attention Signal—A two-tone, attention-getting sound lasting about 23 seconds. The attention signal trips alarms on EBS receivers and alerts all listeners that emergency information is about to be broadcast {9}.

edit—(1) To modify or alter program material by rewriting or re-recording portions of it. (2) A tape machine operating mode with the machine in the play mode without the transport moving the tape past the heads {12}.

effective radiated power—The usable transmitted power of an FM or TV station; the transmitter output power, minus any power losses in the feedline, multiplied by the gain figure of the antenna {15}.

electricity—The flow of electrons.

Electronic News Gathering, ENG—The use of tape recorders and radio links to bring news reports from the field into the radio station {2, 9, 13}.

Emergency Broadcast System, EBS—A voluntary network of radio and TV stations used to alert the general public to any emergency situation affecting the safety of people or property. The EBS can be activated at the local, regional, or national level {9}.

engineer—(1) The person responsible for the operation of the equipment. (2) A person qualified to repair, maintain, and design electronic equipment {2}.

erase head—The tape recorder head that removes previously recorded material from the tape as it passes by {2}.

erasing—Making a tape recording disappear from a tape by putting a random and noiseless magnetic pattern on it {2}.

fading signals—Radio signals varying downward in strength, making reception difficult or impossible {2}.

fail-safe system—Used in broadcast automation systems to make sure something gets on the air in case of system failure. Usually the fail-safe system has a special cart machine with music and jingles reserved for emergency use only {14}.

fast forward—Quick tape movement through the tape path with the tape moving from the supply reel to the takeup reel {2}.

features—Brief radio programs designed to inform or entertain the audience {1, 11}.

Federal Communications Commission, FCC—The agency of the United States Government established to regulate the use of radio and television transmitters {3}.

feedline—The cable that delivers the radio signal from transmitter to antenna {15}.

filaments—One of the parts of a transmitter tube. The filaments must be given time to get hot before a transmitter is put on the air (solid state transmitters have no filaments) {15}.

fill music—(1) Music used to keep programming on schedule. (2) Music played by an automation's fail-safe system when all other available audio sources stop functioning {14}.

first audio—The beginning of program material on the record or tape. Does not include any leader announcement recorded on the tape that is not intended for broadcast {2}.

flutter—A rapid variation in the speed of a tape caused by an undesirable mechanical problem in the tape machine {2}.

FM broadcast band—The band of radio frequencies extending from 88 megahertz to 108 megahertz used by FM stations {1, 15}.

FM broadcasting—The transmission of radio signals intended to be received by the public that uses the frequency modulation method of transmission {1, 5}.

format—(1) An established operating procedure; (2) A station's style of programming {1, 4, 8}.

frequency—(1) The location on a radio dial of a radio station. (2) The number of electronic cycles per second of a radio signal {1, 5}.

frequency meter—A meter or counter that reads out the operating frequency of a radio transmitter {5}.

frequency modulation, FM—A method of combining an audio signal with a radio signal by varying the frequency of the transmitter while holding its signal amplitude constant {15}.

fresh news—The reporting of news that has happened very recently or that still has high audience interest {7}.

frills—Extra program events that make a radio program more interesting (or more complicated) {11}.

gaffer's tape—Strong, cloth-backed adhesive tape; term used primarily in TV and theater; same as gray tape or duct tape {13}.

gate—(1) The opening or slot in the front of a cart machine into which a cart is placed for playback or recording {2}. (2) An electronic circuit used in computer logic.

go button—A lever or push button used by the announcer to signal the automation system to immediately proceed to the next scheduled program event {14}.

golden throat—A humorous or critical name for a radio announcer who either has an especially good voice or for an announcer who uses too much voice inflection.

good operating practice—Using proper procedures and skills {10}.

guide—An arm, roller, or flange in the tape path that holds the tape in an accurate relationship with the tape head {2}.

ham radio—Also called Amateur Radio; an amateur radio service with many educational benefits for broadcasters. Ham radio is not the same as Citizens Band Radio. For more information contact the American Radio Relay League, 225 Main Street, Newington, CT 06111 or call (203) 666-1541.

handheld radio—A radio transmitter and receiver small enough to be carried in a person's hand; used for communication between news reporters and the radio station {2}.

header—A voice announcement at the beginning of an audio tape containing information for the combo operator playing the tape. A header is never intended for broadcast {14}.

health and welfare information—Emergency information relating to the physical well-being of people yet not urgently relevant to the protection of life and property {9}.

hit record—A very popular musical recording.

hub—The round center of a tape reel around which the tape is wound {2}.

ID announcement—An announcement of the radio station's call letters followed by the city served by that station. The call sign and city served are stated on the license document {4}.

inflection—The varying pitch of an announcer's voice. Proper inflection helps convey meaning and is an important part of proper grammar. Good inflection improves an announcer's style; poor inflection is annoying enough to cause listeners to retune the radio and stop listening to your station {6}.

informants—Members of the public who supply newsworthy information to a radio station; also called *stringers* {9}.

in-phase audio—Two perfectly synchronized audio signals, such as in multichannel recording or stereo broadcasting {16}.

input—The entry point of a signal into a piece of equipment.

input selector—The switch that connects several audio sources to an input {3}.

inside joke—A humorous remark that can be understood only by a few people. A broadcast-related inside joke should never be told on the air because the audience will not understand or appreciate the humor.

interference—The reception of two or more radio signals on the same frequency, making them difficult to understand {15}.

intermediate power amplifier, IPA—A radio frequency amplifier between the low-powered exciter and the final power amplifier stages in a transmitter {15}.

ionosphere—A layer of the earth's atmosphere that reflects radio waves back to earth. The ionosphere is made up of charged electrical particles created by the interaction of the sun's radiation with the atmosphere {15}.

jack—An electrical receptacle used for the interconnection of audio circuits in a radio studio {3}.

jack field—Many jacks mounted together in one panel {3}.

jingle—A short musical tune or song used in radio commercials and promos. A jingle package is a set or library of jingles {1, 11}.

job contract—A written agreement between an employer and an employee {8}.

job description—A listing of duties, responsibilities, and work schedules; may also include information about pay rate, holidays, job benefits, etc. {17}.

job interview—A conversation held between an employer and a person seeking employment. Both parties are seeking information about the other {8}.

key—A switch; the switch that routes audio from a mixing channel to the audition, cue, or program channels {3}.

kilovolts—Thousands of volts; kilo- is the metric prefix meaning thousands of {15}.

kilowatts—Thousands of watts {15}.

lead-in—(1) On a tape, a spoken announcement recorded on the beginning of a tape that identifies the program material contained on that tape; also called a header {14}. (2) To music, the introduction to a musical program event {6}. (3) To news, a phrase or sentence that draws the listener's attention to the story that follows {7}.

left channel—One of two audio channels in a stereo broadcast; the audio signals that should come from the left-hand speaker or headphone when you are listening. To verify which is right and left, listen to a symphonic recording—the strings are supposed to be mostly in the left channel {16}.

left-minus-right, L-R—A subtractive combination of the left and right channels. Stereo receivers need this information in combination with the left-plus-right audio signal to reconstruct separate left and right audio signals {16}.

left-plus-right, L + R—An additive combination of the left and right channels; The mono or main channel stereo signal.Stereo receivers need this information in combination with the left-minus-right audio signal to reconstruct separate left and right audio signals {16}.

lethal high-voltage—Voltages high enough to cause serious injury or death if touched. Always be very careful around electrical equipment that is open for servicing {5}.

level—(1) The loudness of an audio signal. (2) "Give me a level" means to feed program material or speak into the microphone so that the operator can determine the proper volume setting on the board {3}.

limiter—A fast-acting AGC amp that prevents audio signals from being louder than a specified level {3}.

live break-in—An interruption in regular programming when the announcer reads a special news bulletin or an emergency message {14}.

live tag—A short message given live by the announcer at the end of a recorded spot {11}.

local availabilities—Specific network program events that might be covered so that the local station can air its own spots instead. A see *cutaways* {13}.

local station—(1) A radio station that has its studios and transmitter near you. (2) A radio station having a format that appeals to the nearby community, often participating actively in community events with live broadcasts. (3) A radio station that has a relatively small signal coverage area {1}.

log—(1) A record of performance. *Program log* is a written record of the scheduled program events and what time they actually ran on the air.(2) *Transmitter operating log* is a written record of the transmitter's performance as indicated by meter readings that are taken periodically. (3) *Maintenance log* indicates what special measurements and equipment adjustments have been conducted by the station's chief engineer {1, 5, 15}.

log book—A notebook containing a collection of log sheets of each day's operations {5, 15}.

loop—See *broadcast loop* and *dedicated line*.

lowercase—On a news wire teletype, contains the letters (in capitals) that are used to print out new copy.

The uppercase contains numbers, punctuation marks, and other special symbols.

magnetic tape—A plastic ribbon coated with a metallic oxide that can store magnetic patterns of audio signals {2}.

main channel audio—The mono channel containing a combination of both left and right audio signals {16}.

mark—Used in a time countdown to signify "zero seconds" or a reference point {13}.

master copy—The original or first-generation recording; the highest-quality recording of a program from which any duplicates are made {11}.

master volume control—A pot connected to the output of the board allowing the operator to control the board's output signal level {3}.

megahertz—Millions of cycles per second; a unit of radio frequency vibrations or oscillations {15}.

meter—A measuring and indicating device that displays values of voltage, current, power, volume level, frequency, etc. {15}.

metric prefixes—Words that combine with electrical units that multiply or divide the number being represented; kilo = thousands of (x 1000), mega = millions of (x 1,000,000), milli = thousandths of (x 0.001) {5}.

mike, microphone—A device that responds to sound waves in the air, producing small electrical currents {3}.

milliamp—1/1000 of an ampere {15}.

mini-drama—A commercial that uses a short-story format to sell the product. Mini-dramas can be serious or humorous {11}.

modulation—The process of combining an audio signal with a radio frequency signal (see *AM* and *FM*) {3, 15}.

modulation monitor—A special receiver in a radio station that samples the transmitted signal and provides a meter that indicates the modulation percentage of the audio {15}.

modulation percentage—The loudness of the audio signal being transmitted, with 100% being the loudest modulation level permitted on negative peaks {3, 15}.

monitor—An amplifier and speaker system that allows the operator to listen to an audio signal {3}.

mono, monaural, monophonic—An audio source producing a single audio signal or combining two or more audio sources into one {16}.

multibay antenna—An antenna having several radiating sections stacked above each other {15}.

multiplex transmission—A complex signal containing

several channels of information; usually requires special receiver decoder circuits to recover all information {16}.

multitrack recording—A recording having two or more separate audio signals {12}.

multivoice spot—An announcement using more than one voice {11}.

musical beds—A selection of music specifically timed and edited to be played during a spot {11}.

natural sound—Sound recorded at a real-life event; not a sound effect that is made to sound like something else {11}.

nemo—A term used to indicate a remote audio source; used by some commercial network personnel. See *remote broadcast*.

network—The interconnection of several radio stations so that they all receive program material from a central source. The network might be over telephone lines, microwave links, satellite, or via tape recordings {1}.

news copy—Radio script containing news for broadcast {7}.

news director—The person responsible for operating the news department of a radio station {9}.

news reporter—A radio station employee responsible to find newsworthy information and bring it to the station in a form suitable for broadcast. A reporter who is paid by the story used is called a *stringer* {9}.

news tips—News information supplied to a reporter by a member of the public {9}.

news wire—A teletype network that supplies news information {7}.

next event button—A manual control on a broadcast automation system that allows the announcer or operator to signal the computer to move on to the next scheduled program event.

noise—Unwanted signals.

nondirectional antenna—An antenna that radiates a signal equally well in all horizontal directions {15}.

normalled—The automatic connection of two jacks in a patch panel when no patch cord is inserted into either of them {3}.

off duty—Not present or ready for work.

off-mike—Sound waves coming from a direction to which a microphone is not sensitive {2}.

oldie—A musical recording that was popular in the past {4}.

on duty—Present and prepared to work.

on-mike—Sound waves coming from a direction to which a microphone is sensitive {2}.

on the air, on-air—Being broadcast; also called "hot."

on-the-spot reporting—A reporter who witnesses and reports a news event while it happens.

open reel—The oldest tape machine format, using two separate plastic or metal reels. The tape unwinds from the supply reel, passes through the tape path, and is wound around the takeup reel {2}.

operator—The person who controls the equipment operation {1}.

out-of-phase audio—Audio signals that are not properly synchronized. Signals that are out of phase tend to cancel each other {16}.

output—The exit point of a signal from a piece of electronic equipment {3}.

over modulation—Audio signals that are loud enough to result in transmitter modulation peaks in excess of 100% {3, 5}.

overtime work—Work in excess of 40 hours per week, or as defined in the job contract {8}.

oxide coating—The magnetic powder glued to the plastic backing of an audio tape {2}.

pacing—The speed of an announcer's speech; also the length of silences between program events. A fast-paced show has little or no silence in it {1}.

Part 73—That part of the FCC's Rules dealing specifically with broadcasting {10}.

patch—A temporary connection between pieces of equipment using a patch cord plugged into jacks {3}.

patch bay—See *jack field* {3}.

patch panel—See *jack field*.

pause—An operating mode of a tape machine. The machine is in the play mode, but the tape is not being moved through the tape path by the transport.

peak limiter—The audio processor stage that will not allow the volume peaks to exceed a specified level, usually 100% modulation {3}.

personality—A radio personality; an announcer who is also an entertainer. Personality radio programs feature the announcer rather than music or other program events, although they are included {4}.

phase—The time delay between two electrical signals {15}.

phone patch—The interconnecting device between the audio console and the telephone line {2, 3, 13}.

pie chart—A circular format chart in which program events are represented by slices of the circle {4}.

pilot tone—A special inaudible tone broadcast by a

stereo radio station that is used to help stereo receivers decode the stereo information and turn it back into discrete audio signals. It is also used to control the muting circuit in a stereo receiver so that the listener hears nothing but usable stereo broadcasts {16}.

pinch roller—Or pressure roller. A rubber or plastic cylinder in a tape machine that holds audio tape firmly against the rotating capstan {2}.

plates—(1) The button on tube-type transmitters that puts the carrier on the air. (2) One of the parts of a vacuum tube {15}.

platter—The large, round, metal plate on a turntable on which the record sits while being played {2}.

play, playback—The operating mode of a tape machine that moves the tape through the tape path, senses the magnetic pattern on the tape, and converts it into an audio signal {2}.

playback amplifier—An electronic circuit that collects the weak electrical signals from the playback head of a tape recorder and makes those signals strong enough to be heard or used in other ways {2, 12}.

playback head—The part of a tape machine that senses the magnetic patterns on the tape {2, 12}.

plug—A short promotional announcement {8}.

poles—The ends of the horseshoe-shaped tape recorder head; the poles touch the tape {12}.

police monitor—A scanner. A radio receiver used in a radio station's newsroom to listen to communications between mobile police and the base station. Some states have laws restricting who can use police monitors, especially those mounted in automobiles.

pot—A potentiometer; the volume control. A mechanical or electronic device that varies the signal level passing through it when adjusted by the audio console operator.

power amplifier, PA—The last amplifier stage in a transmitter {5, 15}.

presence—The high-frequency components of speech sounds; the sounds made by the consonant letters, especially c, g, j, p, s, t, x, and z {2}.

printout—The printed page produced by a teletype or a copying device {7}.

priority information—Information concerning the safety of life or property {9}.

production library—A large set of record albums containing sound effects and jingles used in producing commercials {11}.

production notes—Remarks written into a radio script that tell announcers what voice inflections to use or tell operators what sound effects, music, and special production techniques to use {11}.

program channel—The audio console stages dedicated to audio signals that are to be broadcast {3}.

program event—A segment of a radio program, such as a musical selection, a spot, an announcement, etc. {1}.

program log—The written record of scheduled program events to be broadcast, and the operator's notes and entries indicating what actually was broadcast {6}.

programming—The program events selected for broadcast {1}.

promo, promotional announcement—A spot produced by a radio station which advertises the station itself in some way {1, 11}.

PSA—Public service announcement; a radio spot promoting a product or service for which the station receives no money {1, 11}.

pulling materials—The process of locating the records, tapes, and scripts that will be used on the air, and collecting them together for convenient access by the operator and announcer {8}.

radio link—Communication between two locations by means of radio signals {2}.

radio personality—A radio announcer who is interesting and entertaining to the audience {4}.

radio wave propagation—The way radio waves travel through space. Propagation studies can predict the usable signal coverage area of a radio station's transmitter {15}.

record amplifier—An electronic circuit that takes an audio signal and makes it strong enough to be fed through a tape head, rearranging the magnetic patterns on magnetic recording tape {12}.

record head—That part of a tape machine that is fed an audio signal and produces a magnetic pattern on an audio tape {2, 12}.

records—Phonograph recordings; audio signals preserved as wavy grooves in the surface of vinyl discs {1}.

reel to reel—see *open reel*.

remote broadcasts—A radio program originating from a location other than the radio studio; sometimes called *nemo* by commercial network personnel {13}.

resonance—The magnification of sound waves in an air space {6}.

rewind—Fast backwards movement of the audio tape, going from the take-up reel to the supply reel {2}.

re-write—Editing written copy to make it more suitable for broadcast {8}.

right channel—One of two audio channels in a stereo broadcast; the audio signals that should come from the right-hand speaker or headphone when you are listening. To verify which is right and left, listen to a symphonic recording—the strings are supposed to be mostly in the left channel {16}.

rotating spots—Two or more spots recorded on the same cart {7}.

routine information—Information beneficial to the public but not immediately important to the protection of life or property {9}.

routing switcher—A collection of switches that allow versatile interconnection of audio inputs and outputs. A routing switcher performs the same function as a patch panel but needs no cords, plugs, or jacks {3}.

satellite—A radio receiver and transmitter orbiting the earth in space and relaying radio signals over a wide area of the earth's surface {2}.

satellite feeds—Receiving network signals via satellites orbiting in space. Broadcast satellites are in a geosynchronous orbit 22,300 miles above the earth's equator, allowing satellite receiving dishes to be permanently aimed at a fixed point in the sky {13}.

saturation—(1) Unable to deliver any additional signal output {15}. (2) The ratio of commercial minutes sold to the total available commercial time in an hour {4}.

SCA—See *subsidiary communications authorization*; also see *sub-carrier audio channel* {16}.

script—Written words plus production notes about special effects that are to be used during a radio program {7, 11}.

script files—A file cabinet containing radio scripts used in the past. A script file is important for commercial spot scripts because a sponsor will often ask for an updated version of a spot used months or years ago {11}.

segue—Pronounced SEG-way; to program events played with no silence or interruption in between; means the same as ''back to back.''

sequencer—A computer used to control the airplay of a scheduled series of program events. A sequencer can be mechanical, but most use computer technology that can hold hundreds of program event commands at a time {14}.

SFX—Abbreviation for sound effects {11}.

short-hop remote link—A small portable radio transmitter and receiver used in place of temporary telephone lines. A short-hop link can carry a radio signal from a remote location where phone lines are not available, such as a boat race course five miles out to sea {13}.

shuttling—Fast winding of an audio tape, either rewind or fast forward modes of operation.

sign-off—The radio announcement informing the listeners that the station is going off the air {5, 15}.

sign-on—The radio announcement informing the listeners that the station is beginning broadcast operations {5, 15}.

silence sensor—A circuit used to detect dead air, or unwanted silences. An automation system uses a silence sensor to enact emergency procedures because silence usually indicates a failure of some sort {14}.

single-bay antenna—An antenna having one radiating structure {15}.

slop time—A portion of the broadcast format left unscheduled to allow for delays in broadcasting the scheduled program events {13}.

solid-state transmitter—Uses all solid-state or transistorized amplifiers instead of vacuum tubes {15}.

sound bite—An excerpt of a news interview; a portion of a recorded news event.

sound effects—Abbreviated *SFX*. Sounds that are created to sound like something else. Real-life sounds that are collected and recorded for use in production sessions later {11}.

source—Point of origination of audio signals.

speaker muting—Automatic disabling of a studio speaker when a nearby microphone is turned on {3}.

spec spot—Speculation spot; a radio commercial produced for demonstration purposes only {2}.

spindle—The metal shaft around which a record or tape rotates {2}.

splice—(1) A physical cutting, rearranging, and reattaching of portions of recording tape. {12} (2) The connection between two wires.

splice finder—A special cart machine that locates the splice in the cart's magnetic tape and cues the cart to start right after the splice, ensuring that the recorded message will not have audio dropouts caused by recording over the splice {12}

split-band proc—An audio processor that divides audio frequencies into groups (low, midrange, high) and processes each group separately {3}.

sponsor—A person or company that buys commercial time on a radio station {11}.

spot—A brief radio announcement; usually a commercial message {11}.

spot erasing—Using the erase head on a reel-to-reel tape deck to remove a few seconds out of the middle of a recording while leaving the remainder or the recording undisturbed {12}.

spot reel—A long tape containing commercials, PSAs, and promos. Not often used today with modern broadcast automation systems because multiple-deck cart machines are much more versatile {14}.

stacked bays—See *multibay antenna* {15}.

stale news—Old news; news that has become familiar to the listeners and is no longer interesting {7}.

standing wave ratio—A measure of a station's antenna system performance, always expressed as a ratio such as 1.5 to 1. The lower the reading, the better; the meter scale begins at 1 rather than zero; and ideal reading is 1 (expressed as 1:1). Anything up to 1.5:1 is no problem, and most transmitters can tolerate an SWR reading up to 2:1 before problems develop {15}.

starting groove—The outermost groove on a record. The starting groove contains no audio information {2}.

station breaks—A scheduled interruption in a network broadcast when local stations play local spots, station ID announcements, etc. {13}.

stereo—An audio source that has two channels of audio signals {1, 2, 12, 16}.

studio time—The time an operator spends occupying a studio. Due to limited facilities, studio time must be used efficiently {8}.

stylus—The diamond point that sits in the groove of a record. The stylus detects the wavy patterns in the record groove that represent audio information {2}.

subcarrier audio channel—Abbreviated SCA channel. A specially encoded audio channel that rides ''piggy back'' on stereo broadcasts, usually containing either the L-R stereo information or totally unrelated separate programming {16}.

subsidiary communications authorization—Abbreviated *SCA*. Some stereo transmitters are capable of transmitting several unrelated channels of audio at the same {16}.

supply reel—The reel of tape on the left side of a tape machine, which is full of tape to be played or recorded {2}.

SWR—See *standing wave ratio* {15}.

tails out—A reel of tape that must be rewound to the beginning before it can be played {14}.

take-up reel—The reel on the right side of a tape machine that receives tape that has been played or recorded {2}.

tape bias—A special signal added by a tape recorder to audio signals being recorded onto magnetic tape. The bias signal gives the magnetic particles on the tape an extra push, helping overcome their reluctance to take on a new pattern {12}.

tape delay loops—Special cart machines using tape carts to delay program material for several seconds before putting it on the air. Delay loops are used to ensure that profanity or other unwanted comments do not get on the air during phone-in talk shows {12}.

tape echo—A special effect in which a tape recording is made by a record head, picked up a fraction of a second later by the playback head, and then fed back to the record head, giving a reverberating or echoing sound {12}.

tape format—The physical layout of the recorded tracks on a tape {2}.

tape lifter—A movable guide that either lifts the tape away from the heads or holds it up against the heads, depending on the design of the tape machine {2}.

tape monitoring—The process of listening to a tape recording with the playback head while the recording is being made. Monitoring a tape while recording it gives the operator instant assurance that the recording is being made properly {12}.

tape path—The route taken by a magnetic tape as it moves from the supply reel to the take-up reel; the tape path includes guides, heads, pressure pads, capstan and pressure roller, tensioners, and end-of-tape sensors {2}.

telco—Abbreviation for telephone company {13}.

teletype—An electric typewriter or printer controlled by signals arriving in the studio over a telephone line or radio link {7}.

The Boss—Your work supervisor; usually the radio station's general manager {8}.

three-head tape machine—The normal setup for broadcast quality reel-to-reel machines. The three heads are erase, record, and playback {2, 12}.

throw-away lines—Phrases or sentences that help draw the listener's attention but need not be completely understood {7}.

thumbwheels—Ten-position, edge-mounted switches used in old-fashioned mechanical broadcast automation systems. Rows of thumbwheels were scanned mechanically to indicate which of ten possible program events was to be selected next {14}.

time-check announcements—Special messages sent on a network or remote line to ensure that everyone's clock agrees or to give a countdown until the beginning of a broadcast {13}.

tone arm—The movable arm on a turntable that holds the stylus and cartridge needed to detect sound information on the record {2}.

Top 10—The ten most popular records. The Top 10 is

usually selected based on the number of records sold in stores.

top of the hour—The beginning of the hour; when the minute hand points up to the 12 {4}.

tower—A tall, slender metal structure used by radio stations as a part of the antenna system {5}.

track—The area of a magnetic tape that is scanned by a tape head. Some tape formats have several tracks on one tape {2}.

traffic spotter—A news reporter assigned to watch city traffic patterns and give live reports for the benefit of motorists and commuters. Traffic spotters often work from helicopters or tall buildings.

transistorized transmitter—See *solid-state transmitter* {15}.

transmittal sheet—A list of instructions explaining how to update the FCC Rule book by deleting obsolete pages and replacing them with new pages {10}.

transmitter log—See *log*.

tube-type transmitter—A radio transmitter with amplifier circuits that use vacuum tubes {15}.

uncued cart—A tape cart that has not been allowed to run until automatically stopped by the cart machine at first audio {8}.

undermodulation—An audio signal level being fed to the transmitter that is too low to result in modulation peaks of 85% to 100% {5}.

union—A labor union. A group of employees who work together to negotiate the terms of their job contract with the employer {8}.

union dues—The money paid to the union by employees for the services rendered by the union {8}.

union representative—An employee of the labor union that handles contract negotiations with the employer on behalf of the employees {8}.

update—A report of the latest news details.

uppercase—The teletype's numbers, punctuation marks, and special symbols; the lowercase contains the letters.

vertical tower—A tall, slender metal structure associated with broadcast transmitters. The entire tower serves as the antenna for AM band transmitters, while the tower merely holds a smaller antenna high in the sky for FM and TV transmitters {15}.

virgin tape—Magnetic tape that has never been used. Used tape can be bulk-erased so that its magnetic pattern is completely random and silent, making it sound like virgin tape {12}.

volt—Unit of electrical force {15}.

volume—Signal level; loudness.

volume unit, VU—The unit of measurement of audio signal levels; a VU meter is calibrated in decibels, indicating signal levels as compared with the zero VU reference point (100% modulation level) {3}.

VSWR—Voltage standing wave ratio. See *standing wave ratio* {15}.

VU meter—A meter used to measure the loudness or level of an audio signal.

warm-up—(1) *Voice warm-up* involves exercising and preparing the announcer's voice before going on the air {6}. (2) *Transmitter warm-up* involves turning on the power to the transmitter, allowing all operating voltages to stabilize before putting the carrier on the air {15}.

warning lights—Lights that turn on to indicate that a microphone is on or that a studio is in use {3}.

watt—The electrical unit of power. Transmitter output power is often expressed in kilowatts, or thousands of watts {15}.

weak signals—Signals that are not strong enough or loud enough for reliable use {1}.

weather bulletin—Weather news containing information of immediate importance to the safety and protection of life or property {9}.

weather radio—A radio receiver that is tuned to a weather service transmitter, from which continuous weather information is available {9}.

weather service—The agency responsible for gathering weather information and issuing weather forecasts and warnings {9}.

weather wire—A teletype connected to the weather service {9}.

wire service—A teletype connected to a news distribution network {7}.

woof—Means the same as *mark* or *zero* when giving a time-check countdown; indicates a reference point in time {13}.

wow—Describes a turntable or tape machine that is not running at the correct speed. Happens when a record or tape is so tightly cued that first audio occurs while the machine is still getting started and has not reached normal speed {2}.

Bibliography and Suggested Reading

The publications listed here are ones that the author has found helpful. Inclusion of these specific books and magazines is *not* intended to be an endorsement of these publications over any others. They are listed alphabetically by the author's last name.

Not all of the publications listed below deal specifically with the subject of radio broadcasting. Some deal heavily with television, while others are useful in the broader area of electronic communication. Where possible, full mailing addresses have been included. In any event, your local bookstore can order these books for you.

Baker, Sheridan. *Practical Stylist*. Thomas Y. Crowell Company, 10 E. 53rd St., New York, NY 10022.

Broadcasting Publications, Inc. *Broadcasting and Cablecasting Yearbook*. 1735 DeSales Street N.W., Washington, DC 20036.

Chester, G. et al. *Television and Radio*. Prentice-Hall, Inc., Route 9W, Englewood Cliffs, NJ 07632.

Hilliard, Robert L., ed. *Radio Broadcasting*. Hastings House Publishers, 260 Fifth Avenue, New York, NY 10001.

Hyde, Stuart W. *Television and Radio Announcing*. Houghton Mifflin Company, 1 Beacon Street, Boston, MA 02108.

Oringel, Robert S. *Audio Control Handbook*. Hastings House Publishers, Communications Arts Books, 260 Fifth Avenue, New York, NY 10001.

Settel, Irving. *Pictorial History of Radio*. Grosset & Dunlap Publishers. Distributed by Book Sales, Inc., 110 Enterprise Avenue, Secaucus, NJ 07094.

Shrader, Robert L. *Electronic Communication*. McGraw-Hill Book Company, 1221 Avenue of the Americas, New York, NY 10020.

Summers, Robert E. and Summers, Harrison B. *Broadcasting and the Public*. Wadsworth Publishing Co., 10 David Drive, Belmont, CA 94002.

Wells, Alan, ed. *Mass Media and Society*. Mayfield Publishing Company, 285 Hamilton Avenue, Palo Alto, CA 94301.

Learning more. A successful broadcasters never stops learning about the industry. Reading trade magazines and books are one way of broadening your exposure.

Wilson, Mark, ed. *The ARRL Handbook* (for Amateur Radio operators). American Radio Relay League, 225 Main Street, Newington, CT 06111.

The following magazines are commonly found in radio and TV stations. These publications have informative articles covering all aspects of broadcasting including FCC news updates. They also have exceptionally well produced advertising about the the latest advances in broadcasting equipment. The job ads in the back of the magazines are very helpful to persons seeking employment in broadcasting.

Broadcasting, published weekly. Broadcasting Publications, Inc. 1735 DeSales Street, N.W., Washington, DC 20036.

Broadcast Engineering, published monthly. Intertec Publishing Corporation, Inc., 9221 Quivira Road, P.O. Box 12901, Overland Park, Kansas 66212.

Broadcast Management and Engineering, published monthly. Broadband Information Services, Inc. 295 Madison Avenue, New York, NY 10017.

Radio World, published semimonthly. Industrial Marketing Services, Inc. 5827 Columbia Pike, Suite 310, Falls Church, VA 22041.

INDEX

Other Bestsellers of Related Interest

RADIO-ELECTRONICS® STATE OF SOLID STATE—by the Editors of *Radio-Electronics*

Have you ever wished that you'd clipped some of those solid state projects and explanations of solid state theory from *Radio-Electronics* regular monthly column, "State of Solid State?" Or do you simply need some hands-on guidance in the use of today's digital ICs? If you can answer "yes" to either of these questions, you won't want to miss this collection of articles from *Radio-Electronics'* popular monthly feature. 168 pages, 111 illustrations. Book No. 2733, $9.95 paperback only

HOW TO BE A HAM—3rd Edition
—W. Edmund Hood

Completely revised, this guide will bring you up to speed on the latest innovations in operating practices and equipment availability, as well as the newest FCC rules, regulations, and licensing requirements. Find out about the basics of radio electronics and antenna theory, pipelines, setting up your first radio "shack," effects of weather on transmission, the fundamentals of wave propagation, and more! 320 pages, 95 illustrations. Book No. 2653, $13.95 paperback only

Prices Subject to Change Without Notice.

Look for These and Other TAB Books at Your Local Bookstore

To Order Call Toll Free 1-800-822-8158

(in PA, AK, and Canada call 717-794-2191)

or write to TAB BOOKS, Blue Ridge Summit, PA 17294-0840.

Title	Product No.	Quantity	Price

☐ Check or money order made payable to TAB BOOKS

Charge my ☐ VISA ☐ MasterCard ☐ American Express

Acct. No. _____ Exp. _____

Signature: _____

Name: _____

Address: _____

City: _____

State: _____ Zip: _____

Subtotal $ _____

Postage and Handling
($3.00 in U.S., $5.00 outside U.S.) $ _____

Add applicable state and local
sales tax $ _____

TOTAL $ _____

TAB BOOKS catalog free with purchase; otherwise send $1.00 in check or money order and receive $1.00 credit on your next purchase.

Orders outside U.S. must pay with international money order in U.S. dollars.

TAB Guarantee: If for any reason you are not satisfied with the book(s) you order, simply return it (them) within 15 days and receive a full refund.

BC